In Good and Generous Faith

CHRISTIAN RESPONSES TO RELIGIOUS PLURALISM

Kenneth Cracknell

THE
PILGRIM
PRESS

Cleveland

To the memory of Wilfred Cantwell Smith (1916–2000)
and of Jacques Dupuis SJ (1924–2004)

First published in North America 2006 by
The Pilgrim Press
700 Prospect Avenue, Cleveland, Ohio 44115
thepilgrimpress.com
© 2005 Kenneth Cracknell

Originally published by
Epworth/United Methodist Publishing House (UK)
4 John Wesley Road, Werrington, Peterborough
PE4 62P, England

11   10   09   08   07   06   5   4   3   2   1

LIBRARY OF CONGRESS CATALOGING-IN-PUBLICATION DATA

Cracknell, Kenneth.
In good and generous faith : Christian responses to religious pluralism /
    Kenneth Cracknell.
        p.   cm.
    Includes bibliographical references and index.
    ISBN 0-8298-1721-2
    1. Christianity and other religions. 2. Religious pluralism—Christianity.
I. Title.

BR127.C292 2006
261.2—dc22

                                                2005030026

ISBN-13: 978-0-8298-1721-8
ISBN-10:0-8298-1721-2

Contents

Abbreviations

BCC   British Council of Churches

CCBI   Council of Churches in Britain and Ireland

CWME   Commission on World Mission and Evangelism

DFI   Sub-unit on Dialogue with People of Living Faiths and Ideologies

DWME   Division of World Mission and Evangelism

IMC   International Missionary Council

LXX   Septuagint

OIRR   Office of Inter-Religious Relations

WCC   World Council of Churches

Acknowledgements

All quotations from the Old and New Testaments are from the New Revised Standard Version, copyright 1989 by the division of Christian Education of the National Council of Churches of Christ in the USA, and are used by permission of the National Council of Churches of Christ in the USA.

'Ambivalent Theology and Ambivalent Policy: The World Council of Churches and Interfaith Dialogue' first appeared in *Studies in Interreligious Dialogue* 9 (1999), pp. 87–111. Some of the material in Chapter 5 first appeared in the chapter 'Dialogue is Evangelism; Evangelism is Dialogue', in Inus Daneel, Charles van Engen and Hendrik Vroom (eds), *Fullness of Life for All: Challenges for Mission in the Early 21st Century,* Rodopi, 2003; The Bossey Declaration: Religious Plurality and Christian Self-Understanding is reprinted by permission of the Officers of the Commission on World Mission and Evangelism, Faith and Order, and the Office of Inter-Religious Relations (now the Team for Interreligious Relations and Dialogue) of the World Council of Churches.

FOREWORD

One of the most significant challenges for Christians in the twenty-first century will be our engagement with other religious traditions. While this challenge is not new, it has been intensified and reshaped by changing circumstances. As a disparaged minority, the focus of early Christians in engaging other religions was mainly on defending their own right to exist. With the political establishment of Christianity in the Holy Roman empire (ca. 400 C.E.) this changed dramatically. For the next 1500 years most Christians had little direct contact with members of other religions, and the relating that did occur was largely hegemonic—either as the majority culture in the Christian West imposing severe restrictions on Jews and on indigenous religions in colonized areas, or as restricted communities themselves in the Christian East under Islamic control. Over the last 150 years things have been changing again, particularly for Christians in North America and Europe. As a result of spreading political disestablishment of religion, and several waves of immigration, we are much more likely than our predecessors to have active participants of other religious faiths as our neighbors and family members. Moreover, with the emergence of global media we are exposed to the beliefs and practices of the range of world religions on a regular basis.

This increased contact has helped to reveal some of the caricatures, and simple lack of knowledge, of other religions that have been common among Christians. It has opened our eyes to the beauty and wisdom that can be found in every major religion, helping us appreciate why these religions remain compelling for many. But these new circumstances have also forced us to confront the negative legacy of earlier hegemonic relationships—as reactionary groups have often invoked religion to justify their violent actions. The fear sparked by events like the attack on the World Trade Center can easily reinforce false stereotypes of other religions and increase the difficulties of living together in an ever-shrinking world.

In this context Christians must surely accept the reality of an enduring religious plurality, and our role in promoting peaceful and respectful coexistence among people of all faiths. But how best might we contribute to this goal? Too often the answer suggested is framed within either a paternalistic liberalism that assumes all religions teach the same thing, no matter how much they protest this characterization, or a strong relativism that protects the diversity of religions by dismissing all comparative universal claims. Neither of these models is conducive to the type of dialogue among serious adherents of alternative religions that can lead to mutual respect. There is growing consensus that we need instead an approach that weds humility and conviction, where participants are equally open to learning from others and to sharing their own convictions.

One of the great values of Kenneth Cracknell's book is its embodiment of this desired wedding of humility and conviction—demonstrating that it is not an impossible ideal! Cracknell models throughout the "good and generous faith" that he commends as the character of authentic Christian engagement with other religions.

Equally valuable is the central focus of the present work. Unlike those who take the desirability of Christians approaching other religions in a more dialogical manner as self-evident, or those who dismiss such a desire as mere "political correctness", Cracknell demonstrates in a series of arguments that it is in keeping with sensitivities deeply grounded in the Christian tradition. His treatment of key biblical passages and central theological themes will be of great help to others seeking to understand religious plurality in Christian terms.

But the greatest contribution of this articulation of a "good and generous faith" is its challenge to the frequent assumption that Christians must choose between dialogue and evangelism as the goal in engaging those of other faiths. Cracknell recognizes that the possibility of conversion is always resident in authentic dialogue, and argues that such dialogue is the most appropriate approach to evangelism/mission for our time. Indeed, the deep hope undergirding his book is that it might help Christians in the twenty-first century recover the self-confidence to share the good news of Jesus Christ with their neighbors and friends with humility and deep courtesy.

I commend the book to you with the same hope!

RANDY L. MADDOX
Professor of Theology and Wesleyan Studies
Divinity School
Duke University

PREFACE

Nearly thirty years ago, after teaching in Nigeria (the home of Muslims and Christians and followers of traditional religion) and then in the English Midlands (one of the great areas in Britain for the migration of Hindus, Muslims and Sikhs, from India, Pakistan, Bangladesh and Africa), I was asked to become the first Secretary of the Committee for Relations with People of Other Faiths of the then British Council of Churches. Part of the job description at that time stated rather quaintly that the person to be appointed 'must love congregations'. I happily acceded to that notion (after all I had been a Methodist minister since 1957), and have felt it to be integral to all that I have been about since 1978. For ten years I travelled throughout both Britain and Ireland and, through my connections with the World Council of Churches and the Conference of European Churches, more than sixty other countries. I formed a number of impressions from meeting these churches and congregations. Among these was that, when confronted with central issues of religious diversity, Christians all around the world seemed to have just one scripture verse in their armoury, John 14.6: 'I am the way, and the truth, and the life. No one comes to the Father except through me.' Working primarily among Protestants with their profound respect for Scripture I saw the need to develop biblical studies for the congregations indicating the quite extraordinary resources that the Christian scriptures offer for understanding God's presence in the world of religious faith. I shared much of this material in *Towards a New Relationship: Christians and People of Other Faith,* published by the Epworth Press in 1986. Much of this biblical exegesis is not easily available in other places, yet still remains relevant to the preaching and teaching ministry of the churches. Revised and updated it forms the basis of the first and fifth chapters of this book.

But serious theological work had to be done, too. Happily there was already a significant body of scholarly literature from both Roman Catholic and Protestant sources, all of it pointing to what then was called 'an inclusivist Christology'. In the UK I found myself in the company of eminent British theologians who had come to espouse this view, and from 1979, as a member of the World Council of Churches Sub-unit on Dialogue with People of Living Faiths and Ideologies, I encountered Roman Catholic and Eastern Orthodox theologians who also held such views. I was persuaded then, as I still am, that only some form of Logos- or Spirit-Christology is adequate to the interpretation of God's activity in the world of religion. Some of this I shared in *Towards a New Relationship*. In the midst of this activity I offered my own interpretation of John 14.6, setting the verse in the context of the Johannine Logos teaching. A revised and extended version of this forms Chapter 2 in the present book.

Undoubtedly one of the greatest privileges of my life was to work with the WCC in a programme called 'My Neighbour's Faith – and Mine'. The process of consulting the churches throughout the world culminated in a week-long consultation in Baar, Switzerland, in 1990, at which an invited gathering of specialist theologians and scholars from Orthodox, Roman Catholic and Protestant traditions formulated a declaration affirming the presence of Christ in other religious traditions. My task at Baar was to produce the draft document. Later this Baar Declaration would become the basis for the most recent WCC Statement, printed in this book as Appendix 2: The Bossey Declaration: Religious Plurality and Christian Self-Understanding.

People in the congregations also raised practical issues: of sharing spirituality, of the possibility of interfaith worship, of interreligious marriages, of education in multi-faith settings, and both the WCC and the BCC had working parties addressing these topics. These essentially developed themes set out in the *WCC Guidelines for Dialogue with People of Other Faiths* and the BCC's *Relations with People of Other Faiths: Guidelines on Dialogue in Britain* (1981, revised edition 1983). From close engagement with these questions emerged the two chapters in *Towards a New Relationship* dealing with spirituality and ethics. In twenty years since they were first written many new approaches have surfaced, because of the vast increase in interfaith activity, locally, nationally and internationally. The chapters in this book on ethics and spirituality have been substantially revised in the light of the findings of conferences and assemblies associated with the new multi-faith networks and associations that have arisen since 1986.

Working with congregational groups, Bible classes, adult schools, lay leadership schools and so on led me to reflect on the crucial importance of the ministers and clergy in constructing a welcoming and open theological atmosphere for interreligious meeting. I became convinced that my job description 'must love congregations' had to lead to loving their pastors also, and that there must come a profound change in theological education or, as it is known in some circles, 'ministerial formation'. My colleague Christopher Lamb and I edited a volume in 1986 entitled *Theology on Full Alert,* which urged not only specialist formal teaching about the world's religious traditions and instruction about the theology of religion as essential to the curriculum, but a wide-ranging reform of the theological curriculum. This envisioned that all major subject areas would be conscious of religious pluralism, so bringing to bear the insights of Old Testament, New Testament, church history and systematic theology upon interfaith understanding. At the same time we asked that extensive programmes of visiting synagogues and mosques, temples and gurdwaras involving real personal encounters should be made available to students and faculty alike. And whenever possible ministerial students should learn about other faith traditions from the lips of people who belonged within them. *Theology on Full Alert* contained case studies from teachers around the world who were already implementing such ideas. In the last twenty years programmes of this kind have become widespread (I teach in a divinity school where Judaism is taught by a Jewish professor, who is a full member of our faculty, and where visiting scholars teach Islam, Hinduism, Buddhism and Sikhism). But the more this is done, the greater is the pressure to confront the questions of mission and evangelism, for ministerial students are keenly aware of Jesus' command, 'Go and make disciples of all nations' (as indeed are very many members of their future congregations).

As a direct consequence of the need for adequate missiological teaching I resumed my academic work on mission history, examining the attitudes of missionaries towards non-Christian religion throughout the history of the Church. Eventually I focused on the missionaries of the late nineteenth and early twentieth centuries, examining particularly the report of Commission Four of the World Missionary Conference in Edinburgh 1910. Missionaries all around the world were asked by this Commission: 'What attitude should the Christian preacher take towards the religion of the people among whom he labours?' Overwhelmingly their responses used words like 'sympathy', 'appreciation', 'the broadest charity', using expressions like 'seeing the good, the beautiful and the true in the native faiths'. One veteran missionary was on record as saying, 'We shall never gain the non-Christian world until we treat its religions with justice, courtesy and love.' Those last four words gave me the title of my 1995 book, *Justice, Courtesy and Love: Theologians and Missionaries Encountering World Religions, 1846–1914*. Their successors in the twentieth century were often equally affirming of the faith of other people, entering deeply into not only the Muslim, Hindu, Sikh, Jain, Buddhist or Confucianist thought worlds but also the religious world of Africa and traditional peoples in the Americas and the Pacific region. The older missionaries whom I met only in their writings, and the twentieth-century missionaries whom I often met through the WCC Commission on World Mission and Evangelism and the BCC Conference for World Mission, were frequently exemplars of the principle of justice, courtesy and love in interreligious relationships. Such men and women led me to the formulation that 'mission is dialogue; dialogue is mission': in other words to understand that all sharing of the good news of Jesus Christ has to be done with humility and with deep courtesy. The fifth chapter of this book, 'To Bear an Authentic Witness: A Missiology for Religious Pluralism', reflects on this concern.

The publication of *Theology on Full Alert* had an almost immediate effect on the course of my life. The authorities of the British Methodist Church said in effect, 'OK, if you want to reform theological education, put your money where your mouth is, and go and get your hands dirty by doing it.' So it was that I left the BCC in 1978 and became Senior Tutor at Wesley House in Cambridge, and eventually President of the Cambridge Theological Federation, moving on from Cambridge in 1995 to Brite Divinity School in Fort Worth, Texas, where I currently teach. One of the duties of academics is to keep abreast of the current literature in their field, and subsidiary to that, to share its riches with the rest of the world. This I have tried to do through a series of bibliographies that may be found on the internet at http://www.brite.tcu.edu/directory/cracknell. Another way is through adding extended notes to the text. To be sure no one reader will read all the notes, but from time to time they may set a person on a transformative course of study.

Much of what appears in this book has been tried and tested in the classrooms of the Cambridge Theological Federation and of Brite Divinity School and I record my appreciation to my students in both places. To Brite I offer my particular thanks for its rich resources that have enabled me to produce this book.

The book is dedicated to the memory of two of the finest exponents of the new relationships to which all Christians are called. Both honoured me with their friendship and guided me over the years through their writings. The first is Wilfred Cantwell Smith, who as a missionary from Canada discovered in India the faith of other men and women, becoming one of the world's leading scholars of comparative religion. Wilfred Smith knew that the time has come for 'we all' to be talking about 'us all', as all human beings reflect upon what God has been doing for the whole of humankind. The second is Jacques Dupuis, a Belgian Jesuit missionary to India and professor in the Gregorian University, who saw Christ in the religions of the world. Both were men of good and generous faith.

INTRODUCTION

This book has been written primarily for Christians who know they have a problem: how are they to relate to their fellow human beings who are devout followers of other religious ways and paths without a sense that they are some how being unfaithful to Jesus Christ?

The last fifty years have seen unprecedented migrations, bringing, for example, seven million Muslims to the United States and two million Muslims to the United Kingdom. Huge aircraft are capable of carrying three or four hundred people from Japan to Paris, India to Saudi Arabia, Africa to New York, Pakistan to Manchester, China to Melbourne. People once known to one another only through newsreels and slide shows now live next door to each other and mingle in the supermarkets, attend the same schools and use the same community facilities. In places where once Christianity apparently reigned supreme, Hindu temples and Sikh gurdwaras dot the landscape and minarets vie with spires in city centres and suburban skylines. Television brings instantaneous pictures of worshippers in Iraq, of pilgrims in Mecca or India, of funeral rites in Sri Lanka. Chat rooms on the internet have thousands of cross-cultural conversations going on at any moment, and surfing the web can lead one into the virtual reality of contrasting religious customs and ritual practices.

All this has brought about massive changes in attitudes and perceptions. People of different cultures know each other at a personal level, invite each other into their homes, ask each other to share in their religious festivals. With personal encounter comes new knowledge that conflicts with old prejudice: stereotypes crumble and fall away. What once was so glibly said about Jews or Muslims or Hindus (or whoever else) is falsified in the light of friendship and understanding.

Christians (as indeed people of all the other traditions) have had few resources from their past to guide them in this radically changed world. For Christians the heart of the difficulty lies with the theologies that they have inherited from the past ages of monoculturalism and ethnocentrism. The only religious pluralism known to medieval Europeans appeared in the form of the Jews, who were at best merely tolerated, at worst persecuted and expelled from wider society. In early modern Europe, a kind of religious pluralism did manifest itself in forms of Protestant faith, which were equally persecuted. When some of the followers of these Protestant movements established new colonies where they could organize society the way they wanted it, their vision did not include tolerance for those who differed from them. Most of the theologies of Europe and North America were formulated against such backgrounds and for this reason are distinctly unhelpful for understanding the diversity of religion. Neither the Roman Catholic slogan *extra ecclesiam nulla salus* (outside the Church no salvation), nor the fervent declaration of Martin Luther that 'all worship and religion outside Christ is the worship of idols', nor the icy clear logic of Calvinism that the elect constitute a predetermined number, and that those not elected cannot come to Christ and cannot be saved, offers anything to contemporary Christians in understanding the presence of people of other religious traditions.

But this book is written from the conviction that all is not lost: that there are enormous resources in the Bible and in the history of the Church that offer ways for Christians to understand religious pluralism without repudiating the truth that is in Jesus Christ. The argument of this book is that there is abundant guidance from Scripture and tradition, properly interpreted, to enable puzzled Christians to live with good and generous faith.

So I offer five chapters that deal with the Bible, with theology, with spirituality, with ethics, and with mission and evangelism. Since I have in mind that my first audience will be those who regularly take part in the worshipping life of the Church and revere the Bible as source and inspiration for their daily living, much of Chapters 1, 2 and 5 is properly biblical exposition. In Chapter 1 we will reconsider the notion of salvation history as it finds expression in the churches' lectionaries and courses of study, and ponder why so much of the biblical record is omitted from the schemes drawn up by theologians and liturgists for reading in church, and thus neglected by preachers and teachers. Here we ask what biblical material might suggest to us a new 'salvation history'. Chapter 2 is written out of much experience with church groups over the last thirty years. Even if they asked me in the first place to talk to them about Islam or Buddhism, the question that was always on their minds concerned the uniqueness or finality of Jesus: 'I am the way, and the truth, and the life. No one comes to the Father except through me.' Sometimes the questioners directed the answer away from themselves, asking me to guide them in helping a family member or fellow congregants. Sometimes the questioning was truculent: 'Do you or don't you believe that Jesus is the way, the truth and life?' to which I could only reply, 'Yes, I do, but that won't help to you understand what is meant by this verse.' For John 14.6 is actually in its scope all-embracing and universal, neither divisive nor exclusivist. Chapter 2 is an exposition of an inclusive Christology for religious pluralism.

Less frequently in congregational groups and rather more often with groups of clergy and/or theological students, after my presentation on interfaith dialogue, the dominant question appeared to be about the churches' evangelistic task. Matthew 28.16–20 was usually quoted: 'Go therefore and make disciples of all nations.' 'Yes,' I would reply, 'but there is vastly more to what making disciples means here than people normally think.' On occasions there was time available to deal with the so-called Great Commission in some detail but more often time ran out. Chapter 5 enables me to set out a missiology rather more adequate to a context of religious pluralism than the old models of confrontation and proclamation.

The other two chapters reflect on ethics and spirituality. Chapter 3 is an attempt to distill some of the findings that been achieved in the past thirty years by both monolateral (just Christian) and multilateral (interreligious) conferences and assemblies concerned with the way we have to behave to another in the context of religious pluralism. To be sure there are many straightforward biblical precepts to guide us, ranging from the straightforward injunctions 'Neither shall you bear false witness against your neighbour' (Deut. 5.20), and 'You shall love your neighbour as yourself' (Lev. 19.18), to incidents in the life and teaching of Jesus. But many of the ethical situations that confront us are full of problematic issues, highlighted for many people by the events of September 11, 2001. We shall consider some of these deeper moral issues in attempting 'An Ethic for Religious Pluralism'.

Christians around the world are being continually invited to share in acts of worship or forms of spirituality that originate in any one of the great world religious traditions, or for that matter in traditions that go far back into the history of humankind. The natural disquiet here turns upon St Paul's rhetorical questions in 2 Corinthians 6.14–15: 'What partnership is there between righteousness and lawlessness? Or what fellowship is there between light and darkness? What agreement does Christ have with Belial? Or what does a believer share with an unbeliever? What agreement has the temple of God with idols?' Such questions may create a sense of 'bad faith' for Christians visiting a Hindu temple, accepting prasad in the Sikh gurdwara, sitting in Zen meditation beneath a statue of Kwannon, or studying Sufi texts. But here we have more difficulty in looking to the Christian scriptures to guide us. Neither Old Testament nor New Testament knows anything of the Buddha or the Indian saints, of Confucius or the Japanese masters. Chapter 4 offer some guidelines for 'A Spirituality for Religious Pluralism'.

Originality is not a virtue for a Christian theologian, and in no sense is this book simply spun from the insubstantial fantasies of my own imagination. On the contrary I continue to ask myself if there is anything in these pages that is not derived from some other place. My notes will give some clues as to the written sources I have used, but much more in these pages is the result of the conversations I have had with men and women of most of the major Christian traditions, coming from churches in every part of the world. In all six continents Christians have been asking themselves how they can remain faithful to Jesus Christ and yet affirm the presence of God with other men and women. That this has not been an easily resolved question for any of them can be seen from Appendix 1 to this book, which tells the story of the struggle of the World Council of Churches to find an affirmative theology of religion. In these last two years, a group of scholars from three areas of its life, the Commission on World Mission and Evangelism, Faith and Order, and the Office of Inter-Religious Relations (now the Team for Interreligious Relations and Dialogue), has once more taken up the task of setting out an ecumenical position concerning God's dealings with humanity. This group met in Bossey, Switzerland, in the autumn of 2003 and in the autumn of 2004, producing the document *Religious Plurality and Christian Self-Understanding* that is printed as Appendix 2. I was privileged to be part of this group and I hope that *In Good and Generous Faith* may be seen as a small contribution in support of this statement.

Are you envious because I am generous?

— *Matthew 20.2*

For Christians, involvement in dialogue produces constant reappraisal of our understanding of the Biblical and theological tradition. Dialogue drives all communities to self-criticism and to re-thinking the ways in which they have interpreted their faith traditions. Dialogue brings about change in the experience of faith, helping people to deepen and grow in their faith in unexpected ways. (WCC, *Ecumenical considerations for dialogue and relations with people of other religions*, 2002)

1

All the Peoples of God

A SALVATION HISTORY FOR RELIGIOUS PLURALISM

In this chapter we will reconsider the conception of salvation history as it finds expression in the churches' lectionaries and courses of study. In the way the story is most often told a great deal of important material is omitted from the teaching schemes worked out by the churches' theologians and liturgists. As a consequence many aspects within the biblical tradition are never brought to the attention of Christian congregations. We shall try to recover some of these great themes and show their importance for a different kind of salvation history.

WHAT IS SALVATION HISTORY?

Salvation history is a method for reading and interpreting the Bible. With 66 books written in three languages, collected at various periods and in various locations, the Bible presents enormous problems to the reader.[1] But how can Christians find any sense of unity in such a wide variety of material? One answer is to choose one of the Bible's many themes as a hermeneutical key, a principle through which the 66 books

may be given their proper place in the story. Such hermeneutical keys
were forged from theological convictions that arose from close attention to one or another part of the biblical corpus. Thus intense study
of the Letter to the Romans led Martin Luther to his 'discovery' that
salvation was by faith through grace alone and to his emphasis on the
teaching of St Paul. In the later part of the nineteenth century many
Christians were challenged by what they saw as the biblical teaching
about the 'social gospel' and focused on the Old Testament prophets
and the Synoptic Gospels, especially the Sermon on the Mount. Before
the end of the nineteenth century both evangelicals and liberals had
created their own 'canons' within the canon, privileging certain parts
of the scriptures over others.[2] This often led to pastors and preachers
using only a slim selection of the biblical books in their sermon preparation, often as few as 15 or 20 of the 66. This can hardly be called
'declaring the whole word of God'.

In the twentieth century another significant hermeneutical key was
forged to bring a sense of unity to the content of the 66 books. This
is commonly known by its German title, *Heilsgeschichte,* the literal
meaning of which is 'salvation history'. The Swiss scholar Oscar Cullmann was a prime exemplar of this approach. His famous book *Christ
and Time* (1949) sees the event of Jesus as standing in the middle of
history.[3] The shape of this history is like an hour-glass: large at the
top then narrowing down to a very small aperture, then widening out
again. This story of the redemptive community begins with the covenant with Abraham and all the people of Israel. It includes the events
of Passover and Exodus and the covenant at Sinai. Twelve tribes were
involved in these events, but then begins what Cullmann calls 'pro-
gressive reduction'. In the eighth century ten tribes were lost, leaving
but two. In the exile to Babylon the faithful community narrowed
down still further. In the Suffering Servant of Deutero-Isaiah and the
Son of Man in the book of Daniel we see the beginnings of the idea
of the Remnant, narrowing down still further to the small communities who waited for the consolation of Israel, like the circles described

in the first chapters of Luke. Then it becomes limited to one person: the one faithful Israelite, Jesus of Nazareth. But after Easter Day the story of redemption changes completely. It becomes ever wider. From the tiny company of the first apostles it expands to the ingathering of the day of Pentecost. Then the movement from Judaea and Samaria reached out into Asia Minor and on into Europe. In the eighteenth and nineteenth centuries the birth of the worldwide missions took the gospel message to the ends of the earth, and the gospel will progress until every knee shall bow and all creation confess him as Lord. Cullmann wrote in 1949:

> *Thus the entire redemptive history unfolds in two movements: the one proceeds from the many to the One; this is the Old Covenant. The other proceeds from the One to the many; this is the New Covenant. At the very mid-point stands the expiatory deed of the death and resurrection of Christ . . . Common to both movements is the fact that they are carried out according to the principle of election and representation. This principle then is decisive for the present phase of development which proceeds from the mid-point. The Church on earth, in which the body of Christ is represented, plays in the New Testament conception a central role for the redemption of all mankind and thereby for the entire creation.*[4]

Cullmann is in good faith expounding what he understands to be the 'gracious process' in the saving activity of God. Based on this 'principle of election and representation' he can speak of the history of one people as determinative for the salvation of all people. 'Out of sinful humanity God chose one community, the people of Israel, for the salvation of the world.'[5] In his next chapter Cullman reinforces this idea of the single community by stressing the Greek adverb *ephapax*, one and for all, acknowledging that the prophetic view that sees salvation as effected in a single history is 'foolishness'.[6] Yet, says Cullmann, this is the 'essence of the Primitive Christian proclamation'.[7]

THE PROBLEMS OF THIS 'SALVATION HISTORY'

In his recent book *From East and West: Rethinking Christian Mission*, D. Preman Niles highlights some of these words of Cullmann. He comments that what is worrying about this scheme is the ontological status given to those within 'salvation history' and the implied negative condition of everyone outside it. Others are outside this process because of their sin and can only be incorporated into the elite people of God through conversion. This position, says Niles, has quite astonishing consequences even within the framework of biblical thought. He instances some of them. Where for example in this salvation history are Hagar and Ishmael, through whom Muslims and particularly Arab Muslims claim their inheritance of faith as the descendants of Abraham and Sarah?[8]

But, perhaps more importantly, Niles also sets the Asian questionmark against seeing salvation history as Cullmann sets it out. The whole population of Asia from the Middle East to East Asia makes up two-thirds of the population of the world, yet two centuries of Western mission activity has made Christians of just 2.5 per cent of the population of Asia (there were of course millions of Christians in Asia before the beginning of Western missionary work). *Heilsgeschichte* is bound to be 'an unfulfilled dream', says Niles, because 'mission as the propagation of the Christian faith to gather more adherents has come to an end'.[9]

The Asian situation raises other questions that Western Christians (who include North Americans and as well as Christians from English-speaking parts of the southern hemisphere) need to take rather more seriously. For Asia the experience of religious pluralism is not a new thing as it is for the West, but has been part of everyday life for centuries. Christians in Asia have a quite different experience: as the Indian Theological Association put it in 1989: 'As we perceive the sign of the Absolute Presence also in the lives of our brothers and sisters around us professing various religions, we ask in the light of the divine truth revealing itself what we should affirm about these religions, and how we [should] understand the purpose and meaning of the wonderful religious variety around us and its role and function in the attainment of salvation . . .'.[10] Since there are no Western parallels, Western theologians in general have no history of thinking about affirming such religious variety and become easily content with one or other version of *Heilsgeschichte*.[11]

The Sri Lankan theologian Wesley Ariarajah sees the issues here as turning upon the doctrine of creation. Indeed the theologies that have adopted the kind of salvation history we have been describing have little to say about 'creation'.[12] Ariarajah writes:

> *In much of protestant theology creation just sets the stage or becomes no more than a prelude to the 'fall' and the consequent drama of salvation. An undeveloped theology of creation lies at the heart of the protestant inability to deal with plurality. Today there is a new interest in creation but it is more in relation to the natural environment than to the peoples who fill the earth. Since Asian and African (and many other) cultures and histories are all equally beyond the framework of the Biblical drama of redemption they are made secondary and subsidiary in God's purposes.*[13]

The plea therefore is for another version of salvation history that affirms God's presence throughout creation. This will have to look beyond the single biblical pattern discerned by Cullmann and his many Western colleagues and offer a different telling of biblical story. What is set out now is a biblical salvation history that sees creation as God's first act in redemption. Unlike *Heilsgeschichte* it starts way back before the call of Abraham, and so to speak, long before the disobedience of Adam and Eve and the curse that befell them as a result. Therefore it offers a much broader theological perspective within which to see the redemption of all the peoples of the world.

THE REDISCOVERY OF THE DOCTRINE OF CREATION IN THE NINETEENTH CENTURY

The first Western theologian to concern himself, in good and generous faith, with the world's religious traditions was Frederick Denison Maurice (1805–71). In *The Religions of the World and their Relations to Christianity* he wrote with appreciation of the role and personality of Muhammad as 'a witness of God', even of 'Mahomet's witness for the gospel'; of the 'Hindu desire for spiritual oneness with the divine and their insight into the meaning of sacrifice'; of 'the Buddhist side of Christianity'; of 'Christian Buddhism' and of the 'wisdom and power of the Buddha'. Maurice was utterly convinced that it was vital to 'preserve the precious fragments of truth' that may be lodged in other religions. It was fundamental, he argued, to true religion, that Christians should 'think with delight' on any facts in past or present ages which were indications of the desire to do the will of God, as 'indications of God's will however perverted by man's ignorance or selfishness'.[14] Maurice was able to put these perceptions into a broader theological framework. He had become convinced that the creation narrative in Genesis 1 was the starting-point for all Christian theology (and not the story of the fall in Genesis 3), and had spelled this out in his great work *The Kingdom of Christ* (1838, revised 1842). In *The Religions of the World*, Maurice's clearest expression comes in this passage:

> We turn to the earliest of the Jewish records, and find it declared that God made man in his own image, and gave him dominion over all the other creatures he had formed. Before a word has been said about the difference of one people from another, here is a broad fundamental assertion respecting man as man. Perhaps you will say, 'Yes; but this is set at naught by one which immediately follows it; the fall of Adam is the real, though the creation of Adam of man may be the nominal, beginning of the history.' As we are examining the record to find what they actually confirm, I consider the simplest, nay, the only honest method, is to take them where they seem to begin, not to assume a starting point of our own.[15]

Nowhere in the Bible, Maurice insisted, was it ever suggested that 'the constitution of God was nullified, destroyed or even at all affected by the evil acts of man'. Certainly the very first man forgot that he was made in the image of God, and 'denied the law after which he was created'. But that altered nothing in God's being.

> But neither the first man nor any of his successors could make this degradation or disobedience anything else than an anomaly and a contradiction. The worst man in Scripture is never represented as evil in any other sense than he fights against the law under which he exists, and of which his very transgression is the continual witness. And therefore in the Bible God is ever represented as addressing himself to the creature whom he had formed, as awakening in him by his voice a consciousness of his right condition.[16]

Consequently Maurice is able to affirm the pluralism and diversity in God's dealings with all humanity bringing forth, as he writes in a different context, 'a wonderful testimony, borne from the ends of the earth, from such a medley of strange people, so different in their thoughts, so incoherent in their utterances'. There is, says Maurice, a life-giving Spirit, meant for all humanity; which all may possess together, which alone can bring our universe out of chaos, unity out of vision. This is the Spirit who brooded upon the face of the waters, and still, we may add, renews the face of the earth.

THE COVENANT THAT IS CREATION ITSELF

Creation is already a covenant of grace. So different from Maurice, and proceeding within a totally different theological framework, Karl Barth (1886–1968), the great Swiss Protestant theologian of the twentieth century, expounded this view in his *Church Dogmatics*. Under the twin headings: 'Creation as the external basis of the Covenant' and 'the Covenant the internal basis of Creation',[17] Barth sees these twin themes as expressions of God's eternal purpose in Christ to elect the entire human race into a reconciled relationship with God-self. All human beings are the object of this reconciliation *(Versöhnung)* and the covenant made in creation is with them all. Barth refers continually to the judgement of Genesis 1.31: 'God saw everything that he had made and behold it was very good.'

> *Creation may be good, and is good, because the God is good who in actualizing it also justifies it. In echoing this divine judgment . . . the creature may recognize himself and his fellow creature as good. Creaturely goodness is the benefit of creation. Hence the recognition of creaturely good is the recognition of the benefit inherent in creation on the basis of the self-disclosure of the Creator.*[18]

The covenant made with human beings rests on this understanding of creation. 'In virtue of its being and nature the creature is destined, prepared and equipped to be a partner of this covenant. This covenant cannot be seriously threatened or attacked by the nature of the creature or its surroundings nor by any attributes of man and the world. By its whole nature man is destined and disposed for the covenant.'[19]

To be sure Barth nowhere refers to religious pluralism, and indeed on his own first principles he would see all religious manifestation as avoiding the issue of grace.[20] Our point here is that Barth not only is a stranger to those who see the fall as the starting-point of Christian theology, but offers Christians the opportunity to see themselves as standing alongside men and women everywhere who exist within, and because of, the covenant of creation, the covenant of grace.

THE COVENANT THAT PERSISTS THROUGH
THE GENERATIONS

One of the great themes in the biblical beginning of the story of redemption is found in a sequence of teaching that is linked by the word 'generations', *tol^edoth* (Gen. 2.4; 5.1; 6.9; 10.1; 11.10; 11.27[21]). This sequence begins with the conclusion of the magnificent liturgical or Priestly account of the creation of the world, in Genesis

1.1–2.4: 'These are the generations [tol*doth*] of the heavens and earth when they were created.' At this point is inserted the Jahwist account of creation and fall and the story of Cain and his descendants which continues to the end of chapter 4. But then in Genesis 5.1, the Priestly writers take over with a ringing declaration: 'This is the book of the generations of Adam' (my translation, *zeh sepher tol*doth* 'adam*). This 'book' tells us of the new line of Seth, the true descendants of Adam, in place of the aberrations of Genesis 4.17ff. The *tol*doth* of Seth are listed: Enosh, Kenan, Mahalalel, Jared, Enoch, Methuselah, until Lamech the father of Noah. In 5.29 we are given an interpretation of Noah's name: 'Out of the ground that the Lord has cursed this one shall bring us relief from our work and from the toil of our hands.' Noah, as his name suggests, is a redemptive figure.[22] After the interspersion of the story of the *n*philim* and the growth of wickedness in the earth in Genesis 6.1–8, the Priestly narrative resumes in 6.9: 'these are the generations of Noah' (my translation, *'elleh tol*doth* noach*). Then follows the interweaving of both Jahwist and Priestly Material concerning the flood. This ends with the Jahwist's affirmation: 'I will never again curse the ground because of humankind, for the inclination of the human heart is evil from youth; nor will I ever again destroy every living creature as I have done' (Gen. 8.21). This also is a promise of redemption.

The Priestly narrative then resumes in Genesis 9.1, with its depiction of a universal or cosmic covenant with all humanity, that is with Noah and his descendants. This is a covenant of both preservation and redemption.[23] God's intention to make this covenant is first mentioned to the redemptive figure, Noah, before the Flood, Genesis 6.18, 'But I will establish my covenant with you . . .', and for this the ark was to be the instrument of preservation. Like other Old Testament covenants the covenant with Noah is established by the more powerful partner in the bargain; all that humanity can offer in return is its evil imagination, see 8.21 again. Yet despite the presence of evil in the human heart, the image of God is not lost. The covenant is made with those who still bear the image of God, see Genesis 9.6, cf. 1.26–7 and 5.1–3, all material from the Priestly tradition that uses the Hebrew terms *tselem* and *demuth*, 'image' and 'likeness'. These qualities are not erased because of the transgression of Adam and Eve. The covenant with Noah is a covenant for ever, a *b^erith 'olam*, in 9.16. Like other Old Testament covenants it has its sign, *'oth*. Here the sign is the bow (*qesheth*), usually translated as though it was a rainbow, but that means something closer to a war-bow with its terrifying arrows of destruction.[24] Here the war-bow is now reversed and points towards the heavens (*ha-shemayim*), that is so to speak at the heart of God. The Asian theologian C. S. Song writes of the Noachic covenant thus: 'God binds himself with a covenant as a sign of his repentance as well as his promise. The covenant is thus the reality of God's pain-love for his creation.'[25] As it points away from humanity the bow will function as a reminder to God, if God should ever forget the everlasting covenant just enacted (*liz^ekhor b^erith 'olam*) (Gen. 9.16). And God says: 'When the bow is in the clouds, I will see it and remember.' In this way the prologue of Genesis makes it clear that long before the call of Abraham, the divine redemptive purpose was already at work among peoples and nations. They are seen as all having their common ancestor in Noah. In Genesis 10 the compilers of the Genesis material turn to these nations in the form of genealogies (*tol^edoth*) of the sons of Noah.

As with other chapters of the Bible made up of genealogical lists, Genesis 10 hardly appears in church lectionaries or selections for daily Bible study. This is not only because it makes for rather tedious reading, but also because its does not reflect the *Heilsgeschichte* pattern previously decided upon. Consequently the vision of Genesis 10 is largely unfamiliar to most Christians. It is however strikingly important. First, Genesis 10 teaches that the expansion over the then known world of 'with their own language, by their families, in their nations' (*lil^eshono, l^emish^ep^echotham, b^egoyehem*) in 10.5 was part of God's 'pluralist' plan. It is clear they were to flourish with God's blessing, in the case of Nimrod in 10.9, 'before the Lord' (*liphne jhwh*). Second, the common ancestry of the peoples is repeatedly asserted and their destiny to live in harmony in spite of racial and linguistic differences is implied. Third, Genesis 10 clearly has a different view of the origin of language from Genesis 11.1 ('Now the whole earth had one language [*saphah*] and the same words'). In Genesis 10 the languages of humankind were created by God, who appears to be committed to diversity. Fourth, because all humanity belongs to the families (*mish^ep^echoth*) of the sons of Noah (*b^ene Noach,* 10.32), the basis for biblical universalism is to be found in this chapter.

TWO WAYS OF READING GENESIS 11.1–9

As we have just noted, Genesis 11 begins: 'Now the whole earth had one language and the same words.' At first sight this is a contradiction of what we have just been looking at in chapter 10. The exegetical and lectionary tradition normally pays no attention to this discrepancy, and treats the Babel story as showing God's continuing action in judgement against sinful humanity, consequent upon their expulsion from paradise in chapter 3. The plurality of languages of humankind is a punishment for hubris: 'Come, let us build ourselves a city, and a tower with its top in the heavens, and let us make a name for ourselves' (11.4). There is however an alternative way of reading these verses, familiar in Jewish exegesis.[26] This sees the story as being primarily concerned with the human resistance 'to the divine will that the children of men be dispersed over the whole world'.[27] The key concept here is the instruction given to humanity in Genesis 1.28, 'Be fruitful and multiply, and fill the earth'. What is taking place at Babel is stagnation, for the people are refusing to move on. Armed with a false sense of unity given to them by the use of 'one language and the same words' they planned, as Preman Niles puts it, 'to move upward and make a name for themselves through the construction of a tower reaching to the sky'.[28]

The point of the story therefore lies not in the creation of languages but in God's intention to scatter the peoples over the face of the earth (11.9).[29] Among these peoples are the descendants of Shem with whom the remainder of the chapter is concerned. The listing of the *tolᵉdoth* of Shem ends with the settlement by Terah and his son Abram in Haran (Gen. 11.31–2). The stage is only now set for the *Heilsge-schichte* redemption story which begins with God's special salvation activity through the one in whom all the families of the world will bless themselves (Gen. 12.3; cf. Rom. 4.1–25; Gal. 3.29).

When Christians recover the importance of the *tolᵉdoth* theme for religious pluralism, they find that it was never lost in Jewish exegesis of the Bible. Here for example is the record of a discussion among Jewish scholars in the second century of the Christian era. The question had been put 'What is the greatest scripture in the Torah?' One scholar present answered, 'You shall love your neighbour as yourself' (Lev. 19.18). Rabbi Akiba responded, 'This is the greatest principle in the Law.' But then Rabbi Simeon Ben Azzai said the sentence, '"This is the book of the generations of Adam [*zeh sepher toledoth 'adam*]" is even greater than the other' (*Sifra* 89). What he meant by this is complemented by a sentence from the Mishnah: 'Again but a single man was created for the sake of peace among mankind, that none should say to his fellow, "My father was greater than your father"' (*Sanhedrin* 4:5).

These reflections represents authentic traditions of the Jewish people who have always known that the world was created for the sake of the covenant — not just the covenant with their father Abraham but also the covenant with Adam and all his descendants, with all human-ity: Jesus ben Sirach, the writer of the book known as Ecclesiasticus, summed this up a century before the coming of Christ:

The Lord created human beings out of the earth.
He made them in his own image.
He gave them dominion over beasts and birds.
He filled them with knowledge and understanding, and showed them good and evil.
He set his eye upon their hearts to show them the majesty of his works.
And they will praise his holy name, to proclaim the grandeur of his works.

He bestowed knowledge upon them and allotted to them the law of
life.
He established with them an eternal covenant. (Ben Sirach 17.1,
3, 5, 7 and 8–12)[30]

Our Jewish counterparts have also glimpsed the redemptive purpose
in God's creating: as in this passage which speaks of God's yearning
for humankind:

In the beginning, two thousand years before the heaven and earth,
seven things were created: the Torah written with black fire on white
fire and lying in the lap of God; the divine throne erected in the
heavens – paradise on the right side, hell on the left side; the celes-
tial sanctuary in front of God – having a jewel on its altar graven
with the name of the Messiah; and a voice which cries aloud, 'return
O ye children of men'. *(emphasis mine,* Peshikta 54a)

THE UNIVERSAL COVENANTS AND THE
COVENANT WITH ISRAEL

In the *Heilsgeschichte* sense the first eleven chapters of the book of
Genesis formed but a prelude for 'salvation history'. The 'real' history
starts with Abraham. But in setting out a 'salvation history for religious pluralism' we move in a different direction. God's great saving
acts — the calling of Abraham, the deliverance from Egypt, the giving of the commandments, the entry into the promised land — make
full sense only in the context of God's dealing with all the nations of
humankind; indeed it is for the sake of these nations that the covenant with Abraham is made: 'by you all the families [*mishᵉpᵉchoth*]
of the earth shall bless themselves' (Gen. 12.3). Israel has a mission to be a blessing (*bᵉrekah*) for the world. But too often religious
nationalism and particularism led to the setting on one side of this
mission. Yet at times when Israel became exclusivistic and turned in
upon itself there were many voices raised in protest, and they are to
be found throughout the Hebrew scriptures.

Two ways of examining this material are open to us. One is to look at the many instances in the biblical literature where 'the nations' are spoken of appreciatively. The second is to examine the places where clearly outsiders to the covenant with Israel are seen as exemplars, instructors, or in modern jargon dialogue partners with the Jewish people. We begin by examining the many instances where the biblical record affirms the nations or peoples.

THE 'NATIONS' IN THE PSALMS

'Gradually . . . the custom became established of reserving the noun "people" for Israel, the elect people of God, the People *par excellence;* and of designating other peoples by the word "nations" with a depreciative nuance.'[31] Though there is truth in this judgement, close examination of the word *'am,* people, in the Psalms shows that it may be used for the 'people of Israel', but not exclusively so; other groups may be called by this term as in Psalm 18.43, 'You delivered me from strife with the peoples, *'ammim.' 'Ammim* may be used synonymously with goyim and le *'ummim* as, for example, in Psalm 9.5, 8 and 12. In Psalm 47.1 we have, 'Clap your hands, all you peoples [*kol-ha 'ammim*], shout to God with loud songs of joy'; in 47.3, 'He subdued peoples [*'ammim*] under us, and nations [*le'ummim*] under our feet'; and 47.8, 'God is king over the nations [*goyyim*]'. Then in 47.9 the Massoretic text reads: *n*e*dibe 'ammim n*e *'esaphu } am 'elohe 'abh*e*raham.* Translated word-by-word, this means, 'leaders of peoples gather themselves people of the God of Abraham'. Here is a sample of what the translators of modern English versions have done with this: 'the rulers of the nations assemble with the people of the God of Abraham' (GNB); 'the leaders of the nations rally to the people of the God of Abraham' (Jerusalem Bible); 'the princes of the nations assemble with the families of Abraham's line' (NEB). Compare with these the NRSV: 'The princes of the peoples gather as the people of the God of Abraham', and the KJV: 'The princes of the people are gathered together, even the people of the God of Abraham.' Limits of space forbid me to go into the reasons that may have been used to justify the first three of these translations: we can note however that they are consonant with salvation history as *Heilsgeschichte,* in which it is possible for the outsider to join the single redemptive people.

However, a consistent reading of the Psalms leads us to think that the NRSV has the correct rendering. The concept of all the nations being the peoples of the God of Abraham is in line with Psalm 82.8: 'For all the nations [*ha-goyyim*] belong to you', and with Psalm 87, where we have the graphic picture of the Lord registering his peoples (*'ammim*). 'Among those who know me I mention Rahab and Babylon, Philistia too, and Tyre, with Ethiopia' (87.4). As their names are called so God declares: 'Of Zion it shall be said, This one and that one were born in it' (87.5). Psalm 87 is speaking of the eschatological pilgrimage of the nations to the city of Zion, the centre and the navel of the earth. Many other psalms see the same vision of the gathering of the peoples on the holy mountain of God, e.g. Psalm 96, 97, 98, 99 and 100, for 'He will judge the world with righteousness and the peoples with equity' (Ps. 98.9). 'For the Lord is great in Zion, he is exalted over all the peoples' (Ps. 99.2). While certainly there are some psalms which express vindictiveness towards the nations, such as Psalm 149.7 or Psalm 147.20, the general theme is God's future or eschatological act: 'the nations [*goyyim*] will fear the name of the Lord and all the kings of the earth your glory' (Ps. 102.15). So that at that time 'the name of the LORD may be declared in Zion, and his praise in Jerusalem, when peoples [*'ammim*] gather together, and kingdoms [*mamelakhoth*], to worship the Lord' (Ps. 102.21–2).

There is a very striking feature of this eschatological expectation in Psalm 102, where there is a reference to a people that has as yet to come into existence. Here is a random sample of contemporary versions as they translate Psalm 102.18: 'a people yet unborn shall praise the Lord' (NEB); 'a race still to be born . . .' (Jerusalem); 'a people not yet born' (GNB); 'a people yet unborn' (NRSV). This unanimity is remarkable, but one may wonder if full justice has been done to the profundity of the Psalmist's insight. The words '*am nibera*' mean literally 'a people to be created'. Notice here the special Hebrew root *br'* which is used normally for decisive acts on the part of the Creator God, as, for example in Genesis 1.1, 21, 27 and in Isaiah 65.17, 'I create a new heaven and a new earth', and 65.18, 'I am about to create Jerusalem as a joy, and its people as a delight'. As with Isaiah this Psalmist is concerned about a new people, fresh created. So the KJV translators were wiser than our contemporaries in writing 'the people which *shall be created* shall praise the Lord' (emphasis mine). Thus in Psalm 102.22 the vision is clear: all humankind will 'declare in Zion the name of the Lord, and in Jerusalem his praise, when peoples ['*ammim*] gather together, to worship the LORD' (KJV). In the new heaven and new earth all humanity is to be gathered. We shall see this theme taken up again in the vision of Revelation 21 and 22.

THE 'NATIONS' IN THE LATER PROPHETS

A similar vision of a time to come when all God's peoples will be created anew is found in three places: in the writings of Isaiah, in the book of Jonah, and in the book of Malachi, and we shall look at each of these. In general, however, the theme of the activity of God among the nations in the prophetic literature needs no great spelling out. Amos rebuked his hearers for thinking they were special by telling them that the Lord had brought the Philistines from Caphtor, and the Syrians from Kir (Amos 9.7). In eighth-century Jerusalem Isaiah proclaimed that Assyria would become the rod of God's anger against his own godless nation (*goy*), and people ('*am*) of his wrath (Isa. 10.6). See too Jeremiah 18.7–10, where the constant intervention of God in the affairs of the nations is also described. Much of this material is associated with messianic Zionism. As in the Psalms, the nations will go up as pilgrims to Zion (see Isa. 2.2–4; Jer. 16.14ff.). Zechariah says, 'Many peoples and strong nations shall come to seek the LORD of hosts in Jerusalem . . . In those days ten men from the nations of every language shall take hold of a Jew, grasping his garment and saying, "Let us go with you, for we have heard that God is with you"' (8.22–3). This is the vision of Isaiah 2.3: 'Many peoples shall come and say "Come, let us go up to the mountain of the LORD, to the house of the God of Jacob; that he may teach us his ways and that we may walk in his paths".' To be sure, this is not a clue to living with religious pluralism, portraying as it does an eschatological vision in which the views and attitudes of one people are vindicated in a kind of centripetal mission: they do not have to go to the nations, the nations will come to them.

Chapter 19 of Isaiah, however, gives a remarkable nuance to this vision. In 19.16–24 we have a series of prose fragments that have been appended to the harsh oracles against Egypt in verses 1–15. Though it is impossible to date these fragments with any accuracy, their view-point is not merely historical. Assyria had presumably long ago ceased to exist yet both Assyria and Egypt became figures for all the nations who are called to share in the covenant made with Abraham. Note that in that day there will be an altar to the Lord in the centre of Egypt, and as a further 'sign and witness' there will be 'a pillar to the Lord at its border', for says Isaiah, the Lord will make himself known to them in their own land and 'he will listen to their supplications and heal them' (19.22). 'On that day Israel will be the third with Egypt and Assyria, a blessing in the midst of the earth, whom the Lord of hosts has blessed, saying, "Blessed be Egypt, my people, and Assyria the work of my hands, and Israel my heritage"' (19.24). Israel will then share in a larger community of faith. Indeed, this union of all human-kind in the service of God, also expressed in 2.2–4, is precisely the centre of the Christian hope for all peoples.

Alongside this vision of Isaiah which has been called a religious peak in the Old Testament,[32] we place some comments on the book of Jonah. The prophet Jonah (his name means, literally, a 'dove') was given a message of judgement against Nineveh, a city that was for the Israelites the symbol of military power and aggression. Jonah proclaimed the downfall of Nineveh, but then the people repented, to the very great displeasure of the Israelite prophet.[33] Then God repented, and 'changed his mind about the calamity that he had said he would bring upon them' (3.10).

In the story Jonah found this very hard to take, and he sulked. This led God to rebuke Jonah, 'And should I not be concerned about Nineveh, that great city, in which there are more than a hundred and twenty thousand persons who do not know their right hand from their left, and also many cattle' (4.11). The message of the book of Jonah is even more far-reaching than just a proclamation of free forgiveness: in Edmond Jacob's words, 'The nations will know in their turn that God is not only the master of universal history, but that he is merciful and compassionate, and that his kingship is fulfilled in his love. From that point onwards there is no need to go to Jerusalem; it is possible to be at the same time a citizen of Nineveh and a worshipper of Yahweh.'[34]

With these two passages in mind we turn to Malachi 1.11: 'From the rising of the sun to its setting my name is great among the nations, and in every place incense is offered to my name, and a pure offering; for my name is great among the nations, says the Lord of hosts.' Some scholars have sought to interpret these words as referring to the worship of proselytes, or to worship offered by Jews in the diaspora, or even as some kind of syncretistic ideal. Others have avoided the plain sense of the words by projecting them into the future. In the context of Isaiah 19 and the book of Jonah this could be seen as an eschatological hope: the days are coming when there will be a pure offering among all the nations. (There are notable modern versions of the Bible that reflect this interpretation by translating *gadol sh^emi baggoyim* as 'my name will be great'.[35]) But a more careful examination of the context shows that Malachi is contrasting the bad behaviour of his audience with how much better things are done elsewhere in the world, of which he is fully aware (we should not fail to note that a Persian word for governor, *pechah,* is used in verse 8). His point is to compare the unworthy offerings of his hearers, in verses 7ff., with the better practices in surrounding nations. Malachi was asserting that in their religious activity, as for example in the Persian (Zoroastrian) worship of Ahura Mazda, they worshipped the one true God with a 'pure offering' (*minchah t^ehorah,* v. 11). The inadequate and insincere offerings that were being offered in the Jerusalem temple were in stark contrast to those of the nations surrounding Israel: 'For I am a great

King, says the Lord of hosts, and my name is reverenced among the nations [sh*e*mi nora' baggoyim]' (v. 14). Malachi's rhetorical purpose is clear, but so too is his claiming for the God of Israel worship that is not offered to his name but validated by a pure heart.[36]

These are appropriate sources for understanding religious pluralism. In the prophetic writings all nations and peoples are the objects of God's activity; God created them and God will redeem them. In the end-time they will be gathered every one to God, not simply as incorporated into the people of Zion but as themselves, smitten and yet healed, made, with Israel, a genuine part of God's new eschatological people, united with the same God who promised Abraham that all the nations should be blessed.

GOD AND PEOPLE OUTSIDE THE COVENANT

Many readers may readily agree that God rules over the affairs of the nations with deep personal care and concern. But they could be considerably more reluctant to affirm unequivocally that God has actually 'spoken' to men and women outside the special covenant people.[37] But there is considerable evidence within the Hebrew scriptures that God has done precisely this, and that those who shaped the biblical tradition were not in the least surprised that this should be the case. I want now to set out some of the biblical material that deserves careful reflection. I use for convenience the anachronistic term 'dialogue partners', not least because it adequately conveys the idea that these people accompanied the Jewish people in their religious quest.

DIALOGUE PARTNERS IN THE TORAH

The Genesis story tells us of Melchizedek, King of Salem (14.17ff.).[38] He is described as priest of God Most High, 'El-'Elyon. He blesses Abram, as he then was, in the name of God Most High. The Genesis writer clearly understands this as an authentic action on behalf of the Lord. But the situation is even more intriguing. Some firm historical traditions lie behind the record here. As a Canaanite priest Melchizedek naturally invokes his own deity by name: 'Blessed be Abram by 'El-'Elyon, maker of heaven and earth.' Abram, two verses later, uses the terminology known to him, i.e. he uses the word YHWH, to which he adds 'El-'Elyon, creator of heaven and earth. In this latter formulation the phrase 'El-'Elyon appears to be descriptive, especially in apposition to 'maker of heaven and earth'. Melchizedek, the Canaanite priest, seems to be employing 'El-'Elyon as a personal name. This terminology is independently attested.[39] But this is worth pondering. As one scholar has commented 'That later religious Hebrew literature should have identified 'El-'Elyon with Yahweh, quite probably on the basis of this passage, is readily understandable. But this appears to be the only late reflex of Gen.14. The narrative itself has all the ingredients of historicity.'[40] If this is the case Abraham is accepting a blessing from the non-Israelite priest, and offering him tithes in return. The implications of this are spelt out for us by a writer concerned with Christian missiology: 'Even while God was calling the patriarchs away from their country and their kindred to be the parents of a unique elect people, this was being done in such a way as to show the positive contribution from secular environment and pre-existing "pagan" religions. A message is being flashed to us that religion is never a new and pure creation by God but a synthesis of the best under a new inspiration from God.'[41]

A few chapters later, in Genesis 20, we find the poignant story of the encounter of Abraham and Abimelech. Abraham tries to claim that Sarah is his sister. Few commentaries focus their attention upon Abimelech, choosing rather to dwell upon scriptural impartiality in relating the failings as well as the virtues of its heroes. But Abimelech is clearly portrayed as a man of high moral quality. He has acted, as he says, 'in the integrity of my heart' (b^etam l^ebabi, 20.5). God speaks to Abimelech in a dream, and agrees 'Yes, I know that you did this in the integrity of your heart' (b^etam l^ebabka, 20.6). When Abimelech meets Abraham again, he asks him, 'What have you done to us?' Abraham replies, significantly, 'Because I thought, there is no fear of God at all in this place.' It is the same 'fear of the LORD' (yirath YHWH) that 'is the beginning of wisdom' (Ps. 111.10). It is also the quality predicated of Job, who was blameless (*tam*) and upright (*yashar*) and who feared God (*yira''elohim*) (Job 1.1). The Torah thus adds its testimony that in Abimelech the 'fear of God' is found beyond the boundaries of Israel, and certainly where Abraham did not expect it.

A further witness to the faith of people outside the boundaries of the covenant people is in Exodus 18, where there is the account of Jethro, Moses' father-in-law. He is described as 'the priest of Midian' (18.1). His story is fascinating in terms of the history of Israel's religion, and gave rise to the so-called Kenite hypothesis, i.e. that YHWH was originally the God of the Kenites, and that YHWH first revealed himself to Moses at the Burning Bush (Exod. 3.16). This hypothesis may be the explanation of verse 11: 'Now I know that the Lord is greater than all the gods.' H. H. Rowley, the Baptist Old Testament scholar of a previous generation, was among those who accepted the Kenite hypothesis, and he says about Jethro's words: 'His joy at the manifestation of Yahweh's surpassing power would be more intelligible if Yahweh was the God he served.'[42] But whether or not YHWH was a Kenite god, there are obvious implications in the inclusion within the Torah of this story of a priest of Midian offering a true sacrifice on behalf of the people of Israel. But we may note nevertheless that some later editor has discerned the oddity of this story. For clearly Exodus 18 has been displaced from its original context (see Exod. 17.1–16 and 19.1ff.). It has been suggested that this later editor took offence at the notion of a Midianite priest sacrificing to God at Sinai after God had revealed himself to Israel and had anointed Aaron to the priesthood (see Exod. 28 and 29). To avoid the issues raised by this, the editor has moved this post-covenant happening to its present position as chapter 18. But what is to be emphasized is that the tradition is quite assured: YHWH was known and worshipped outside Israel.

In Numbers 22–4 we have the early and intriguing narrative about Balaam, the son of Zippor. In 22.8 the name of YHWH is placed upon the lips of a non-Israelite soothsayer. (From this text it is apparent that those who were responsible for the book of Numbers in its final form found no difficulty in allowing that non-Israelites had fundamental insights into the will of God, as in 22.38: 'the word God puts in my mouth, that is what I must say'.) J. H. Hertz, a former British Chief Rabbi, quotes with approval this judgement: 'This recognition of God's revelation of His purposes concerning Israel to a non-Israelite is striking evidence of the universality of Judaism.'[43] We need only add 'and the universality of God's activity among the nations'.

DIALOGUE PARTNERS IN THE PROPHETS AND THE WRITINGS

In Ezekiel 14.14 and 20 we have a reference to three righteous figures: Noah, Daniel and Job. Noah we have already discussed, but the other two men are non-Israelite figures. Daniel is first mentioned in a long epic text from Ras Shamra ('the legend of Aqhat'[44]) in which Daniel is said to be a king who dispenses justice: 'He judges the cause of the widow, and vindicates the cause of the fatherless.' Dani'el means 'God has judged', and we can see that in the prophetic tradition he was held up as a paragon of wisdom and justice, even though he was a Syrian and a non-Jew.

The book of Job has as its setting the land of Uz. Most likely this was Edom, though some have reckoned it to be elsewhere, maybe north of Transjordan (east of the Lebanons). But in any case Job is portrayed as a man of the desert, a Bedouin sheikh. Whatever date we give to the book of Job or however strongly it may be insisted that in its final form it is the product of the culture and theology of Israel, the epiphany of God (the tremendous 'answer to Job' out of the whirlwind in 38.1–42.6) is presented as taking place outside the borders of Israel, 'I had heard of you by the hearing of the ear, but now my eye sees you' (42.5) spoken by a man who does not belong to Israel and who yet, in Jacques Dupuis's words, represents 'a climax of holiness'.[45] Job also demonstrates that true righteousness is possible outside the Covenant: 'I put on righteousness, and it clothed me; my justice was like a robe and a turban. I was eyes to the blind, and feet to the lame.

I was a father to the needy, and I championed the cause of the stranger' (29.14–16).

Alongside Job we may put the name of Ruth, on any reckoning one of the 'holy pagans' of the Old Testament even before she speaks the moving and beautiful words to her Israelite mother-in-law, 'Where you go I will go; where you lodge I will lodge, your people shall be my people and your God my God' (Ruth 1.16). But there are other figures in the Old Testament who live outside the Covenant. These can just be listed with no further comment at this point: Abel, Enoch, Nimrod, Lot, the Canaanite women Shua and Tamar (Gen. 38.2), Asenath (Gen. 41.50), Pharaoh's daughter (Exod. 2.5), Rahab (Josh. 2), Ithra the Ishmaelite (2 Sam. 17.25), the Queen of Sheba (1 Kings 10.1–10) and, we may add, the sailors in the story of Jonah who call upon the name of the Lord (Jonah 1.14).

So the three elements that make up the Hebrew Scripture, the Torah, the Prophets and the Writings, show in their own ways that God is at work and touches men and women outside Israel. As we turn now to the theme of 'wisdom', we discover a theology that made explicit Israel's sense of God's universal activity.

THE WISDOM TRADITION AS 'DECENTRALIZED UNIVERSALISM'

The French scholar Lucien Legrand summed up the evidence we have presented of God's activity beyond the abrahamic covenant in the phrase 'decentralized universalism'. This is in contrast to the 'centralized universalism' that often prevailed in the OT prophetic literature, where conversion to YHWH consists in turning to Israel. Legrand wrote that 'decentralized universalism is the primary context, for Israel's calling takes place in a world where men and women are deeply conscious of the presence of God'.[46] Supporting this judgement is the body of literature within the Israelite scriptures that acknowledges the crucial role of sages and wise men and women within all the nations and peoples. Such persons appear throughout the ancient Near East as the aides and counsellors of rulers, members of courts, and instructors in morals and ethics. Jesus ben Sirach tells us of his travels and exchange of ideas with such people in Israel's surrounding cultures. These circles associated with 'wisdom' offer a counterbalance to Jewish exclusivism. They were recognized as doing this by the people who determined the Jewish canon at the end of the first century of the Christian era. Wisdom literature makes up three books in the Hebrew canon: Job, Proverbs and Ecclesiastes. Two other books from the Wisdom tradition are present in the Apocrypha, the book refused by the non-Hellenistic Jews. They are the books of Wisdom and Ecclesiasticus (Ben Sirach). In tone and substance these five writings are books of 'decentralized universalism' discoverable in all the nations. In Proverbs 8.14–21, personified Wisdom says of herself,

> *I have good advice and sound wisdom; I have insight, I have strength. By me kings reign, and rulers decree what is just; by me rulers rule, and nobles, all who govern rightly. I love those who love me, and those who seek me diligently find me. Riches and honour are with me, enduring wealth and prosperity. My fruit is better than gold, even fine gold, and my yield than choice silver. I walk in the way of righteousness, along the paths of justice, endowing with wealth those who love me, and filling their treasures.*

We shall return to Wisdom and the Wisdom literature in our next chapter when we see the use to which such texts were put in the formation of Christology in the early centuries of the Church.

GODLINESS AMONG THE NATIONS IN THE NEW TESTAMENT

Support for the hour-glass view of salvation history can certainly be drawn from writings within the New Testament. For example, we find a clear understanding that in the days before Jesus there had been a faithful minority or 'remnant' in Israel, loyal to the old ways and cherishing the hope of the Messiah. In Luke this is made explicit when we are introduced to representatives of this faithful remnant like Zechariah and Elizabeth, 'both of them were righteous before God, living blamelessly according to all the commandments and regulations of the Lord' (1.6); like Simeon, 'righteous and devout, looking forward to the consolation [*paraklēsis*] of Israel' (2.25); and like Anna the daughter of Phanuel, who 'began to praise God and to speak about the child to all who were looking for the redemption [*lutrōsis*] of Jerusalem' (2.38). Also emerging from these circles was John the Baptist, who proclaimed the imminence of the arrival of a saviour and called the people to repent. Both Luke's and Matthew's Gospels have genealogies tracing Jesus' ancestry, in one case to Adam and in the other to Abraham, thus rooting him firmly within Israel, and setting him in the context of a divine plan. For many New Testament writers Jesus was the climax of a story that God even then was bringing to a fulfilment.

But to follow this 'salvation history' too closely might be to overlook God's parallel activities among the nations; to believe, in other words, that according to Matthew's narrative of Jesus' life and work, God was concerned only with the 'lost sheep of the house of Israel' and their deliverance (Matt. 10.6).[47] There are however many indications that Jesus transcends this narrowed-down understanding of his activity. Thus the Lucan narrative frequently presents a Jesus who deliberately counters the view that God was concerned only with this 'house of Israel'. So as Luke tells us, when Jesus preached his first sermon in Nazareth he truncated the Hebrew text of Isaiah 61.1, 'The Spirit of the LORD GOD is upon me, because the LORD has anointed me; he has sent me to bring good news to the oppressed, to bind up the brokenhearted, to proclaim liberty to the captives, and release to the prisoners.' The next verse in the Hebrew text reads 'to proclaim the year of the LORD's favour, and the day of vengeance of our God' (61.2). What such favour and vengeance entail is made clear in verse 5: 'Strangers shall stand and feed your flocks, foreigners shall till your land and dress your vines; but you shall be called the priests of the LORD, you shall be named ministers of our God; you shall enjoy the wealth of the nations [*goyyim*] and in their riches you shall glory' (Isa. 61.5–6).

According to Luke, Jesus stopped reading before he came to the words 'the day of vengeance' and then omitted all the following vindictive oracles against the foreign nations. In Luke 4.22, Jesus' words are described as *logoi tēs charitos,* 'gracious words', in the NRSV. They would be better translated 'words of grace' because their implications of pardon and forgiveness towards Israel's enemies were not remotely attractive to Jesus' hearers. They demanded to know who gave Jesus the right to proclaim God's pardon to their enemies ('Is this not Joseph's son?', 4.22). Luke then indicates the substance of the remainder of the sermon: the prophet Elijah was sent to Zarephath in Sidon, a Phoenician port city in modern Lebanon (1 Kings 17.8ff.) and the prophet Elisha received a soldier with leprosy from Syria (2 Kings 5.1ff.).

God is thus presented as being just as concerned with the gentiles as with the 'lost sheep' of Israel. Jesus acknowledges no middle wall of partition between them, and is presented in all four Gospels as a willing participant in conversations with a Roman centurion/military police captain (Matt. 8.5–12; Luke 7.1–10) with a woman from Syrian Phoenicia (Mark 7.24–30; Matt. 15.21–8) and with a woman from Samaria (John 4.1–30). None of these men or women is presented either as without a sense of God or as beyond the compassion of God. Indeed in Matthew's Gospel the Roman officer is described as presenting a paradigm of faith: 'Jesus was amazed and said to those who followed him, "Truly I tell you, not even in Israel have I found such faith [*tosautēn pistin*]"'(Matt. 8.10). In Luke's view Jesus clearly expects that there will be many more instances of faith like this that will come from the east and the west. We should note that faith in this context, as well as in the story of the Syrian Phoenician woman, is not an assent to some catechetical formula, but more akin to the meaning of faith (*'emunah*) in its Hebrew sense, a profound human quality of trust and commitment.[48] Its meaning here is on a level with hope and love, as in 1 Corinthians 13.

THE NATIONS IN THE ACTS OF THE APOSTLES

Luke was the only Gospel writer to write a second volume. He gives us in the Acts of the Apostles the first book ever written about church history. He is at once a careful historian and a theologian of penetrative insight with both a story to tell and a message to convey. On one side the message is dispiriting. From where he was sitting, it appeared that the generality of the Jewish people had not been inclined to accept the Christian message (though many did, see Acts 2.37ff.; 18.18; 19.8; 28.23). On the other hand he was exhilarated by the numbers of gentiles who joined the Church. Though nowhere does he give up hope for the Jewish people, Luke's ringing conclusion is, 'this salvation of God has been sent to the Gentiles [*tois ethnesin*]; they will listen' (Acts 28.28) thus fulfilling the missionary instruction given by Jesus in Acts 1.8: 'you will be my witnesses in Jerusalem, in all Judea and in Samaria, and to the ends of the earth'. These two texts frame the story of Acts, presented by Luke as a Spirit-led progress first into Samaria, then into the Greek-speaking world of Syria and Asia Minor; then into Europe, first Macedonia and then to the Greek mainland; and after sundry vicissitudes on into the capital city of the Roman empire itself.

But our interest here is not in retelling this story but in noting some of Luke's underlying assumptions about the nature of this gentile audience and of its prior commitment to goodness and godliness. We re-examine three well-known stories from this standpoint.

THE CONVERSION OF PETER IN HIS ENCOUNTER WITH CORNELIUS, ACTS 10–11

Luke is much concerned with the status of the Roman centurion Cornelius in the sight of God prior to the time of his becoming a Christian. Explicit and precise descriptions of Cornelius' pre-Christian manner of life are given in three places in Acts 10 and 11. Let us emphasize some of these expressions: he is a 'devout man who feared God', who 'gave alms generously to the people' and 'prayed constantly to God' (10.2). The messenger Cornelius sent to Peter described him as 'an upright and God-fearing man, who is well spoken of by the whole Jewish nation' (10.22) and Peter himself affirmed Cornelius as a man whose 'prayer has been heard' and whose 'alms have been remembered before God' (10.31). These are the NRSV translations and we note that many of them exactly replicate words used in the Septuagint to describe saints of the Old Testament.[49] As Peter begins his exposition of the Christian message in 10.34, he is recorded as expressing an authentic biblical judgement concerning 'good people' who live outside the Covenant. 'I truly understand that . . . in every nation [*ethnos*] anyone who fears him and does what is right is acceptable to him'. Those who live according to the pattern of the truth in the Torah are God's people even though they live outside the boundaries of Israel.

On the subject of the account in Acts 10 and 11 of the launching of the mission to the gentiles, Krister Stendahl has written, 'The slowness and resistance of the Church when it comes to such momentous new insights and new steps is described not primarily as a critique of the Church. It means to show the glories and the greatness in new applications of God's love and lack of partiality, this beyond the limits to which one was accustomed.' Later Stendahl adds, 'The Cornelius story shows that it is not easy for God to teach the Church that He does not practise partiality. To many of us the signs are strong that He has many ways of working in his world.'[50]

PAUL AND BARNABAS AMONG RURAL PEOPLE IN LYSTRA, ACTS 14.8–18

In Acts 14 we see the apostolic message encountering the paganism (in its strict sense of 'the religion of country people', Latin *pagani*) of the rural hinterland of Asia Minor. But what Paul has to say to these people who were ready to make him and Barnabas into gods is extremely impressive. Even those most remote from civilization may be aware of God; even the most superstitious of peoples are not without some clue as to God's graciousness. We need only instance Acts 14.16–17, 'In past generations he allowed all the nations to follow their own ways, yet he has not left himself without a witness in doing good – giving you rains from heaven and fruitful seasons, and filling you with food and your hearts with joy.' We note in this verse the term *euphrosunē*: 'joy', 'gladness', 'good cheer'. In similar contexts in Hebrew the word would be *simchah* (as Numbers 10.10, and in many other places; cf. Acts 2.28, quoting Psalm 16.11, 'You will make me full of gladness with your presence'). 'Rain from heaven, the provision of food and the joy of life all point to the reality of the one God.'[51] They become what a twentieth-century anthropologist called 'the sacraments of simple folk'.[52] Furthermore, Luke's tone here is quite other than that of Paul in Romans 1.18–23. There is no suggestion here that this revelation of God in creation had to work to the condemnation of these rural people. Even their mistaking Paul and Barnabas for Zeus and Hermes had within it elements of implicit faith.

PAUL'S MEETING WITH THE ATHENIAN PHILOSOPHERS

From the 'simple folk' of Lystra we turn to their exact opposites, the extreme sophisticates of Athens, the city where Plato, Socrates and Aristotle had taught. In Acts 17.6–32 there is the account of Paul before the philosophers who met in the Areopagus (the Hill of Ares/ Mars). The story of Paul's encounter is often told like this: Paul was there unintentionally, having escaped mob activity in Beroea, and while he was waiting for Silas and Timothy to catch up with him, he went on a sightseeing tour of the city. His spirit was provoked 'to see that the city was full of idols' (Acts 17.16). Therefore he 'argued' or 'disputed' in the synagogue and the marketplace with the result that he caught the attention of the Stoic and Epicurean philosophers who 'took hold of him' and brought him to the Areopagus (Paul all unwillingly as it were, in the midst of taunts and jeers). Despite all this Paul makes the most of his opportunity by attacking their superstitions, 'for', he says, 'as I went through the city and looked carefully at the objects of your worship, I found among them an altar with the inscription, "To an unknown god". What, therefore, you worship as unknown, this I proclaim to you.' Then, according to this style of exposition, he made a bad mistake. He tried to use intellectual arguments to win these intellectuals to Christ. This was a total disaster and he left Athens a chastened and a wiser man. It is no surprise therefore that when he got to his next port of call and began his ministry in Corinth he had this thought uppermost: 'I did not come proclaiming the testimony of God to you in lofty words or wisdom. For I decided to know nothing among you except Jesus Christ, and him crucified' (1 Cor. 2.1–2). The gospel message is discontinuous with Greek philosophy.

We will tell the story another way that shows a quite different understanding. In being 'full of idols' Athens was no different from any other Mediterranean city, including Tarsus his home city, but Paul was able to use this as the presenting reason for his 'disputing' in the synagogue and the marketplace. He attracted the attention of those Stoic and Epicurean philosophers with time on their hands who brought him to the Areopagus (probably an area of the Agora where there was the 'painted stoa', or portico: a favourite meeting-place for intellectual discussion[53]). The stage was now set for a confrontation between major systems of ancient thought and the new teaching of Christian faith. Luke portrays Paul as a little like a second Socrates, who also taught in the Agora.

Despite the apparent all-pervasive idolatry in Graeco-Roman cities there is little or no evidence that sophisticated philosophers had any investment in the gods. For example Epicurus (341–270 bce) had taught that human life was free from any interference by the gods. Life was an accident of nature in which there was nothing but atoms dancing in a void. Life ended with death. Nevertheless humans had to live soberly and responsibly, striving both for bodily health and for freedom from anxiety. The Stoic movement was also founded in Athens in the fourth century before Christ, taking its name from the 'painted stoa' we have just mentioned. The Stoics did not believe in the gods, any more than the Epicureans, but did have a heavy commitment to divine immanence in the form of universal reason. Reason, *logos,* permeated and ordered all things. All human beings had been endowed with the divine spark of reason, the *logos spermatikos.* Like the Epicureans, the Stoics thought that life was to be lived virtuously and rationally, and that human beings were to accept what life brought them without emotional turbulence. Such thinkers were Paul's conversation partners in Athens.

Paul began his speech by addressing the 'Athenians' as 'extremely religious' (NRSV).[54] The term here, *deisidaimonesterous,* is somewhat ambiguous, because it can mean superstitious, 'addicted to the worship of gods' (this is the way the RSV translated it in 1946 in conformity to the older interpretation of this encounter). The majority of recent commentators think, however, that it must have positive connotations here: it serves to establish a point of contact.[55] His audience would understand what Paul is talking about because they are persons of faith: 'as I went through the city and looked carefully at the objects of your worship, I found among them an altar with this inscription, "To an unknown god". What therefore you worship as unknown, this I proclaim to you' (17.23). Paul does this, first asserting a truth held by both Stoics and Epicureans: God does not 'live in shrines made by human beings nor is God served by human hands as though he needed anything'. Their own teachers had taught this much, and Paul and they shared common ground. Then boldly Paul quotes without attribution from their own Stoic or Epicurean teachers, 'In him we live and move and have our being' and 'we too are his offspring'. We can but guess who these teachers were. Perhaps one was Aratus of Soli, about 270 bce, who wrote: 'Let us begin with Zeus, streets and markets, oceans and harbours are full of him; we all need him, and we are of his family.'[56] His near contemporary Cleanthes of Soli has the words 'we are born of thee' in a hymn to Zeus.[57] From Epimenides we have these words (they are put into the mouth of Minos, the son of Zeus): 'The Cretans carve a tomb for thee, O holy and high, liars, evil beasts and slow bellies! For thou art not dead for ever, thou art alive and risen; for in thee we live and are moved and have our being.'[58]

The next verse, too, would have carried the assent of his listeners: 'being then God's offspring we ought not to think that the deity is like gold or silver or stone, a presentation by the art and imagination of man'. So far we have a perfect missionary sermon, based on the assumption that the problem before the Athenians is not human perversity but human ignorance. It is only then at verse 31 that controversy breaks out. Not surprisingly the announcement that history will end in an eschatological judgement, and that the judge will be a man raised from the dead, was simply too much for many of the people at the Areopagus. The more aggressive among them 'mocked' or 'scoffed'. But we notice that another part of the audience said 'we will hear you again about this' (17.32). Perhaps for some this meant postponing a decision without being overly hostile, but this could also mean that there were some who truly wished to pursue the matter by further dialogue. There is a third group who immediately became Christian believers, and aligned themselves with Paul: Dionysius a leading member of the Areopagus, a woman named Damaris, probably a woman of high social standing, and some others. This is hardly the story of a failure in communication.[59]

On the contrary, Luke was showing us a method for sharing the Gospel across cultural boundaries.[60] We note in 17.17 the presence of the word *dielegeto* the Greek verbal form of dialogue, even though the translations obscure this by using such words as 'argued' and 'disputed'. Since there is no true English word 'dialogued', words like 'discussed' or 'reasoned' should be used here. We should not think Paul to have been as hostile as verbs like 'argued' and 'disputed' make him sound. By his use of the ancient philosophers and the generally Hellenistic tone of his speech Luke sees Paul as setting a pattern that we shall return to when we discuss a missiology for religious pluralism in the last chapter of this book, see pp. 143ff.

The eschatological vision of the nations
in the book of Revelation

In the last section of this chapter we reflect upon a biblical vision of the way God's purposes in creation will be fulfilled. It is, to be sure, both optimistic and inclusive, in contrast with the apocalyptic passages to be found elsewhere in the New Testament. But as we have shown already in many other parts of the Bible, Christians do not need to commit themselves to a vision of judgement and exclusion in which most of God's children will perish in the flames of eternal separation. The book of Revelation is the surprising vehicle for a positive and gracious understanding of human destiny.

We need to explain why. As the most paradoxical of all the biblical writings the book of Revelation made its way into the canon only with the greatest difficulty. Intended to be read as one single letter, and not as a series of 'revelations',[61] it contains two very different sets of images picturing the final destiny of human beings. Some of these portray, or imply, a very limited salvation, suggesting that only faithful Christians will be gathered in heaven (14.9–10; 20.11–15; 21.7–8). But numerous other images suggest that God's final victory will embrace all people and all creation (1.7; 4.3; 5.13; 14.14; 15.4; 21.5; 21.22–22.3). Because John is what we might call today a 'dialectical theologian', he deliberately uses both sets of images: on the one hand exciting pictures of the ultimate triumph of God, but on the other dire portrayals of what will be the consequences of choosing to reject the truth and of living in allegiance to false gods. Both are realities: the reader is not invited to ignore either one or the other, nor are commentators invited to harmonize them. But for our purpose here the focus is on the 'universalism' of the book of Revelation.[62]

Among the great images of God's ultimate victory is the vision of the new heaven and the new earth in Revelation 21.1–22.5. This it seems is where 'salvation history' has been leading to all along, the eschatological fulfilment and renewal of the world. Immensely important issues arise out of this text and we offer some brief comments on some of them.

The vision is of a city ❋

It would be natural to expect that at the end of the human race is a return to Eden, a going back to the paradise from which they had been expelled. There the consequences of human disobedience would be reversed and expunged, humankind might be again as though the fall never happened. That such an idea has been attractive in religious history can be seen in the Qur'anic descriptions of the Islamic paradise, where those who have succeeded on their individualistic path to success enjoy their rewards as individuals. In this biblical vision there can be no nirvana world in which humans are freed from the mortal ills of earthly existence. On the contrary, John insists that the renewed and transformed life of the city of God will be a shared experience of community: to be sure without physical danger (represented by the sea, no more floods or tsunamis 21.1); without tears, death, mourning, crying, pain (21.4); and without the kinds of people who have deliberately chosen to do evil (as listed in 21.8 and 27). The image is of a great city where there is room for all (the purpose of the symbolic dimensions set out in 21.16). This is a city in which there is no temple, since the purpose for which any temple is built no longer exists: the worshippers no longer need a specific place or time to encounter God. The city and the temple will be coterminous: they are where God is present with all God's peoples.

The salvation in this city is for all the peoples of God ❋

God's dwelling (*skēnē*) will be with all humankind: for 'He will dwell with them; they will be his peoples' (*kai skēnōsei met' autōn kai autoi laoi autou esontai*, Rev. 21.3). Although many modern versions prefer to read a singular as though they were translating, *laos,* people, the textual evidence is clear. Though there is some manuscript evidence for the singular reading, which makes the text conform to Ezekiel 37.27, two authoritative texts, the Codex Sinaiticus and the Codex Alexandrinus, have *laoi* instead of *laos.* The plural form is the much more difficult one, and we ought to follow that principle of textual criticism which suggests that more weight should be given to the 'more difficult reading'. One can easily see the power of Ezekiel 37.27 to influence a scribe to inadvertently write *laos* for *laoi;* it is less easy to imagine the same scribe altering *laos* to *laoi*. The NRSV is correct in using the plural form, peoples.

We have seen the eschatological strand in the Old Testament witness: there will be a time when all the 'peoples' of God will be gathered together. We recall the eschatological pilgrimage of the nations to Zion and its temple in Zechariah 14.26. The plural form, 'peoples' in Revelation 21.3, leads us on to the gathering of the nations (*ethnē*), in the City of God (Rev. 21.22–22.2). In this city the glory of God is its light: 'The nations will walk by its light, and the kings of the earth will bring their glory into it.' These kings are the very people who have been represented as so hostile to God in the earlier pages of Revelation.

THE GLORY AND HONOUR OF THE NATIONS IS
PRESENT IN THE NEW CITY

The nations and peoples will bring into the city their glory (*doxa*) and their honour (*timē*) (21.24, 26). We may interpret both 'glory' and 'honour' to be the highest values and achievements of the cultures of the world. John does not hold the view that the world will end in nothingness, and that all human efforts will have been mere whistling in the wind. Nor does he think that ultimately God will save a handful of martyrs and let the rest of humankind perish in the abyss of non-being. In his vision the City of God is to be the fulfilment of all efforts by humans everywhere to live in the best of faith: to build worthwhile human habitations, to occupy themselves with transcendent values, create great music, art and architecture. As two recent commentators write: 'Not only religious works but all the efforts of all human history to construct a good society are taken into the eternal city. Nothing good is lost.'[63] To be sure the dross and unworthy elements in the cultural traditions and religious practices of the nations will be abandoned: 'nothing unclean will enter [the city], nor anyone who practises abomination or falsehood' (21.27). But the noblest ideals and achievements of humankind will be redeemed from all imperfections, reinvigorated and transformed by God's love. 'Nowhere', said another commentator, 'do we find a more eloquent statement than this of the all-embracing scope of Christ's work.'[64]

A TREE WHOSE LEAVES ARE FOR THE HEALING
OF THE NATIONS

We should also take note of the 'Tree of life' in Revelation 22.2, the leaves of which are for the healing of the nations (*eis therapeian tōn ethnōn*). This tree with healing leaves has always been something of a problem to the exegetes concerned about taking the eschatological details at their face value. An earlier commentator makes the point for us: 'the best sense is undoubtedly made by understanding this as during the millennium. There would be no nations to be healed when the eternal and final City is established.'[65] The author of the book of Revelation however is not trying to make this kind of sense. What he is remembering are the words of Ezekiel 47.12, where Ezekiel describes trees growing on both sides of a river, whose 'leaves will not wither nor their fruit fail, but they will bear fresh fruit every month, because the water for them flows from the sanctuary. Their fruit will be for food and their leaves for healing.' Then his vision widens. It now embraces not only the restored Jewish community gathered out of the hands of the nations (Ezek. 39.25), whose life was to be centred upon the rebuilt temple described in Ezekiel 40–8, but those very oppressor nations themselves. They too are in the City. Furthermore the vision of the book of Revelation makes it clear that the nations are not to be understood as disembodied spiritual wraiths. They will retain their social and geopolitical dimensions even in the new City. In the end-time, John implies, the nations will still be recognizable entities, still themselves, bearing the wounds of their hostility to God and to each other. Just as the Christian doctrine of the resurrection of the body points to human individuals being recognizably themselves in the age to come, so too the peoples and nations will still be distinctively themselves: smitten, chastened, but being healed by the leaves of the tree. The tyranny of Genesis 3 will be at an end: the whole creation will open once more to the grace and love of God: no flaming sword, turning every which way, guards the way to the tree of life (see Gen. 3.27). All humanity will then live in the presence of God and the history of God's saving acts will have come to fulfilment.

A SALVATION HISTORY FOR RELIGIOUS PLURALISM

We have suggested in this survey that all human history, from creation to end-time, in every phase and among all nations and peoples, must be understood as a single 'history of salvation'. Embedded in the purpose of creation is the reconciliation of all humankind to God. Now we need a way of understanding how God has communicated with humanity through all this history, and in every part of it. The earliest Christian theologians turned to the great concepts of 'the Word of God', 'the Wisdom of God', and 'the Spirit of God' that, as we have begun to see, were used to testify to such communication taking place and to show that God has never ceased to 'speak' with all the children of God. So we move to our next chapter to reflect this story. We shall see how the Christian message of the Word/Wisdom/Spirit of God becoming flesh among us enhances our understanding of how to live with good and generous faith in the midst of religious pluralism.

2

The Universal Presence of the Word

A CHRISTOLOGY FOR RELIGIOUS PLURALISM

There are currently many suggestions for a theology for interfaith dialogue, and there are several good introductions to these themes for those who wish to explore them.[1] But it appears to me that still the most helpful approach is that of a Word/Spirit/ Logos Christology, especially in the light of the biblical testimony that God has moved and still moves among the nations in self-revelation. In this chapter we shall try to set out this understanding of God's activity. There are two sections. In the first part we look at the doctrine of the Logos or Word as it emerged in the early Church, how it was lost, and then later rediscovered in the nineteenth century. This forms the theological background for the exposition of John 14.6 'no one comes to the Father but by me' in the second section. Some readers may prefer to omit the first section and proceed to the second part, perhaps returning to the first later.

We begin with an exposition of the explicit teaching of the New Testament concerning a Christology which is inclusive, all-embracing, cosmic and universal in its scope, illuminating all the processes of creation and history and human creativity in culture, arts, music, science and literature. It is a Christology of the Word, or Logos, of

God, to which the Fourth Gospel bears its astonishing witness in John 1.1–8. There are not too many indications in the first three Gospels that prepare us for the presentation of Jesus as the manifestation of a pre-existent being who enters this world from an eternal realm where he has dwelt with the Father.

There are three main theories as to the historical antecedents of the term Logos in John 1.1. For many interpreters the idea of the Logos is simply taken over from the OT usage. The Hebrew word *dabar* is almost always translated *logos* in the Septuagint, i.e. the LXX, and refers either to a divine oracle in the mouths of a prophet, the 'word of the Lord', or to the agency of God's action, whether in creation as in Psalm 33.6, 'by the word of the Lord [*dabar* YHWH] the heavens were made', interpreting Genesis 1; or liberation, 'he sent out his word and healed them, and delivered them from destruction' (Ps. 107). The word of God has its distinct reality full of power and intentionality: the Word that goes forth from the mouth of God 'shall not return to me empty, but it shall accomplish that which I purpose, and succeed in the thing for which I sent it' (Isa. 55.11). As the dynamic expression of God, the Word is God turning to human beings in self-revelation; God calling human beings to a communion of life; God at work to save and to heal.

Other interpreters see the Logos idea as having its deepest roots in the Jewish Wisdom tradition (see the first chapter). There are poems to 'Wisdom' (Hebrew *hochmah,* Greek *sophia,* both feminine nouns), in the book of Proverbs, in Ecclesiasticus (Ben Sirach), in Job and in the book of Wisdom. Proverbs 8.30 is the most telling example. Here 'Wisdom' says that when God 'marked out the foundations of the earth, then I was beside him, like a master worker ['*amon*]; and I was daily his delight, rejoicing before him always, rejoicing in his inhabited world and delighting in the human race'.[2] Other Wisdom texts, Job 28.27, Sirach 24.90, also affirm the pre-existence of Wisdom, but there are many other examples where the presence of Wisdom throughout the universe is affirmed. So the book of Wisdom calls her 'a breath of the power of God, and a pure emanation of the glory of the Almighty' (7.25), and speaks of her mission 'to renew all things'; 'in every generation she passes into holy souls and makes them friends of God and prophets' (7.27). She is the source of perfect conduct, who teaches the fear of God and justice (Prov. 3.7; 8.13; Sirach 17.14). She looks for a dwelling with humankind, but her seeking is in vain; although she comes to her own (all human beings), her own do not accept her (Sirach 24.6). For those who find her she is life itself, and those who ignore her injure themselves, indeed she declares, 'all who hate me love death' (Prov. 8.35–6). In a pre-Jesus sense she is 'the way, and the truth, and the life', universally present in the history of humankind.

The Wisdom literature also makes a close connection between the Wisdom (*hochmah*) of God, and the Spirit (*ruach*) of God. The book of Wisdom says that 'the spirit of the Lord has filled the world' (1.17; cf. Job 34.14–15), and matches the Psalmist's expression, 'When you send forth your spirit, they are created; and you renew the face of the ground' (Ps. 104.30). Almost as an exposition of these words the book of Wisdom affirms:

> *You love all things that exist, and detest none of the things that you have made, for you would not have made anything if you had hated it. How would anything have endured if you had not willed it? Or how would anything not called forth by you have been preserved? You spare all things, for they are yours, O Lord, you who love the living. For your immortal Spirit is in all things.* (11.24–12.1)

A third possibility is that the concept of the Logos came from the circles of Jewish-Hellenistic philosophy in the Mediterranean world that were particularly associated with the Jewish philosopher and exegete Philo of Alexandria (c.20 bce–c.50 ce). For Philo the Logos represented both the creative power through which God orders the world and the rational principle behind all phenomena; at the same time the intermediary through whom human beings can know God. In so far as God may be apprehended and experienced, the Logos is what is knowable about God.[3] In the second instance the Logos is truly a divine hypostasis (a refraction or manifestation of God), God's first born, through whom God creates the world. Thus in Philo's allegorical exegesis of the Septuagint, it was the Logos that spoke to Moses at the burning bush and who is symbolized throughout as the 'high priest'.[4]

With these explanations fresh in our minds, we read again the first verses of John's Gospel:

> *In the beginning was the Word, and the Word was with God, and the Word was God. He was in the beginning with God. All things came into being through him, and without him not one thing came into being. What has come into being in him was life, and the life was the light of all people. The light shines in the darkness, and the darkness did not overcome it.* (vv. 1–4 NRSV)

As we compare this declaration with the possible sources we cannot fail to hear echoes of the earlier writings, but none of these possible sources gets anywhere near the idea in 1.1 and 1.14 that God was the Word (*theos ēn ho logos*) and that the Word could become flesh (*ho logos sarx egeneto*).

THE FOURTH GOSPEL AND THE TEACHING OF ST PAUL

The New Testament uses the idea of pre-existence in relation to Jesus Christ in many places, from an almost passing remark of Paul in 1 Corinthians to the developed Pauline understanding of Colossians, the view of the Letter to the Hebrews, and material in the book of Revelation. There are also signs of a Wisdom Christology in the synoptic tradition. We go first to Paul. Among his earliest writings this often unnoticed passage occurs:

> *I do not want you to be unaware, brothers and sisters, that our ancestors were all under the cloud, and all passed through the sea, and all were baptized into Moses in the cloud and in the sea, and all ate the same spiritual food, and all drank the same spiritual drink. For they*

drank from the spiritual rock that followed them, and the rock was
Christk. (*1 Cor. 10.1–4, emphasis mine*)[5]

In equating a legend of a rock that followed the Israelites in the wanderings with Christ, Paul clearly presupposes the idea that Christ was
working in the world a long time before he was manifested as Jesus.
In Colossians 1.15–20 we have a 'Christ-hymn' in two stanzas, joyfully
praising Jesus Christ as 'the image of the invisible God, the firstborn
of all creation, for in him all things in heaven and on earth were created' (vv. 15–16); 'He is before all things and in him all things hold
together [*sunestēken*]' (v. 17). In the second stanza, Jesus is called the
'beginning, the firstborn from the dead' the one in whom 'all the fullness [*plerōma*] of God was pleased to dwell, and through him God was
pleased to reconcile to himself all things [*ta panta*]'. Such praise-lan-
guage announces that God has always been at work in a creation that
was, and is essentially, God's domain; it has never fallen in the hands
of the 'evil one'. Equally importantly it points to the cosmic scope of
the reconciling action of Jesus. No person, no thing, can abide outside
this universal purpose. Other places where this central Pauline insight
is found include 1 Corinthians 8.6: there is 'one Lord, Jesus Christ,
through who are all things and through whom we exist'; and Romans
11.36: 'For from him and through him and to him are all things. To
him be the glory for ever. Amen.'

The writer to the Hebrews also declares that Jesus is 'Son' (in the
Greek text there is no article[6]) who is appointed 'the heir of all things'
(Heb. 1.2). The writer affirms that it was through the power of this
Sonship that God created the worlds (v. 2). This 'Sonship' 'reflects the
glory of God', bears 'the exact imprint of God's very being', and upholds
the totality of everything that exists, i.e. the universe (*ta panta*), 'by his
powerful word' (1.3).

There are very few indications of the pre-existence of Christ in the
synoptic Gospels, but the thought is not unfamiliar. Personified Wisdom language does appear in Matthew 11.19, 25–30, and in 12.42,
when Jesus' detractors are complaining that 'the son of Man has come

eating and drinking' and mocking him. 'Look, a glutton and a drunk-ard, a friend of tax collectors and sinners!' Jesus appeals to 'Wisdom', saying she 'is vindicated by her deeds' (11.19). This appears to be the trigger for the profound meditation that follows about why God has hidden the secret of his teaching from the wise and understanding and has revealed them to babes: 'yes, Father, for such was your gracious will. All things have been handed over to me by my Father; and no one knows the Son except the Father, and no one knows the Father except the Son and anyone to whom the Son chooses to reveal him'. Here the parallels with the Lady Wisdom are exact: God alone knows Wisdom (Job 28.12–27; Sirach 1.6–9), the Father alone knows the Son. Only Wisdom knows God (Wisd. 9.1–18), only the Son knows the Father. As Wisdom reveals the purpose of God (Wisd. 10.10) so the Son is the revealer of God's hidden truths. And then just as Wisdom calls upon men and women to take up her yoke in Sirach 51.23–30, so Jesus tells his hearers to take upon them his yoke, 'and learn of me for I am gentle and humble in heart, and you will find rest for your souls' (11.28). 'For Matthew, Jesus is not merely the messenger of divine wisdom but he identified with the heavenly wisdom of God; he speaks not only for wisdom as other prophets did but as the divine Wisdom.'[7] In 12.42 Matthew reinforces this 'wisdom Christology' by reminding his reader of how the Queen of the South came from the ends of the earth to hear the wisdom of Solomon, yet in Jesus Christ 'something greater than Solomon is here!'

These themes are explored in a letter that is part of the Pauline writings, namely the epistle to the Ephesians. According to its magnificent Confession of Faith (Eph. 1.21–2), God has made Christ Jesus now,

> *far above all rule and authority and power and dominion, and above every name that is named, not only in this age, but also in the age to come; and he has put all things under his feet and has made him the head over all things* [ta panta] *for the church, which is his body, the fullness* [plerōma] *of him who fills all in all.*

Christ shares God's role as ruler of the universe, and the destiny of the universe is to become the Church in its fullness: where all tears have been wiped away and death is destroyed, where all people are reconciled, where history has been brought to the consummation of a faithful, loving communion. To be sure this may sound triumphalist, even vainglorious, given what we know of the state of the world and its very fallible churches, but we should rather see in these words a confession of the overwhelming difference Christ has already made through his redeeming love and the sense that ultimately this redeeming love will prevail, utterly and completely, to the ends of the earth and to the end of time.

We may also learn from the theology of Ephesians that there is no place where Christ is not already present. This has historically been a hard lesson for Western Christians to digest. The older models have spoken, for example, of a Church outside of which there no salvation, extra ecclesiam nulla salus, or of 'Christendom', the domain of Christ, beyond which there is only heathen darkness. Missionaries were called to take Christ to souls in desperate darkness, and their hymns spoke of the real absence of Christ from his world.[8] But the message of Ephesians is crystal clear:

> But each of us was given grace according to the measure of Christ's gift. Therefore it is said, 'when he ascended on high, he made captivity itself a captive; he gave gifts to his people'. When it says, 'He ascended' what does it mean but that he had also descended into the lower parts of the earth? He who descended is the same one who ascended far above all the heavens [pantōn tōn ouranōn] that he might fill all things [ta panta]. (Eph. 4.7–10)

To the straightforward question, 'Where is Christ now?' the answer is 'here, and everywhere'. To the proposition that we should take Christ to heathen lands, the only response can be that we go to meet him there (but this anticipates our later chapter on 'a missiology for religious pluralism').

These then are the grand themes of the New Testament that show us we must learn to speak of the pre-existent Christ who fills the universe. They form the basis of Christian Trinitarian theology, and challenge the Christian community when it falls into a kind of Jesus worship that becomes a unitarianism of the Son.[9] Jesus is always more than a personal saviour who offers a private religious experience, however intense, or an edifying example of moral virtues and values, however uplifting.

THE LOGOS CHRISTOLOGY OF THE EARLY CHURCH

In the search for an understanding of God's ways in the whole of creation we turn now to some of the very earliest Christian theologians, writing and teaching in Greek in the second and third centuries of the Christian era.

These theologians wrote and taught in a context far different from ours, and they were hardly concerned with religious pluralism as we know it, never having heard of either Confucius or Ramanuja, Muhammad or Guru Nanak. Furthermore they were deeply opposed to many of the religious phenomena that surrounded them in the ancient Mediterranean world, finding no room for an appreciation of the mystery cults and gnostic dualism. Nor did they like the spiritualizing and world-denying forms of middle-Platonism and Neoplatonism. These rejected the possibility of the Word becoming flesh and thus were foes of Christian theology.

But this is hardly the whole picture of the relationship of the early Christians to their environment. They did not repudiate two great spiritual movements of those centuries that have proved themselves to be of comparable depth and power to the Christian message. In the realm of thought, one was Greek philosophy; in the area of politics and society the other was the Roman empire and its legal apparatus. The Christian Church could not repudiate these movements as of no significance in the sight of God. 'On the contrary,' wrote Wilfred Cantwell Smith, 'it presently came to terms with each of them, and was in both cases deeply enriched. Internally to the Christian movement, Christian theology emerged and has continued as in some ways an amalgam of the Christian vision with the one, and the Roman Catholic and Orthodox church in some ways, structurally and otherwise, as an amalgam of Christian vision with the other'. Furthermore Christians have lived their lives in the West in relation to the Graeco-Roman philosophical legacy and in relation to government and state as a parallel involvement to their relation to the Church. 'Christians,' Smith said, 'corporately and individually, have been pluralist throughout — however uncritically, even unwittingly.'[10] Smith's judgement would have the support of many contemporary Asian and African theologians who have not failed to notice the deep syncretism of the Christian message within Western forms of thinking and social ordering.

The first thinkers positively to recognize that they had to find a way of engaging with many other aspects of Graeco-Roman culture, religion and philosophy were the second- and third-century theologians: Justin Martyr (c.100–c.165), Irenaeus (c.130–c.200), and Clement of Alexandria (c.150–c.215). What these people needed above all else was a 'salvation history' that had to do with the whole experience of humankind. Justin, Irenaeus and Clement needed to affirm that God had always been since the creation among all races and people. Doing this was pivotal to their task of showing good reasons why people should give up the customs of their ancestors and adopt what appeared to be a new religion. Formidable opponents of Christianity, like Porphyry and Celsus, objected to the Christian position on the grounds that it was an upstart doctrine, a religion with vulgar new theology.

The first argument employed by the second- and third-century writers was to insist that Moses and the Pentateuch were older than the Greek philosophers and that Greek religion was indebted to them for much of its teaching. So we have the strenuous, if not strained, efforts in Clement of Alexandria, in his *Stromateis,* book 1.20, to prove the priority of Christian doctrine.[11] But then they developed a second line of interpretation, namely that the Word was in the world before Christ

Jesus was born. Reaching towards the Logos-doctrine of John's Prologue, Justin affirmed the 'Son of God, the only one who may properly be called the Son, the Word existing with him and begotten before all creatures, when in the beginning he created and ordered all creatures'. The manifestation of this Word was apparent everywhere, long before the incarnation of this Word. In his *First Apology* 46.1–4, Justin wrote:

> *We have been taught that Christ is the first-begotten of God. He is the Logos in whom the whole human race shares. Those who have lived in accordance with the Logos are Christians, even though they were called godless, such among the Greeks, Socrates and Heraclitus, and others like them: among the barbarians, Abraham, Ananias, Azaria, Misael, and Elijah, and many others, whose deeds and names I forbear to list, knowing that this would be lengthy. So also those who lived contrary to the Logos were ungracious and enemies to Christ, and murderers of those who lived by the Logos, and those who live so now are Christians fearless and unperturbed.*

Justin elaborates this view in the *Second Apology:* for example, 'in moral philosophy the Stoics established right principles, and the poets too have expounded such because the seed of the Word [*sperma tou logou*] was implanted in the whole race'; and 'whatever law-givers or philosophers uttered well, they elaborated by finding and contemplating some part of the Word'. Thus Socrates 'knew Christ in part [*apo merous*], for Christ was and is the Logos present in all things [*ho en panti on*]'. In chapter 13, Justin claims the teaching of ancient philosophers for the Christian Church: 'The truths which men in all lands have rightly spoken belong to us Christians. For next to God we love and worship the Logos, born of the unbegotten and ineffable God, because for our sakes he became man in order to heal us of our wounds by sharing in them. These writers were able to perceive the Truth obscurely [*amudros*], thanks to the sowing [*spora*], of the Logos which had been imparted in them.'

The implications of this are clear, says Jacques Dupuis: all possession of religious truth as well as all righteous conduct come as a personal manifestation of the eternal Word. 'Christianity exists beyond its visible boundaries and prior to its historical appearing, but up to the incarnation, it is fragmentary, hidden, even mixed with error, and ambiguous.'[12] Referring to the great Roman Catholic theologian Karl Rahner, Dupuis asks, 'is this not, but for the expression, the theology of an "anonymous Christianity"?'.[13]

IRENAEUS

The patristic writer with the strongest sense of 'salvation history' is undoubtedly Irenaeus.[14] In his *Adversus omnes Haereses*, he works out a theology of the revealing Logos in this way:

> *Since it is God who works all things in all, he is, by his nature and his greatness, invisible and ineffable to all his creatures,* but not therefore unknown, *for through his Word, all learn there is one sole God and Father who contains all things, who gives being to all things, as it is said in the Gospel: 'No one has seen God at any time; the only begotten Son, who is in the beginning with the Father, he has made him known'. (emphasis mine)*[15]

This is a grander theology than that in Romans 1.18, where Paul wrote that since the creation of the world the 'eternal power and glory' of God 'have been perceived in the things that have been made'. Using their reasoning powers humans can figure out the existence of God, and even some of God's attributes. Irenaeus has no place for such 'natural knowledge': all intuitions of the divine are the work of the Logos. 'Moreover, the Word was made the dispenser of his Father's grace for the benefit of people, for whose sake he carried out such divine plans, showing God to people, presenting them to God and preserving the invisibility of his Father so that the human being should never come to despise God . . .'.[16] The first of these divine plans, or 'economies' was creation itself, in which God gives life to all who live on the earth. Irenaeus implies that this gift of life is personal knowledge, through the Word, of the Giver, for by the means of the creation itself, 'the Word reveals God the Creator'.

Again we stress that Irenaeus is not addressing issues of religious pluralism. Yet his concern for all humanity as addressed by the Word at creation directly meets the interests of Asian and African theologians who are pleading for a better doctrine of creation; at the same time it offers a theological understanding of human beings as those who have the Word firmly embedded within them: 'because the Word implanted in their minds moves them and reveals to them that there is one God, the Lord of all'.[17]

CLEMENT OF ALEXANDRIA

We find the thought of Irenaeus taken up in Clement of Alexandria, for whom all personal knowledge of God is given through the Logos: 'We understand the Unknown by divine grace, and by the Word alone that proceeds from him.'[18] Though Clement can make a distinction between an elementary knowledge of God that can be attained through the use of reason, logos as it were with a lower case l; the Logos with a capital L introduces men and women into things not glimpsed by mortal sense. This revelation, significantly for the understanding of religious pluralism, extends way beyond the Church, and may be found, for example, throughout Greek philosophy. Greek teachers had truly prophesied and seen God, through what Clement calls 'scintillations of the divine Word'. Indeed Greek philosophy constitutes part of the divine economy, even a special preparatory covenant offered to the Greeks, Clement says, 'to fit their ears for the Gospel':

> Before the advent of the Lord, philosophy was necessary to the Greeks for righteousness. And now it becomes conducive to piety; being a kind of preparatory training to those who attain to faith through

demonstration . . . philosophy was given to the Greeks directly and primarily, until the Lord should call the Greeks . . . Philosophy there, was a preparation, paving the way for him who is perfected in Christ . . . the way of truth is therefore one. But into it as into a perennial river, streams flow from all sides.[19]

Even more pertinently to our theme, Clement sees authentic guides for humanity among other nations. These include Indian sages, including Brahmins, and some of the Indians 'who obey the Buddha; whom, on account of his extraordinary sanctity they have raised to divine honour'.[20] These, too, have their place in the divine economy of the Logos.

Clement has his own evangelistic purpose to fulfil in his writings. Just as the 'Law' of the Jewish people was a schoolmaster to lead them to Christ, so too 'philosophy' had to find its completion in the Good News:

Since the Word has come to us from Heaven, we need not go . . . any more in search of human learning to Athens and the rest of Greece, and to Ionia. For if we have as our teacher him who fills the universe with his holy energies in creation, salvation, beneficence, legislation, prophecy, teaching, we have the Teacher from whom all instruction comes; and the whole world, with Athens and Greece has become the domain of the Word . . . We who have become the disciples of God have received the only true wisdom; and that at which the chiefs of philosophy only guessed at, the disciples of Christ have both apprehended and proclaimed.[21]

Despite this clear desire to affirm a qualitative difference between the 'old' apprehension of the truth and that which has come in Christ, Clement is one with Justin and Irenaeus in affirming one universal salvation history: the Word has been present among the whole human race throughout history, and consequently is the ultimate source of the concern for truth and for justice as well as the piety (*eusebeia*) also apparent in the religious and philosophical traditions of the world.

ATHANASIUS

One last testimony from the patristic writers comes from Athanasius (c.296–373), patriarch of Alexandria and primate of Egypt, but a Greek by birth and education. In two small but influential treatises, he set out the Logos doctrine. In his 'Treatise against the Greeks' (*Ad Gentes*), where his intended dialogue partners were thinkers like Porphyry and the Emperor Julian who asserted that God governed the world through intermediaries, Athanasius asserted, 'the all-powerful reason of the Father, penetrating the universe, developing everywhere its forces, illuminating with His light things visible and invisible, allowing nothing to escape from his powerful action, vivifying and preserving all beings in themselves and in the harmony of creation'. Everything has its being in the Logos of God and all things have their place in a universal harmony.

In his 'On the Incarnation of the Word' (*De Incarnatione Verbi*) Athanasius is more concerned with reconciling divine immanence without confounding God and the world. He does this by building his thought upon the Logos who expands himself in the universe as light expands in the air, penetrating all things: 'He gives himself without losing anything of himself, and with him is given the Father, who makes all things by him, and the Spirit who is his energy.' This is an expression of the true God of humanity whose presence and love we feel: the God who communicates while remaining distinct from humankind. The very point of the incarnation of the Word to assert emphatically the solidarity of humankind with Christ, so that all that Christ was and all that he did now belongs to all humanity. The saving force that was in him becomes through the incarnation inherent in the life of humankind.[22]

This broadly is the witness of the Greek theologians. It stands very sharply in contrast to the Latin theologies (which include many forms of Reformation theology) that have placed more emphasis on the exclusiveness of the Church. It is no accident that the saying 'there is no salvation outside the Church' is often quoted in Latin: *extra ecclesiam nulla salus*. The tenets which dominate Western theology — original sin and original guilt (*reatus*); the absolute necessity of baptism; the denial of the freedom of the will; the doctrine of election; the idea of a schism in the divine nature which required a satisfaction to retributive justice before love could grant forgiveness; the notion of atonement as a principle of equivalence; the conception that revelation is confined within the Bible; doctrines of sacramental grace and priestly mediation; the thought of Jesus' Church being identical with any form of ecclesiastical organization — have no place in Greek theology.

The re-emergence of Logos theology in the nineteenth century

It took until the nineteenth century for the theology of the Greek fathers to re-emerge in the West (to be sure the churches of the East never lost it). Henry Scott Holland captures the sense of this nineteenth-century re-awakening precisely:

> *We have lost much of that rich splendour, that large hearted fullness of power, which characterizes the great Greek masters of theology. We have suffered our faith for so long to accept the pinched and narrow limits of a most unapostolic divinity, that we can scarcely persuade people to recall how wide was the sweep of Christian thought in the first centuries, how largely it dealt with those deep problems of spiritual existence and development, which now impress upon us the seriousness of the issues amid which our souls are travelling. We have let people forget all that our creed has to say about the unity of all creation, or about the evolution of history, or about the universality of divine action through the Word. We have lost the power of wielding the mighty language with which Athanasius expands the significance of creation and regeneration, of incarnation and sacrifice, and redemption and salvation and glory.*[23]

The most significant theologians working in the English language to rediscover the significance of Logos theology were Frederick Denison Maurice (1805–71), Brooke Foss Westcott (1825–1901) and Alexander V. G. Allen (1841–1908). Not only did they affect the shape of contemporary theology in Britain and North America, but offered much-needed resources for late nineteenth- and early twentieth-century missionaries who reached out for support to the these three theologians of the Word to interpret what they had found in the spiritualities of other men and women.[24]

So we close the first section of this chapter, aware that we have not dealt with the insights of twentieth-century theology. Some of the more recent theologians who have contributed to Logos Christology are referred to later in this chapter. For the moment it is I hope sufficient to have indicated the long pedigree of Logos/Wisdom/Spirit Christology in the history of Christian thought. Only with this in mind it seems to me that we can adequately deal with the apparent stumbling-block text for religious pluralism, 'I am the way, and the truth, and the life. No one comes to the Father except through me.'

Four ways of interpreting John 14.6

We turn in the second part of this chapter to spelling out some of the practical implications of Logos theology as we confront the text that so often appears to prevent Christians participating in good and generous faith in our multi-faith world. The following are four different treatments of John 14.6, that have been used at various times to help Christian groups to see that far from blocking off conversation with people of other religious commitments, the words of John 14.6 open up ways to a positive understanding of other religious paths.

Here is the full text in which John 14.6 occurs:

'Do not let your hearts be troubled. Believe in God, believe also in me. In my Father's house there are many dwelling-places. If it were not so, would I have told you that I go to prepare a place for you? And if I go and prepare a place for you, I will come again and will take you to myself, so that where I am, there you may be also. And you know the way to the place where I am going.' Thomas said to

him, 'Lord, we do not know where you are going. How can we know
the way?' Jesus said to him, 'I am the way, and the truth, and the
life. No one comes to the Father except though me. *If you know*
me, you will know my Father also. From now on you do know him
and have seen him.' Philip said to him, 'Lord, show us the Father,
and we will be satisfied.' Jesus said to him, '"Have I been with you all
this time, Philip, and still you do not know me? Whoever has seen
me has seen the Father. How can you say, 'Show us the Father'"?
(*emphasis mine*)

THE ANSWER TO THOMAS

The temptation is almost irresistible to want to make John 14.6 into a
doctrinal proposition concerning the eternal destiny of people of non-
Christian faith. But this is a false step. The words of John 14.6 may
not be lifted out of their proper context. The answer to Thomas does
not address the questions 'Can Hindus be saved?'; 'Will Buddhists go
to heaven?'; 'Is my late Sikh grandfather in Hell?' and so on. Much
rather these words must compel readers to address the question of
their own spiritual well-being; of their own knowledge of God.

The whole passage is part of the last discourse of Jesus before his
betrayal and death. The disciples are deeply troubled and perplexed
and John 14.6 appears in the immediate context of a conversation
between Jesus and Thomas. To grasp the significance of both question
and answer we need to look first at the part Thomas plays within the
total narrative structure of the Fourth Gospel. A towering figure in both
this Gospel and early Christian history, Thomas is for John both apostle and witness.[25] We need to rid our minds of the associations of ideas
that often arise upon hearing the name of Thomas. Christian tradition
in the West has labelled him 'Doubting Thomas'. The preconceptions
established by this sobriquet appear to continue to blind many to a
positive reading of his function in the Fourth Gospel, namely that he
is *believing, faithful* Thomas, the disciple who is the most committed
to Jesus, and to obedience to what he understands of Jesus' intentions.

But even until today the commentators on the Fourth Gospel tend to characterize Thomas as 'loyal but literal minded' (William Temple); 'loyal but dull' (C. K. Barrett); 'a type of the unimaginative but loyal disciple' (F. C. Grant); 'doggedly loyal but sceptically minded' (Lesslie Newbigin). In *The Interpreter's Bible*, A. J. Gossip wrote: 'Thomas, who always liked the feel of solid facts beneath his feet, and perhaps had not much poetry in his nature, blurts out, Lord, we do not know where you are going; how can we know the way?'[26] Thomas's loyalty is emphasized, but the possibility that he may be the vehicle for special insight is hardly ever taken into account.

We need to set this passage alongside the other two incidents in which he figures in the Fourth Gospel. We first meet Thomas in the Lazarus story in chapter 11.1–44. In verse 16 he speaks words of profound commitment to Jesus: 'Let us also go, that we may die with him.' The Fourth Gospel depicts Jesus and the disciples as faced with an urgent cry for help from the sisters of Lazarus. But the sisters live in Judaea, which by now has become a dangerous place for Jesus. 'Rabbi, the Jews were just now trying to stone you, and are you going there again?' the disciples ask (11.8). Jesus responds with words about his mission: 'Are there not twelve hours of daylight? Those who walk during the day do not stumble, because they see the light of the world. But those who walk at night stumble, because the light is not in them' (11.9–10). These strange, pregnant words, with their echoes of and cross-references to other Johannine imagery, have to do with death and suffering. Note the associations called up by the words 'twelve hours', 'my hour is not yet come . . .' and then 'my hour is come . . .' (John 2.4; 7.8, 33; 13.1). These are forenotes of the theme of Judas's leaving the supper table: 'and it was night' (John 13.30), as well as of the night scene in Gethsemane. The strange detail of hesitation of the two days' wait in verse 6 is a counterpart to the stories of Jesus' anguish and indecision in the synoptic Gospels. It is also John's version of Jesus' setting his face to go to Jerusalem as in Luke 9:51. According to Mark, Jesus set out in the company of an astonished and frightened group of followers (Mark 10.32). We know, but it is certainly possible that John also knew these traditions, and that he is indirectly commenting on them. In the synoptic tradition, when Peter was told of the sufferings that awaited the Christ (Matt. 16.22; cf. Mark 8.31–3), he is recorded as reproaching Jesus, saying 'God forbid it, Lord! This must never happen to you.' But whether or not John is making this deliberate contrast, it must strike us that there is a very great difference between the response recorded of Peter and the words John attributes here to Thomas: 'Let us also go, that we may die with him.' This response is hardly to be interpreted as 'dull, unimaginative and literal-minded'. Thomas appears to have discerned something of the mystery of redemptive suffering, and of the inner struggles of the one who must so suffer to redeem.

Thomas also is the one into whose mouth is put the supreme affirmation about the person and work of Jesus Christ in this Gospel: 'My Lord and my God' (John 20.28), thus negating any interpretation of Thomas in the Fourth Gospel which underplays his ability to discern mystery. Thomas was very far from being a crass materialist demanding physical evidence of the resurrection. For the question Thomas is asking in 20.25 is about the reality of suffering and death. Thomas, committed as he had been to going to Judaea, 'that we may die with him', is here represented as one who must be assured that the resurrection was not 'docetic illusion' or a conjuring trick on the part of God.[27] 'Thomas does not want proof that what the others have seen is not imaginary, but wants to identify the Lord. The real question therefore is not *what* has happened but *who* has appeared.'[28] John affirms this as a proper form of questioning by having Jesus use in his reply to him Thomas's exact words (20.25, 27). That Thomas is vindicated in his quest for the identity of the Risen One with the Crucified One is shown in his immediate response of faith. We note that Thomas does not, actually, physically touch the wounds: if, in the mind of the evangelist, he had been actually seeking proofs of the grossest and most palpable kind, Thomas does not reach out to prod and to probe, and cries out 'My Lord and my God.'

Now we return to John 14.6. Jesus has just said that he goes to prepare a place for them (14.2), and that the disciples know the way to the place where he is going (14.5). The question here is whether

Thomas stands as a type of all who demand tangible proofs and precise definitions, or as the representative of all who long to understand the nature of the redemption. Thomas in our view is asking, 'Lord, what is your ultimate intention, and how do we follow you in achieving so great a purpose?'

To such questioning there is, and can be, no easy answer. For however necessary it might have seemed to later theologians or commentators that Jesus should have clearly stated the nature of the road by which his disciples can follow in his footsteps, this is almost exactly what Jesus did not do. The nineteenth-century Cambridge scholar F. J. A. Hort is much nearer the truth of the matter in emphasizing the obscurity of Jesus' answer:

> It was therefore impossible that Christ should mean 'I am the Guide' or 'I am the Example' when he said 'I am the Way'. These phrases may exact a slighter effort of thought; but only because they belong at best to a rudimentary and transitory form of truth. It was doubtless hard for those who reclined around that table to understand in what sense one in fashion like themselves could say 'I am the Way'. Perhaps it is equally hard for us who have received Him through the Creeds in His Divine majesty. Whether spoken from the human lips of Jesus or from the highest heaven, the words have a perplexing sound which no Jewish forms of speech suffice to make clear. They must always remain unintelligible as applied to the function of a simple Teacher or Ruler.[29]

Hort was pointing to two conceptual difficulties: first the inherent difficulty of any human being speaking such words, and second to the difficulty of reducing John 14.6 to a set of propositions as though human beings can know exactly what was meant. Just as poetry cannot be reduced to its prose content (otherwise it would have been written in prose in the first place), so John 14.6 cannot be reduced to a set of explicable theological propositions.

Hence the importance of the Thomas dimension when interpreting John 14.6. Whatever else we do with the words 'I am the way, and the truth, and the life', we must hold to the element within them of mystery, of redemptive suffering, of life through death. This redemptive suffering seen in Jesus' life and death is consonant with the anguish of God for his creation, his tender forgiveness for the weak and the broken, his ready pardon for the sinner and the criminal. In the broken and divided world we live in it is as well to remember that John 14.6 may never become a triumphalist slogan through which just a very few of God's children may minister to their own self-esteem, coming to believe that they alone are the specially favoured. When the shaping of the answer to Thomas points to the recognition of pain and perplexity, ambiguity and suffering, sacrifice and self-emptying, it speaks of the 'beyondness' and 'transcendence' of our human understanding. We are in the company of not simply the Rabbi/Prophet of Galilee but of the Word become flesh and dwelling among us, the incarnation of the Logos.

'I AM THE WAY'

Let us continue the quotation from F. J. A. Hort:

> *The claim which [these words] embody includes not merely a set of men moving in a world but the world itself which contains them. They convey a doctrine of Creation and Providence, not merely of historical mission; a claim on the part of the speaker to permanent supremacy in the whole manifold economy of circumstance. They are the practical and ethical expression of an all-embracing truth which we may perhaps apprehend best in the form of two separate doctrines: first that the whole seeming maze of history in nature and man, the tumultuous movement of the world in progress, has running through it one supreme dominating Way; and second, that He who on earth was called Jesus the Nazarene is that Way.*[30]

We shall need to take seriously both these affirmations. Hort has taken us into the heart of the christological question, 'Who is this Jesus? Is he a man for us or is he God for us?'. Christian orthodoxy since the Council of Chalcedon has held that four propositions are integral within the worshipping, praying, witnessing community: (1) Jesus Christ is truly human; (2) Jesus Christ is truly divine; (3) Jesus Christ is one Person; (4) Jesus Christ is ultimately related to the more general action, presence and revelation of God in his world. There is a long and intricate history as to how the worshipping, praying and witnessing Church has sought to hold all these four elements in a proper tension. There have been periods in that history when one or other emphasis has so dominated the others that a serious distortion of Christian theology has arisen and heresy and schism broke out. But in some periods it was the Christian centre that distorted the proper shape of Christology, and taught the divinity of Jesus to the virtual exclusion of his humanity. There have been periods too when it has seemed that the fourth proposition has been seriously underplayed and when the transcendence of God has been emphasized at the expense of God's immanence.[31] While it is with this fourth aspect of the four-fold propositions of Christology that we are primarily concerned, we cannot consider that fourth element in isolation from the first three, even though it is not necessary to enter into a full discussion of how Jesus Christ may be at one and the same time 'perfect in Godhead and also perfect in manhood, truly God and truly man, of a reasonable soul and body; consubstantial (*homoousion*) with the Father according to the Godhead, and consubstantial (*homoousion*) with us according to the manhood; in all things like unto us without sin'.

The Scottish theologian Donald Baillie suggested applying a 'paradox of grace' to the mode of God's acting in Christ. This is based on the wider conception of paradox of grace that attempts to express a Christian experience that every good work and good intention found or accomplished by human beings is the result of the work of God in them. This begins with Paul, 'by the grace of God I am what I am: and his grace which was bestowed on me was not found in vain; but I laboured more abundantly than them all: yet not I but the grace of God which was with me'; to Thomas à Kempis in the fifteenth century, 'overhearing what Christ says about his saints "They glory not of their own merits, for they ascribe no goodness to themselves, but all to me'", and summed up in Harriet Auber's lines:

> *Every virtue we possess,*
> *And every victory won,*
> *And every thought of holiness*
> *Are His alone.*[32]

This is at once profoundly religious and deeply persuasive. Baillie goes on to say that if the saints 'experience the paradox of grace for themselves in fragmentary ways, and are constrained to say, "it was not I but God"', may not this be a clue to the understanding of that perfect life in which 'the paradox is complete and absolute, that the life of Jesus which, being the perfection of humanity, is also and even in a deeper and prior sense, the very life of God Himself'.[33]

Baillie was heavily criticized for never quite succeeding in indicating what was 'continuous' between the 'very life of God Himself' and the life of Jesus. Is it a continuity of grace such as may in principle, if not in fact, be experienced by all other human beings if they were to be able to make themselves as open to God as Jesus was, or must it be an ontological continuity? In the light of our previous discussion we affirm here clearly that it was the eternal Word, the second 'hypostasis' in the Godhead, who was incarnate in Jesus. We have to say that the eternal Word, consubstantial with the Father, dwelt in Jesus.

The eternal Word signifies the general action, presence and revelation of God in his world and in human history. Using Hort's words, 'the whole tumultuous movement of the world in progress has running through it one supreme dominating Way; and He who on earth was called Jesus the Nazarene *is* that Way'.

In this section we ask: Are there signs of the presence of this 'Way' in the religious traditions of humankind? We may begin by pondering the fact that religious people are often profoundly committed to seeing themselves as following 'the Way', with or without the capital letter. Religious traditions are not primarily institutionalized systems but 'ways' and 'paths'. In recognition of this reality, the Dutch Franciscan theologian Arnulph Camps once posed these questions. 'Aren't the Old and New Testaments full of talk about the Way of the Lord? Weren't the first Christians called followers of the Way? (Acts 9.2). Doesn't the first Sura of the Koran talk about the straight Way? Doesn't Hinduism know three Ways to salvation? Doesn't Buddhism talk about the Eightfold Path? Here it seems to me, we have a good starting point for dialogue.'[34]

In Camps' insight there may be an equally good starting-point for a Christian theology of religion that may enable us to enter into that dialogue relationship in good and generous faith. Based upon their understanding of Christ as the 'Supreme dominating Way within the whole tumultuous world in progress', they may enter into fruitful discussion with others who have seen the presence of God, or the divine, immanent in the life of the world. It is not merely that it is of passing interest to see that the other religious traditions have used the term 'Way' or 'Path' as self-descriptions. More importantly, they are claiming their 'paths' and 'ways' have a direct relationship to the action of God in his world.

Therefore we affirm that other religious traditions are counterparts to Christianity. Wherever people take their religious tradition seriously, it determines their life-patterns, sets them ideals and gives them principles by which to live and in times of crisis and danger sustains them, comforts them, encourages them. But a religious tradition can only do this because religious believers can affirm that their tradition's essential teaching bears close relationship to that 'beyondness' or transcendence to which human beings can only respond by faith.

How for example have Jews thought of their way? Judaism is predominantly concerned with *halakhah,* which means, literally, 'walking'. This is the technical term for Jewish teaching concerning all matters of the Law and all the everyday rules for conducting one's life. It is derived from Exodus 18.20: 'teach them the statutes and instructions and make known to them the way [*ha-derek*] they are to go and the things they are to do'. But we mistake this if we interpret this way simply as a form of legalism. One of Rabbi Lionel Blue's books, *To Heaven with Scribes and Pharisees,* bears the subtitle *The Jewish Path to God.* Blue quotes from Moses Maimonides: 'on the dark path on which a man is to walk here on earth just as much light is provided as he wants to make the next step. More would only dazzle, and every side-light bewilders him.' Nevertheless Maimonides' *Guide for the Perplexed* was a work of moral theology.[35] The Jewish way of walking has to do with how God is perceived to be both in his ultimacy and in his relationship to the world.

Islam is the Christian tradition's other partner among the Abrahamic families of faith. This is the *Fatiha,* or Opening Sura of the Qur'an in A. J. Arberry's translation:

> *In the Name of God, the Merciful, the Compassionate.*
> *Praise belongs to God, the Lord of all Being,*
> *the All-merciful, the All-compassionate*
> *the Master of the Day of Doom.*
> *Thee only we serve; to Thee alone we pray for succour.*
> *Guide us in the straight path,*
> *the path of those whom Thou hast blessed,*
> *Not of those against whom Thou art wrathful,*
> *nor of those who are astray.*[36]

The following of the straight path is intimately linked with the perception of God as *Rabb,* the Master of the universe, and to the Muslim understanding of his purposes in cherishing and sustaining the world by his compassion. Furthermore, the codification of Muslim law is called the *shari'ah,* a word that means the path, and more specifically the path which leads to the watering-place.

This sense of the necessity of following a straight path to find *moksha,* deliverance, release from futility, unreality, and the endless cycles of *karma* and rebirth, is understood clearly in Hindu thought. The prayer in the *Brihadaranyaka Upanishad* is familiar to Western Christians:

From the untruth, lead me to reality
From darkness lead me to light
From death lead me to life. (I. iii. 28)

The Indian sages have taught that such aspirations are fulfilled in three *margas*, or paths; the *jnana marga*, or path of know-ledge; the *karma marga*, or the path or discipline of good works and the *bhakti marga*, or the path of devotion.[37] No commentary of mine can begin to touch upon the inexhaustible riches of the Indian religious traditions. But simply as an illustration of the spiritual power that we are dealing with, let us set down first of all the verse from the *Upanishads* which Mahatma Gandhi thought summarized the Hindu tradition: 'Behold the universe in the glory of God (the Lord) and all that lives and moves on the earth. Leaving the transient, find joy in the eternal. Set not your heart upon another's possession' (*The Isa Upanishad*).[38]

A second example comes from India's most beloved Scripture, the *Bhagavad-Gita (The Song of the Blessed One)*. Its compactness (just seven hundred verses) and its vivid poetry make it the most often translated of all Hindu writings. The story turns upon Arjuna, who is hesitating before a great battle for the dominion of the world, refusing to fight because he sees the faces of kinspeople in the other army. Krishna manifests himself to Arjuna as his charioteer to urge Arjuna into battle. Eventually we learn that Krishna is Vishnu, Lord of All. For *bhakti* devotees the primary teaching of *bhakti* yoga lies in the offering of all actions to Krishna (and thus to the Lord Vishnu). Central is the vision given the charioteer Arjuna through the gift of a 'celestial eye'. Arjuna sees the form of Krishna:

Thou art Imperishable, the highest theme
of wisdom, cosmic resting-place supreme,
thou changeless Guardian of eternal Law
the everlasting Spirit, thee I deem. (11.18)[39]

A few verses later Arjuna prays:

> *And to my prostrate body bending low,*
> *O Lord adorable, thy grace bestow,*
> *as father bears with son, as friend with friend,*
> *as lover with beloved, God's mercy show. (11.44)*

Krishna then imparts to Arjuna his divine teaching:

> *However not as you behold*
> *can I be seen in such a guise,*
> *by austerity or Vedas,*
> *by gifts of alms or sacrifice.*
> *Only by undivided love [bhakti]*
> *can I in reality be seen*
> *in such a guise as you perceived*
> *and both be known and entered in.*
>
> *So work for me, intent on me,*
> *be free from ties, have love for me*
> *and lacking hate, whoever is so*
> *to everyone to me shall go. (11.53–5)*

The teaching of India's seers concerning the path to *moksha*, release, liberation, salvation, thus also depends upon theological notions concerning the 'way' in which the created order moves. To the concepts of love (*bhakti*) and grace (*prasad*) we shall return when considering the 'fatherhood' of God in the other religious traditions.

The Pali derivative of *marga* is *magga*, the word which Buddhists use for the Fourth Noble Truth, the Noble Truth of the Way.[40] But other Buddhist terms familiar to Westerners also contain the idea of the Way. The best loved book of the Theravada Buddhist tradition is called the *Dhammapada*, literally 'the path of truth'. Here is a central passage from the *Dhammapada*:

The evildoer mourns in this world and he mourns in the next; he mourns and suffers when he sees the evil results of his own work. The virtuous man delights in this world and he delights in the next; he delights in both. He delights and rejoices, when he sees the purity of his own work. The evildoer suffers in this world and he suffers in the next; he suffers in both. He suffers when he thinks of the evil he has done; he suffers more when going on the evil path. The virtuous man is happy in this world, and he is happy in the next; he is happy in both; he is happy when he thinks of the good he has done; he is still more happy when going on the good path.[41]

A Thai Buddhist insists on the eternal presence of the *dhamma* in this way:

Everyone has the Buddha nature. I can quote the Buddha – the truth is there, the Dhamma *is there whether the Buddha is born or not. And the Buddha is anyone who can transform himself from a selfish being to a selfless being. That is how a person awakes. Once he or she awakes, then know-ledge becomes understanding and understanding becomes love. And I see that in my great religious tradition.*[42]

Some Buddhist scholars can speak of a vision of salvation at the heart of the Buddhist worldview:

Buddhism starts with the culture of man and the elevation of his dignity. A first step in this direction is the insistence on the virtue of maitri, *of the practice of loving–kindness. It is basically the state of friendliness, of being a friend to* mitra *that links man to a society. It is no doubt extended to all grades of life, human and animal, and further extends through time and space, leaving no room for caste, creed or ethnic differences. It is in fact interesting to observe that the future Buddha on whom the salvation of this present world is said to be hinged is named Maitreya. This insists as it were that the salvation of man rests on the mutual love of and respect for one another.*[43]

In Chinese tradition there is the sublime teaching about the *Dao*, or 'Way'. It is particularly interesting to notice that the famous commentary on St John's Gospel by B. F. Westcott, Hort's contemporary and collaborator, actually refers to this Chinese tradition in his note on John 14.6. Writing in 1880, he belonged to that period when awareness of other religious traditions was just breaking in upon Western scholars, and he uses the opinions of one of the nineteenth-century pioneers in the study of other religions. Westcott wrote: 'The use of the corresponding word [sc. "the way"] in the Chinese mystical system of Lao-tse is of interest. "In the mysticism of Lao the term Tao [the way, the chief way] is applied to the supreme cause, the way or passage through which everything enters into life, and at the same time to the way of highest perfection."'[44]

So let us allow Lao-tzu (as he is now usually called) to speak for himself in words which the contemporary Chinese theologian Choan-Seng Song finds significant enough with which to begin his *Third-Eye Theology*:[45]

> *Impenetrable is the darkness where the heart of Being dwells*
> *This being is Truth itself and Faith itself.*
> *From eternity to eternity, they will never perish,*
> *Who saw the beginning of All?*
> *The beginning of All, one only knows through the perennial Spirit.*

Therefore Song affirms, by quotation,

> *Man models himself after the Earth;*
> *The Earth models itself after Heaven;*
> *The Heaven models itself after Tao:*
> *Tao models itself after Nature.*

The *Tao Te Ching* ('the Classic of the Way and its Power') opens like this: 'The name that can be followed is not the eternal way: the way that can be named is not the eternal name.' At the thought of the Tao human lips have no words; the Chinese symbol translated as 'oh!' in the following passage is simply an attempt to render the feeling of awe at the deep and unfathomable nature of the Tao.

> *There was something containing all.*
> *Before earth and heaven it exists;*
> *The tranquil oh! Incorporeal oh!*
> *Alone it stands and does not change.*
> *It goes everywhere and is not hindered.*
> *It can therefore be the universe's mother.*
>
> *I know not its name;*
> *I characterize it by calling it the Way.*
> *Forced to make a name for it I call it the Great.*
> *Great I call the elusive.*
> *The elusive I call the far,*
> *The far I call the returning.*

One conclusion Christians may have to draw from this is that they ought to be more conscious of talking about the Christian path as but one way among many ways. But the reason why these paths and ways have for so long inspired, consoled and encouraged the hearts of human beings is in their discernment that somehow their way is comparable to the way of God in the things that can be felt and apprehended in the created order. So much is affirmed by Paul in Romans.

It is not accidental that in chapter 14, as elsewhere, John used specific notions and terminology derived from the religious traditions of his contemporary world. The Fourth Gospel has itself to be interpreted against the background of gnostic dualism, Stoicism, Platonism, the Hermetic and Mandean literature, in short, what C. H. Dodd called 'the general medley of religious beliefs characteristic of the Hellenistic world'.[46]

So let us not lose sight of the manifold contexts to which Dodd points us. The multiplicity of religious ways and paths was an issue in the New Testament period. It is therefore clear that there is something to be said from John 14.6 about the theology of religions, and about the way in which we may attempt to communicate with a variety of dialogue partners. It is that longings and aspirations of humanity are to be recognized. They reflect the universal condition of all human beings, created in and through the eternal Word of God. Since they are created in and through this Logos it can be no surprise that they have so often sought to understand themselves as following a way which reflects the way of God in the created order. The discernment of the early Christian community in which the Fourth Gospel came to light is that such understandings of the human situation are in the profoundest sense true to reality for, as Hort said, 'the whole seeming maze of history in nature and in man, the tumultuous movement of the world in progress, has running through it one supreme dominating Way'. Here is the element of continuity.

But equally the Christian community believed then, as it must still do, that this Way of God has been most clearly discerned in the way that Jesus followed — the path of rejection and suffering, of abandonment and death. Thomas's question has still to be answered when we speak of Jesus as the Way. This way of Jesus is clearly discontinuous with all religious ways which offer false hopes or minister to human egocentricities whether on the individualist or on the communal level. Whatever path human beings choose is not necessarily a reflection of the way of God; ways which have not discerned somehow the mystery of suffering and the mystery of love are 'untrue to reality', whatever label they carry. For in the end of the day, the one who on earth was called Jesus of Nazareth is the exegesis of that Way (John 1.14). Whoever has seen him has seen the Father (John 14.10). But to say these words 'has seen the Father' raises other vast issues to which we now turn.

COMING TO THE FATHER

'I am the way, and the truth, and the life. No one comes to the Father but by me.' Now we ask, what is it to 'come to the Father' or 'see the Father'? Jesus' central teachings about God as father portrayed the divine being as possessing an infinite quality of love, striking in its intensity and anguish (see the parables in Luke 15: the lost coin, the lost sheep and the lost son). This fatherly love was also totally gracious and limitless in its reach: it included sinners and criminals. Indeed, so far-reaching are Jesus' teachings about the divine fatherhood that it appears often that Christians themselves have not seen its implications. But as far as they have seen, Christians have wanted to affirm that Jesus' understanding of 'fatherness' is unique and insurpassable: no one else to their knowledge has ever taught quite like this.[47]

But this raises a question. Is it in fact true that other religious traditions have never found the Father, in the sense of meeting God as the gracious, the loving, the forgiving and yet the ultimate One, Maker and Sustainer of the Universe?

Franz Rosenzweig (1880–1929) is perhaps less well-known than his contemporary Martin Buber (1878–1965). But it could be argued that his significance for, and contribution to, Jewish–Christian dialogue was greater than Buber's. He was the first among Jewish teachers in the last century to speak of Christianity as having a positive role to play in relation to Judaism. As Hans-Joachim Schoeps has written: 'Starting from this recognition of the other faith in its own depth of belief, Rosenzweig can admit what no Jew before him ever admitted of his own free will — and without this admission, in the future, no further discussion is possible — that not one of the nations of the world comes to the Father except through Jesus Christ.'[48]

But there is a reverse side of this proposition. In Rosenzweig's own words:

What Christ and his church mean within the world – on this point we are agreed. No one comes to the Father except through him. No

one comes to the Father – but the situation is different when one
need no longer come to the Father because he is already with him.
That is the case with the nation of Israel (not the individual Jew) . . .
The nation of Israel elected by its Father, keeps its gaze fixed beyond
the world and history toward that last most distant point where he,
Israel's Father, will himself be One and Only – 'all in all'.[49]

The wider context of these words not only gives a range of astounding insights for the Christian understanding of the continued existence of the People of Israel, but is also the agenda for the unfinished task of dialogue between Christians and Jews. Here these sentences focus our attention on to the Fatherhood of God as experienced in the tradition of Israel, i.e. in the Hebrew scriptures and in the religion and worship of the synagogue.

This begins with the earliest traditions of the Father-God in the Pentateuch, in which the close relationship of God to the patriarchs is constantly stressed: God acts directly in human affairs and guides the people of God. On one hand this understanding of God is tribalistic and clannish, and belongs to a nomadic type of society where all events take place within very limited horizons. On the other hand it is a personal and non-mythological relationship, and is central to the understanding of the salvation-history of Israel. Thus in Exodus 4.22 we read: 'Thus says the Lord, Israel is my firstborn son'; and in Deuteronomy 32.6: 'Is not he your father, who created you, who made you and established you?' We may note that the Pentateuch also implies a doctrine of the motherhood of God in Numbers 11.12: here Moses is asking the Lord reproachfully, 'Did I conceive all this people? Did I give birth to them, that you should say to me, "carry them in your bosom, as a nurse carries a sucking child"?' The rhetoric of this was not lost in Isaiah 46.3 with its feminine imagery: 'Listen to me, O house of Jacob, all the remnant of the house of Israel, who have been borne by me from your birth, carried from the womb; even to your old age I am he, even when you turn grey I will carry you. I have made and I will bear; I will carry and I will save.' The imagery is of course of feminine tender loving care.

It may be true to say that the further use of the title Father is rare in the Hebrew scriptures. But in the Psalms God is frequently compared to a father; or his activities compared to those of a father: 'Father of orphans and protector of widows is God in his holy habitation; God gives the desolate a home to live in; he leads out the prisoners to prosperity' (Ps. 68.5–6). And 'as a father has compassion for his children, so the LORD has compassion for those who fear him. For he knows how we are made, he remembers that we are dust' (Ps. 103.13–14). Equally the Wisdom literature effectively uses the father metaphor for God's relationship with humankind: 'My child, do not despise the LORD's discipline or be weary of his reproof, for the LORD reproves the one he loves, as a father the son in whom he delights' (Prov. 3.11–12). Sirach even addresses God as 'Father and Master of my life' (Sirach 23.1).

But it is in the prophetic tradition where we find the deepest insights into the divine attributes of love, care and compassion that may be postulated of the best of earthly fathers. Thus Hosea uses parenthood imagery: 'I took them up in my arms, but they did not know that I healed them. I led them with cords of human kindness, with bands of love' (Hos. 11.4). Isaiah of Jerusalem allows God to say, 'I reared children and brought them up, but they have rebelled against me' (Isa. 1.2). The same sense of God's disappointment that the love that has been so unstinting has not been returned is found in Jeremiah: 'I thought you would call me, My Father, and would not turn from following me' (Jer. 3.19). The prophetic insight is that, despite this anguish and disappointment, God never ceases to care: 'With weeping they shall come, and with consolations I will lead them back; I will let them walk by brooks of water, in a straight path in which they shall not stumble; for I have become a father to Israel, and Ephraim is my firstborn' (Jer. 31.9). God can, therefore, be directly addressed as Father by Isaiah in 63.16: 'You, O LORD, are our father, our Redeemer from of old is your name' and in 64.8–9:

Yet, O LORD, *you are our Father;*
we are the clay, and you are our potter;
we are all the work of your hand.
Be not exceedingly angry, O LORD,
and do not remember iniquity for ever.
Now consider, we are all your people.

Extra-biblical traditions preserved from the times before the birth of Jesus similarly affirm God's fatherliness: first we note this from the *Testament of Levi:* 'And then shall the Lord raise up a new priest . . . the Heavens will be opened, and from the temple of glory sanctification will come upon him. With a fatherly voice, as from Abraham to Isaac' (18–26) and from the Testament of Judah: 'And after this there shall arise for you a star from Jacob in peace; and a man shall arise from my posterity like the Sun of righteousness . . . and the heavens will be opened upon him to pour out the spirit as a blessing of the Holy Father' (24.1–2). The New Testament scholar James H. Charlesworth, who instances these passages, comments that they indicate that Jesus was not the only Jew of his period who held that God was to be understood as 'Father'.[50]

If we move forward to the Judaism of the Mishnah in the first centuries of the Christian era it is not hard to find the formula: 'Our Father who art in heaven'. This is traditionally linked to Rabbi Akiba, who said that Israel was made clean by the mercy of 'your father in heaven'. Another tract of the Mishnah has the question 'On whom can we depend?' with the answer 'Only on our Father in Heaven' (Sota 9.15).

Present-day Judaism continues to call upon this same God as 'Our Father' (*'abinu*), and Christians visiting the synagogue for the first time are often taken aback to sense how intimately present or 'near' this 'Father' is to the worshippers. I take just one example from the *'Amidah* (the Eighteen Benedictions):

Restore us, our Father ['abinu], *to thy Torah; draw us near, our King, to thy service. Cause us to return to thee in perfect repentance. Blessed art thou, O Lord, who art pleased with repentance. Forgive us, our Father, for we have sinned; pardon us, our King, for we have transgressed; for thou dost pardon and forgive. Blessed art thou, who art gracious and ever forgiving.*

'*Abinu, malkenu*, Our Father, our King', as a form of address mark other prayers of the synagogue, not least in the prayers said at the time of Rosh Hashanah and Yom Kippur, holding as they do the proper tension between majesty and intimacy. We must not be tempted into trying to say everything at this point. What the 'fatherhood' of God means to Christians and to Jews becomes the subject matter for common Christian and Jewish exploration of what it means to pray today after the Holocaust.[51]

The Fatherhood of God in other
Religious Traditions

We turn our attention to teaching about the Fatherhood, and indeed the Motherhood, of God in other religious traditions. Although Franz Rosenzweig insisted that 'not one of the nations comes to the Father except through Jesus Christ', this was an a priori statement. He had no access to other religious traditions. Our current awareness shows that many nations and peoples have called upon God as 'Father', or have perceived in other ways the qualities of love, forgiveness, compassion and sustaining care that we attribute to 'fatherhood', especially as we have seen such qualities evidenced in the Old Testament texts. It is possible to find the Fatherhood (and Motherhood) of God explicitly affirmed both by the use of the word Father (or Mother) and also through the feeling and tone and manner in which prayer is made, where such evocation is to a gracious, loving, forgiving God. We look at three religious traditions which are quite independent of Judaism and Christianity.

In proceeding to look at this evidence we need to bear three considerations in mind. First, the use of the term Father (or Mother) is somewhat rare in other religious traditions.[52] The instances that follow are cited in order to show that such expressions of the religious spirit have occurred.

Second, religious traditions are, as Hendrik Kraemer was at such pains to teach us, 'all-inclusive systems and theories of life, rooted in a religious basis'. They 'therefore embrace a system of culture and civilization, and definite structures of society and state'.[53] They are not merely speculative sets of ideas about the eternal destiny of human beings, for the words in which the religious traditions are passed on carry freight from the total culture and worldview of the people who use those words. Isolated quotations tell us little or nothing of the far-ranging presuppositions which lie beyond the words of the quotations.

Third, the affirmations that follow are present within the traditions, and, most significantly, are increasingly emphasized by contemporary followers of these ways and paths in their own response to religious pluralism. We may hazard our own guesses why this should be so, and indeed, in the light of our Christian understanding, we might find here a confirmation of the thesis that Jesus' teaching becomes the canon or benchmark or touchstone for measuring or assessing the good and the valuable in the old traditions. We choose from among the world's religious tradition just a selection: the experience of the Sikhs, the *bhakti* experience in India and the African experience.

THE 'FATHER' IN SIKHISM

We choose Sikhism for our first example of an Eastern path or way where it is possible to see religious men and women 'coming to the Father' otherwise than through the direct influence of Jesus' teaching. With its 10–12 million followers, Sikhism is an astonishing melding of Sufi Islamic tradition with the devotional traditions of Northern India initiated by Guru Nanak (1469–1539). Though it developed in its first three hundred years from a path of discipleship ('Sikh' means disciple in Punjabi) to become a disciplined quasi-military community at the time of the Moghul occupation of India, it has always retained its strongly devotional theism. Consider this prayer of the tenth Guru, Gobind Singh (1666–1708):

> *O kind Father, loving Father, through thy mercy*
> *We have spent our day in peace and happiness;*
> *grant that we may, according to Thy will,*
> *do what is right.*
> *Give us light, give us understanding, so that we*
> *may know what pleases Thee.*
> *We offer this prayer in Thy presence, O wonderful Lord:*
> *Forgive us our sins. Help us in keeping ourselves pure.*
> *Bring us into the fellowship of those*
> *in whose company we may remember Thy name.*
> *(Through Nanak) may Thy name be forever on the increase*
> *and may all men prosper by Thy grace.*

or this (all these words are to be found in the *Adi Granth* better known as the *Guru Granth Sahib*):

> *O True King! O loved Father! In this ambrosial hour of the morn*
> *we have sung Thy sweet hymns, heard Thy life-giving Word, and*
> *have discoursed on thy manifold blessings. May these things find*
> *a loving place in our hearts and serve to draw our souls towards*
> *Thee.*
> *Save us, O Father, from lust, wrath, greed, worldly attachment and*
> *pride; and keep us always attached to Thy feet.*
> *Grant to Thy Sikhs the gift of Sikhism, the gift of the Name, the gift*
> *of Faith, the gift of confidence in Thee, and the gift of reading*
> *and understanding Thy holy Word.*
> *O kind Father, loving Father, through thy mercy we have spent*
> *the night in peace and happiness; may Thy grace extend to our*

> *labours of the days too, so that we may, according to Thy will, do
> what is right.* (The Sikh Prayer)

The devotional expression matches Sikh theology. This proclaims the
unity of God, 'My God is one, brethren, my God is one' (*Adi Granth*
350); 'This alone is his merit that there is none like him, there never
was, nor will there be another' (*Adi Granth* 349); 'There is no place to
go except God and he is but one' (*Adi Granth* 349). God is intensely
personal. Guru Nanak himself probably favoured the term *Sat Nam*
'Eternal Reality'; among contemporary Sikhs, *Waheguru,* 'Wonderful
Lord', is perhaps the most popular divine name. But the Sikh teaching is clear: 'Your names are countless, O Lord, I do not know their
end, but of one thing I am sure, that there is not another like you'
(*Adi Granth* 87); 'Eternal Reality', God is the gracious one, who hears
prayer: 'Whoever cries out and begs at the Lord's door is blessed' (*Adi
Granth* 349). Sikhism is supremely a religion of grace with a message of good news. Thus Owen Cole interprets the calling of Guru
Nanak as a 'deeply transforming experience, which resulted in the
consciousness of being chosen to undertake the mission of revealing
the message of God's name to the world'. Cole quotes both the *Janam
Sakhi* narrative and one of Guru Nanak's hymns in support of this
view. In the *Janam Sakhi* we are told of Nanak's having been taken to
God's court and escorted into the divine presence. There he was given
a cup of nectar (*amrit*) and told to drink it with the words: 'This is the
cup of adoration of God's name. Drink it. I am with you. I will bless
you and I raise you up. Whoever remembers you will enjoy my favour.
Go, rejoice in my name and teach others to do so. I have bestowed the
gift of my calling upon you. Let this be your calling.'[54] And in the *Adi
Granth* there is this hymn from Nanak himself:

> *I was a minstrel out of work,*
> *The Lord gave me employment.*
> *The Mighty One instructed me,*
> *'Sing my praise, night and day.'*

The Lord summoned the minstrel
To his high court.
On me he bestowed the role
of honouring him and singing his praise.

On me he bestowed the nectar in a cup
The nectar of his true and holy name.
Those who at the bidding of the Guru
Feast and take their fill of the Lord's holiness,
Attain peace and joy
Your minstrel spreads your glory
By singing your word.
Nanak, through adoring the truth
We attain to the all-highest. (Adi Granth 150)

Any Christian theology of religion has to reckon with the question where the Word was when Guru Nanak had this experience. But in this context Christians have still to ponder to ask, in the light of John 14.6, not only where the Word was in this experience, but also what the Word may have revealed of the grace and love of the 'Father' of the Lord Jesus Christ. Further we need not go at this point, save to indicate that this is a substantial issue in Christian–Sikh dialogue.

THE BHAKTI EXPERIENCE OF FATHERHOOD

We have already noted the three Hindu paths *jnana marga, karma marga* and *bhakti marga*. When following the third of these ways, Hindus lay emphasis on loving devotion and self-surrender as the path to union with God, 'the response of love to the Great Lover'.[55] The centuries of *bhakti* exposition of the *Bhagavad-Gita* ('The Song of the Blessed One') have made this work the most famous Hindu scripture as well as the seminal expression of true monotheism in India. From Geoffrey Parrinder's verse translation we cite the following words set in the mouth of Arjuna:

Thou Father of the world, of motionless
or moving things, dear teacher whom we bless
in all the worlds no other equals thee
none greater, unexcelled in mightiness.

And to my prostrate body bending low,
O Lord adorable, thy grace bestow.
As father bears with son, as friend with friend,
As lover with beloved, God's mercy show![56]

The *Bhagavad-Gita* urges the worshipper or *bhakta* to 'Go to him alone for refuge; With all your being, by his grace, You will attain the highest place, And his eternal resting place.'[57] Krishna, the incarnate Lord, replies:

Show love to me, bear me in mind
Offer me worship and revere.
I promise you will come to me
Because to me you are so dear.

Abandoning all things of law
to me you must repair
from every evil ever more
I shall release you, have no care.[58]

How these words have been understood across the centuries of India's spiritual searching there is no need to detail here. But we can illustrate the strength of the tradition by choosing some poems or hymns from the *bhakti* tradition that indicate not only a searching, but also a finding and a 'being found'. Here some stanzas from representative poets. First from Tukaram (1600–49):

How merciful He is! In those who are helpless
He feels His chief delight.

He bears their burden on His head; He undertakes
the care of acquiring and keeping for them.
He suffers them not to stray from the path, He takes
them by the hand and leads them.
Tuka says, This is the reward if you follow him
with absolute devotion.[59]

From Tukaram again:

I proclaim these tidings, since I have power to do so; we are Thy chil-
dren by loving service; we speak the language of close affection. By
dwelling close to Thee we shall do away with doubt and fear. Tuka
says, There is a genuine taste here: how can we go away.[60]

Here is Tukaram's 'casting his burdens on the Lord':

No deeds I've done nor thoughts I've thought
Save as Thy servant I am nought.
Guard me O God, and O control
The tumult of my restless soul.
Ah do not, do not cast on me
The guilt of mine iniquity.
My countless sins, I, Tuka, say
Upon Thy loving heart I lay.[61]

Maharashtra Dadudayal (1601–60) came from Gujarat, and this verse
bears the same marks of filiality, insight into unworthiness and the
need of gracious love and mercy:

Evils without number, countless vices are within me
Many stains within me,
Not a single good deed have I done
No virtue is there in me; no merit is mine:
Yet forsake not thy sinful child, for without thee
where is my refuge?

Desire, pride and anger have misled me since my birth:
O miserable man that I am!
Thou only art my help: Father wash me with the nectar
of Thy rich forgiveness and heal the mind that is sore.[62]

This poetic tradition continues to our own times. Many Westerners have discovered, for example, the work of Rabindranath Tagore, whose *Gitanjali*, or 'Song Offerings', have been through many editions since they were first published in 1912.[63] Here is an example:

This is my prayer to thee, my Lord – Strike, strike at the root of penury in my heart. Give me the strength lightly to bear my joys and sorrows. Give me the strength to make my love fruitful in service. Give me the strength never to disown the poor. Or bend my knees before insolent might. Give me the strength to raise my mind high above daily trifles. And give me the strength to surrender my strength to thy will with love.[64]

Many of the Hindu people now living in West have been nurtured in this *bhakti* tradition. It is, as I noted in the case of the first visits by Christians to the synagogue, something of a surprise for Westerners when they make their first visit to a Hindu temple to discover this form of worship and devotion. Instead of finding gross idolatry and superstition, as they supposed, they come face to face with people who have 'come to the Father'. Some of the most fruitful contemporary interfaith dialogue in the West is taking place with followers of the Gaudiya Vaishnava tradition known more familiarly as the International Society for Krishna Consciousness.[65]

The 'Father' in African traditional religion

Because there are very few written records of its past, Africa has happily been spared the systematizing process that has taken place in the studies and libraries of the nineteenth-century and twentieth-century 'orientalists'.[66] We have no artificial intellectual construction called Africanism examining the sacred books of Africa.[67] Nevertheless, we are discovering afresh how much of the ancient traditions of Africa is still available to us, thanks to the devoted work mainly of Africans themselves.[68]

In these brief paragraphs we call attention to a widespread African awareness of the Fatherhood/Motherhood of God. In this we are indebted to the Kenyan scholar John S. Mbiti's *The Prayers of African Religion*.[69] Five examples will suffice:

> *Our Father, it is thy universe, it is thy will, let us be at peace, let the souls of the people be cool; thou art our Father, remove all evil from our path. (Nuer, Sudan)*

> *O my Father, great Elder, I have no words to thank you, but with your deep wisdom I am sure you can see how much I prize your glorious gifts. O my Father, when I look upon your greatness I am confounded with awe. O great Elder, ruler of all things both in heaven and upon earth I am your warrior, and I am ready to act in accordance to your will. (Kikuyu people, Kenya)*

> *O Mawu Sodza (God) Mother of men, Mother of beasts. If thou givest to man, thou givest truly. If thou deniest to man thou deniest truly. In thy greatness I am great, and I agree to thy will. (Ewe people, West Africa)*

> *God has turned his back on us*
> *The words of men have made him wrathful*
> *And yet he will turn about again*
> *God has turned his back on us.*

> *We are the children of our Maker*
> *And do not fear that he will kill us*
> *We are the children of God*
> *And do not fear that he will kill.*

How, in the time of deprivation,
Will the people live?
In the time of deprivation
I will not fear
Because I have prayed and prayed
The word of the Lord will not be mocked
His good word will ever keep you. (Dinka people, Sudan)

And, because it is becoming familiar to Western readers, here is the confession of faith of the Pygmy people:

In the beginning is God.
Today is God.
Tomorrow will be God,
Who can make an image of God
He has no body.
He is a word which comes out of your mouth.
That word! It is no more
It is past and still it lives.
So is God.[70]

In Africa, as John Mbiti says, God 'remains true, loving, ever ready to forgive and help the people who are his children'.[71] As one who has worked as a Christian missionary in Africa, and, like many others, who has learnt from the people that I served very much about the love of God and his ways with humankind, I am always astonished to see how near Africans had already 'come to the Father' before they ever heard the message of Jesus.[72]

My experience made me ask how God had spoken to the African peoples and led me to research the experience of innumerable missionaries before me. In my *Justice, Courtesy and Love: Theologians and Missionaries Encountering World Religions 1846–1914*, I have recounted their diverse experiences and their answers. One may stand for all of them. He is Robert Allen Hume (1847–1929), a Congregationalist from New England. A man of particularly good and generous faith, he set out his views in his two books, *Missions from the Modern Point of View* and *An Interpretation of India's Religious History.* In the first of these he notes that 'more Protestant reformers have appeared in the religious history of India than in the religious history of Israel; perhaps more than in the Christian Church':

> *While this statement may seem surprising to some, is it not just what we should expect from such a living, righteous, spiritual, living God as has been revealed to us in Jesus Christ? The Lord Jesus Christ never implied or said that God the Father of the spirits of all men had through what Jesus himself said or did become different from what He evermore had been and must be. Jesus Christ came to reveal the Father, not to make God a father.*[73]

Hume instances the reforms of, for example, Hindu saints Kumarila, Rananuja and Chaitanya and the Sikh gurus as 'prompted by God' and affirms that the *bhakti* movement as a whole arose 'under God's influence'. It was 'not strange but natural' that they are counterparts to the doctrines of Christianity in the various phases of Hinduism, 'because the Divine Spirit who taught these truths to Christians was never inactive towards non Christians'. Hume says it should have caused no surprise that people had guessed at God's grace, even without the revelation of Jesus Christ.

Robert Hume was just one among many who voiced the same ideas at the time of the World Missionary Conference in Edinburgh in 1910, and who turned to the Logos doctrine of John's Gospel and the early Greek theologians as a guiding statement.

THE LOGOS BY WHOM WE ALL COME TO THE FATHER

'I am the way, and the truth, and the life. No one comes to Father except through me' is set in a larger context in the total thought of the Fourth Gospel. The immediate context of John 14.6 is the questions of Thomas. We have seen that we cannot avoid the implications of that: now we meet head-on the issue that John 14.6 cannot be taken out of the wider context of John's Christology of the Word.

In John's Prologue the Word plays the central role in both creation and redemption. All that is created is ultimately related to the Word, for it was created not only through him but in him (1.3). The Word is not just instrumental in the creative process, but is also the principle in and through which everything coheres. This is the teaching not only of the Johannine Prologue but also of Colossians 1.16. 'For in him all things in heaven and on earth were created . . . all things were created through him and for him. He himself is before all things, and in him all things hold together.'[74]

The Word's role in both creation and redemption is stressed again in John 1.5. In the Word was life. Here the Greek word is *zoē*, which is used elsewhere in the Fourth Gospel, exclusively for the concept of 'eternal life'. This life, says the Prologue, was the light of all people. Here we come to an interpretative crux. Some scholars have noted that the gift of eternal life is associated only with the coming of Jesus (John 3.1; 5.40; 10.10). To others it appears that the jump from speaking of the role of the Logos in the relation to the whole of creation to the specific mission of Jesus is far too abrupt. It is a matter of great importance how we read the text here, for on our reading depends our acceptance or rejection of the kind of inclusive Christology for which we are arguing throughout this book. It seems that the judgement we make is itself dependent on what we understand to be John's purposes in writing the Gospel.

Many would read the Fourth Gospel above everything else as a missionary document, one which sets out to open up a dialogue, and not to foreclose on the essential discussion of the role of Jesus in the universal salvation history. Let me make this clear by calling attention to the process of communication as described by a twentieth-century Cambridge scholar of comparative religion with strong missionary connections:

He [the missionary] will begin by recognizing that if [his hearers] have enough serious purpose in them to want to talk about religion, or to listen to what he has to say about Christ, they have already within them encountered the Divine Logos, though perhaps unconsciously, have been found by Him, and have been moved by Him to take some step towards further knowledge and towards a deeper and more explicit relationship. This is perhaps what C. F. Andrews meant when he was asked how he approached earnest Hindus, and answered: 'I always take it for granted that they are Christians, and as I talk to them, I often see the light of Christ come into their eyes.'[75]

The same scholar commented that it is 'incredible how rarely commentators on the Fourth Gospel allow themselves to ask: "What did its author hope and expect that its readers would understand from it?"' He added that it is inconceivable that the author should have begun his work with a prologue which, dependent as it is upon the introduction of the technical term Logos, uses that term in a private sense completely misleading to his readers:

It would have been tantamount to some British writer introducing a scientific term like 'relativity' into a theological work, but intending it to mean something quite different from what it would have signified when used by Einstein. To make such a supposition in the case of the Johannine author seems fantastic. Whoever he may have been, when he wrote 'Logos' he meant 'Logos', and he meant it to be taken in the sense in which a contemporary Stoic writer would have taken it.[76]

C. H. Dodd was also clear that in the Fourth Gospel we have a missionary document rather than a work of dogmatic theology in our hands. He wrote that if we try to enter into the author's intention:

it must surely appear that he is thinking in the first place, not so much of Christians who need a deeper theology, as of non-Christians who are concerned about eternal life and the way to it, and may be ready to follow the Christian way if this is presented to them

*in terms that are intelligibly related to their previous religious inter-
ests and experience.*[77]

For these reasons those concerned with the theology of mission and
the theology of religion are most likely to see the first verse of the
Prologue as speaking of the Universal Word at work everywhere. The
function of the Logos is to bring life and light to the world. All human
creatures are within range of that light, however great the darkness,
and in principle the light is stronger than the darkness. This Logos is
the true light that lightens every man that comes into the world. That
light is the light of revelation.

It is, we suggest, essential to an adequate theological response to the
discovery of 'truth', 'revelation', 'faith' and 'love' outside the Christian
community to point to the Logos doctrine, and in this way to speak
of an inclusive Christology. Just as Justin Martyr, Irenaeus, Clement
of Alexandria and Athanasius were concerned that Jesus should not
be seen as an interruption to the world's history, in our time we need
the Logos doctrine also, in order to avoid portraying Jesus Christ as a
'catastrophic and irrational intrusion into a world from which in any
genuinely significant sense God is taken to be absent'.[78]

To be sure the Word takes on a voluntary limitation by becoming flesh
(John 1.18). But she is neither exhausted by nor confined to that action.
We can expect to find 'disclosures' or 'manifestations' of the Word outside the Christian community of faith; as well in other religious traditions as in the natural world, in human history, in music, literature, the
fine arts and in philosophy; as well in scientific discovery as in the
depths of the human imagination.[79]

The eternal Word is everywhere at work, creatively and redemp-
tively. As Wisdom she subsists eternally in God. She is the hypostasis in the Godhead who goes forth in creation, in revelation and in
redemption. As the hypostatic entity in God's self-communication, as
Word, *ruach, dabar* and *hochmah,* it is she, not Jesus, who pre-exists.
This essential Christian orthodoxy should not need to be especially
stressed. Much piety, however, has led Christians to speak about the

pre-existence of Jesus in ways that can be variously described as Jesu-olatry, Christomonism or the Unitarianism of the Second Person of the Trinity.

The idea of the pre-existence of the Logos is no newcomer to recent theology. We use a few examples to illustrate the point. First, from a previous generation we have Archbishop William Temple (1881–1944), in his Readings in *St John's Gospel*:

> *From the beginning the divine light has shone. Always it was com-ing into the world; always it enlightened every man alive in his rea-son and conscience. Every check on animal lust felt by the primitive savage, every stimulation to a nobler life, is God self-revealed within his soul. But God in self-revelation is the Divine Word, for precisely this is what that term means. What is constituted within that divine self-communication, as one element composing it, is the energy of Life; this is what urges all kinds of living things forward in their evolution; and this is what is fully and perfectly expressed in Christ. So it may truly be said that the conscience of the heathen man is the voice of Christ within him — though muffled by his ignorance. All that is noble in the non-christian systems of thought, or conduct, or worship is the work of Christ upon them and within them. By the Word of God — that is to say, by Jesus Christ — Isaiah, and Plato, and Zoroaster, and Buddha, and Confucius conceived and uttered such truths as they declared. There is only one divine light; and every man in his measure is enlightened by it.*[80]

Even here William Temple's language, the language which comes naturally to the believing Christian, can mislead us. Can it really be by 'Jesus Christ' that Isaiah and the rest spoke. Does Temple secretly think of the pre-existence of Jesus? Elsewhere he makes it plain that he does not mean this. In his 1926 book *Christus Veritas* he wrote of the purpose of the divine act of incarnation:

> *That purpose would seem to be twofold — Revelation and Atone-ment. For the former, what is necessary is that Jesus Christ should be*

truly God and truly Man; for the latter what seems to be necessary is that human experience as conditioned by the sin of men should become the personal experience of God the Son — not as an object of external observation but of inward feeling (to use the language of human consciousness). Neither of these requires that God the Son should be active only in Jesus of Nazareth during the days of the Incarnation. 'The light that lighteneth every man' did not cease to do so when He shone in full brilliance in one human life. Jesus did not control affairs in Mars, or in China. But God the Son, who is the Word of God by whom, as agent, all things came to be and apart from whom no single thing has come to be, without ceasing His creative and sustaining work, added this to it, that he became flesh and dwelt as in a tabernacle among us.[81]

From another philosophical tradition, we have the following statement of John Hick (b. 1921) that takes into account what may be said of the Logos in the light of his profound awareness of religious pluralism:

All salvation — that is, all creating of human animals into the children of God — is the work of God. The different religions have their different names for God acting savingly towards mankind. Christianity has several overlapping names for this: the eternal Logos, the cosmic Christ, the Second Person of the Trinity, God the Son, the Spirit. If selecting from our Christian language, we call God-acting-towards-mankind the Logos, then we must say that all salvation, within all religions, is the work of the Logos, and that under their various images and symbols men in different cultures and faiths may encounter the Logos and find salvation.[82]

There is a splendid clarity in these statements from Temple and Hick, which does not mean that we are bound to agree with either of them in every point of detail and probably not at all with their underlying philosophical presuppositions. They indicate how Logos Christology can make sense as a way of describing God's working in all human lives.

But some important matters still remain to be discussed. The first is the human resistance to God, or to the Logos, what the Fourth Gospel points to when it says that the 'light shines in the darkness' (1.5). Even with the most generous of faith, Christians are not to be naive about those religious phenomena that enslave human minds, distort perceptions of reality, and harden people against their neighbours. Men and women have frequently put their trust in things that not only cannot save but ultimately lead to destruction of human well-being. Forms of fanaticism and bigotry have stained and marred most of the world's religious traditions, including the Christian one. Because of the Word's becoming flesh, the 'measure of Christ' can be applied to them.[83] This is because the human life of Jesus of Nazareth is the revelation of the Father. He is the 'one of a kind' (*monogenēs*) from God, and as such the exegesis of God's purposes.[84] In his revelation of God's plan and purpose, Jesus' own life and ministry led frequently to conflict and criticism, and ultimately to crisis and judgement.

But the burden of the whole of this chapter has not been the problem of human wickedness and superstition, but rather its corollary, the far greater conundrum of the persistence against all odds of human goodness and faith. Good and generous faith needs to be able to affirm the presence of truth and justice, integrity and wisdom among humans everywhere. We suggest Christians have the resource they need for this in the Gospel of John's Prologue. To the insistent and inevitable questions that press in upon us as we contemplate good and generous faith in men and women who follow other 'ways' and 'paths', they may respond with genuine gratitude that it is work of God.

We conclude then with one last reflection. If it is the case that all human beings are created in and through the eternal Word, the Logos, we can hardly suppose that it would be the New Testament writer's view that because the Word has become flesh and lived among us, this primary relationship has come to an end. On the contrary, the argument must surely be 'how much the more' are all human beings likely to be related to God through the risen and ascended Christ. Here we should use Scripture to interpret Scripture and notice the force of

Ephesians 4.10: 'He who descended is the same one who ascended far above all the heavens, so that he might fill all things.' The risen and ascended Christ stands in direct relationship to every created thing. That Christ alone is the link between God and humanity may remain intact as the confession of the Church. And in good and generous faith Christians may declare there have been, that there are, a multitude of men and women whose prayers and actions are moulded by other religious traditions who are touched by, illuminated by the Logos, and who in their response actually 'come to the Father'. Christian faith sees this happening through the One who is risen and ascended, and who fills all things, who is the link between God and humankind.

So we may offer an implicit answer that is given in John 14.6 to such questions as: Does God hear the prayers of Jews and Buddhists? Is the devotion of Hindus and Buddhists acceptable to God? Is the worship of Muslims and Sikhs a living link between them and God? And the answer is Yes. 'I am the way, and the truth, and the life. No one comes to the Father except through me', as words spoken by the Logos, carry a further dimension: the Word is the means through which all of us 'come to the Father'.

In the last four sections I have set out four ways I have used in responding to the challenges that questioners have implied by challenging me with John 14.6. In none of these four ways of responding have I sought to explain them away. Taking seriously 'I am the way, and the truth, and the life. No one comes to the Father except through me' actually opens new ways into interreligious understanding. Christians may own a rich and profound Christology for religious pluralism that enables them to share in religious pluralism with a good conscience and generous spirit.

THERE IS NO OTHER NAME

A similar process of exegesis and interpretation could be engaged upon with regard to another much-quoted 'exclusivist' text, that of Acts 4.12: 'There is salvation in no one else, for there is no other

name under heaven given among mortals by which we must be saved.'
The Lucan context in Acts 3–4 is however not so rich in connotation
as that of the Fourth Gospel, and yields less profound material for
reflection. But it is important not to ignore it and thus appear to be
avoiding its 'plain' import as a deterrent to dialogue and an adequate
theology of religion.

Lifted out of its context, Acts 4.12 is a formidable statement: salvation is uniquely through Christ; there is no one else in whom to put
our trust. But the first question must be about the context of this
pronouncement by Peter. Does it allow Christians to build up the
universal dogma that no non-Christian has any hope for salvation? We
will suggest once again that contextual considerations will not permit
its use in this way.

As we read the whole narrative set out in Acts 3 and 4, it becomes
clear that these words are the climax to a series of events arising from
a healing miracle. Peter has said to a man lame from his birth, 'in
the name of Jesus Christ of Nazareth, stand up and walk' (3.6). This
becomes immediately the opportunity for a long polemical utterance
showing that Jesus was the Messiah appointed for the Jewish people
(3.20). This led to the arrest of Peter and John, and their appearance
before the Jerusalem authorities the next day. In 4.9 Peter has been
called to account for 'this good deed done to someone who was sick',
and then to explain 'how this man has been healed'. The context is
polemical, and we need not expect measured theological utterance,
but rather a passionate defence of an act of healing.

In the speech recorded in 4.8–12 it is important to note the Greek
words used for this healing act. In verse 9 it is *sesōstai,* which carries
the meaning 'healed'. In 4.12 two other forms of the same root are
employed: the noun *sōtēria,* healing, as well as salvation; and the passive infinite forms *sōthēnai* of the verb *sōzein,* to heal, make whole,
save. All English translations have problems with these words. For
another striking example see the various renderings of Luke 8.48:
'your faith has made you well [*sesōken se*]' (NRSV); 'your faith has
cured you' (NEB); 'your faith has healed you' (J. B. Phillips); 'thy faith

hath made thee whole' (KJV and RV). In the light of this and because of the healing context, Acts 4.12 should be translated as 'There is healing in no one else' or 'there is no other name by which we must be healed'. If we were to retain the verb 'to save' in this context it would have more to do with deliverance from sickness or demon possession than with the ultimate destiny of the human being.[85]

Further close inspection of the textual evidence confirms that Peter is not making a general statement of universal validity but is appealing to the Jewish leaders that such a healing is reason enough for them to accept their Messiah. In other words this verse should be read in the proper context of Luke's reconstruction of the anti-Jewish polemic of the early Church. It would be highly improper to generalize them beyond that context.

But as with John 14.6 there could remain something positively helpful for us for the dialogue with people of other faiths, were we to reflect further on Acts 4.12. Though it is not available to answer questions about the exclusiveness of Jesus as the bearer of salvation, Acts 4.12 has clearly in it a centring upon Jesus, and no Christian faith can avoid that and still remain Christian. For Christian faith 'Jesus' is the name by which the nature and activity of God is fully revealed. His name is for Christians the saving name because it shows them the chief means by which human beings 'share in the grace and love that is the nature of God himself'.[86] It is this that Christians would perhaps most want to share with their partners in dialogue. But their knowing (and loving) the name of Jesus does not preclude the possibility that the grace and love which Jesus represents for them might be found under names within the other religious traditions. Indeed, rather than pointing to an exclusiveness, Acts 4.12 might help us to think of ways in which the grace and love of God operate in the world without being named at all. The humility and 'unknownness' of Jesus in his early life may point to a humility and 'unknownness' in the activity of God in our own world. Only upon this pattern, which for Christians bears the name of Jesus, will there be healing, wholeness, well-being, salvation for the world: only in this way can any of us be saved.

3

In Order
to Friendship

AN ETHIC FOR RELIGIOUS PLURALISM

The argument of this book is that Christians should look forward to a future in which they will be able to contemplate a plurality of religious traditions with a good and generous faith. Because of the theological framework set out in the first two chapters they should be able to live alongside men and women of other religious paths, without undue anxiety lest, not having been converted to belief in Jesus Christ in this life, the latter should be lost eternally. Our intention in setting out an inclusivist salvation history and an inclusivist Christology has been to enable Christians to behave with a new openness and generosity towards others in the light of their understanding of the purposes of God. Their participation as Christians in interreligious encounter depends upon such an understanding which allows them to be both humble and honest, vulnerable and yet committed, and thus able, in the words of the Fourth Gospel, 'to do the truth' in our time.

The practical implications of this doing of the truth in the light of these understandings emerge, first, in the ethics of our interreligious relationships, and, second, in new forms of spirituality. Insights into both the ethical and spiritual issues that are raised may come both from within and from outside the Christian tradition. There are now rich stores of reflection based upon the ever-increasing interfaith encounters of our time. The practical ground-rules for our behaviour towards one another have been considered and reconsidered by important interfaith conferences and networks and worked and reworked by competent individuals from many different faith backgrounds. When we have looked at these we shall try to set, however tentatively and precariously, these ethical matters within a framework of prayer and spirituality, faith and love.

In surveying contemporary ethical possibilities there are three more kinds of material to draw upon. First there is writing and reflection that deals with ethical questions which are themselves part of the content and subject matter of interfaith dialogue. Such literature very often contains profound insight into the ethical considerations that have to govern right relationships between the religious communities.

In the second category is the kind of writing which illustrates actual interreligious encounter. A considerable amount of this descriptive writing comes from 'within' first-person accounts of deepening relationships and enrichments; but it may also narrate the experiences of other people and groups. There is much thoughtful material of both these kinds, produced by bodies such as the World Conference on Religion and Peace (WCRP), the World Congress of Faiths (WCF) and the International Association for Religious Freedom (IARF). The ethical content of this published material is considerable, but as yet it remains raw material for the reflection of ethicists. Then there were the documents which arose out of the centenary celebration of the Parliament of the World's Religions in Chicago in 1993, where, notably under the leadership of Hans Küng, a statement of a Global Ethic was produced with the overall slogan 'No peace among nations without peace among the religions. And no peace among religions without a greater dialogue among them.'[1]

The third category is that of the genre called 'Guidelines'. These are attempts by responsible groups within the faith communities to set the rules of the game for those who wish to take part in this new activity of interreligious dialogue. Very often such documents are in the nature of efforts to set down the parameters within which dialogue is permissible, with often a strong suggestion that there are boundaries across which participants in such relationships may not step, or thresholds which may not be crossed. Nevertheless, for our purposes this last category will provide us with basic material which may be discussed from the points of view of both descriptive and prescriptive ethics. At the same time we will be constantly reflecting upon how this 'Guidelines' material is consonant with the ethical considerations in the other types of writing. We begin with this 'Guidelines' literature.

'GUIDELINES ON DIALOGUE'

'Guidelines on dialogue' between people of different faith commitments come from all around the world and often reflect quite different situations. Very often they are what is called 'bilateral' in their scope, referring to what should happen between just two partners in a conversation. Other sets of Guidelines are 'multilateral' and tend to refer to the general principles involved in interreligious encounter. For our purposes, we will look carefully at two sets of guidelines of the multilateral type: the *Guidelines on Dialogue with People of Living Faiths and Ideologies,* from the World Council of Churches, 1979, reworked in 2002 as *Ecumenical Considerations for dialogue and relations with people of other religions;* and the British Council of Churches' *Relations with People of Other Faiths: Guidelines on Dialogue in Britain,* 1981, revised 1983. We have not yet so far had a document from the Vatican which is exactly equivalent to the WCC *Guidelines,* but it would be grossly misleading to treat the ethics of interreligious relationships as though the Roman Catholic Church had not made some decisive contributions in interfaith activity. However, the great Vatican II statements *Nostra Aetate* and *Lumen Gentium* are not in themselves formal guidelines for interreligious relationships.

The WCC has had a Sub-unit on Dialogue with People of Living Faiths and Ideologies since 1971.[2] In its earliest years this Sub-unit was greatly involved in the organization of high-level international encounters between leaders of world faith communities. No doubt these early ventures were open to the charge of elitism, and in fact they aroused a good deal of suspicion about the purpose of such dialogue. Was it to shape a new world religion? To eliminate religious differences? To engage in conscious or unconscious syncretism? To offer a substitute for mission and evangelism?

A conference in Chiang Mai, Thailand, in 1977 produced a statement entitled *Dialogue in Community* for the WCC. 'Dialogue', it said, is to be done 'in community', and therefore it is to be focused upon ethical rather than theological concerns. This document became the basis for the first set of guidelines produced by the World Council of Churches in 1979 entitled *Guidelines on Dialogue with People of Living Faiths and Ideologies*. This important statement, reprinted many times and translated into scores of languages, sets out four principles of dialogue: (1) 'Dialogue should proceed in terms of people of other faiths, rather than of theoretical impersonal systems'; (2) 'Dialogue can be welcomed as a way of obedience to the commandment of the Decalogue: "You shall not bear false witness against your neighbour"'; (3) 'Dialogue . . . is a fundamental part of Christian service within community'; and lastly, (4) 'The relationship of dialogue gives opportunity for authentic witness.' Under the last heading the *Guidelines* affirmed: 'We feel able with integrity to commend the way of dialogue as one in which Jesus Christ can be confessed in our world today; at the same time we feel able in integrity to assure our partners in dialogue that we come not as manipulators but as genuine fellow-pilgrims.'

In 1981 the then British Council of Churches (or BCC, now the Council of Churches in Britain and Ireland, CCBI) produced its own set of guidelines, *Relations with People of Other Faiths*. These guidelines were dependent upon the WCC *Guidelines* in that they were a deliberate working-out for one particular national context of the four main WCC themes. The BCC guidelines see four principles of dialogue:

- Dialogue begins when people meet each other.
- Dialogue depends upon mutual understanding and mutual trust.

- Dialogue makes it possible to share in service to the community.
- Dialogue becomes the medium of authentic witness.

In the body of the document the BCC showed itself concerned with prescriptive ethics for the Christian churches in Britain, treating such areas as community relations, pastoral care, religious education and denominational schools, as well as such issues as interreligious worship and the sale of Christian premises to, and the use of church property by, people of other faiths. We can look more closely at these to see how they offer guidance to people of good and generous faith.

DIALOGUE BEGINS WHEN PEOPLE MEET EACH OTHER

This principle echoed the statement in the WCC *Guidelines:* 'Dialogue should proceed in terms of people of other faiths, rather than of theoretical impersonal systems.' Such a formulation reflects the consensus of people involved in constructive interreligious relationships. This widespread agreement has, however, developed in various ways since 1979.

First, there has been a strongly proscriptive element: 'Dialogue', i.e. creative interreligious encounter, is not to be conducted in terms of religious or ideological systems, and this for two reasons. On the one hand the practice of dialogue has led repeatedly to the discovery that no one human being, who belongs to a religious community, is the embodiment or personification of ideas and beliefs set out in textbooks for the convenience of students and other interested 'outsiders'. We are learning not to say to one another: 'As a Buddhist you believe in x', or 'You Hindus believe in the doctrine of y, all the books say so'; or even that 'The Holy Qur'an says you Muslims believe in z.' It is only as we meet any given Buddhist, or Muslim, or Hindu, that we discover that he or she may or may not, for whatever reason, believe x or y or z. Too much book-learning in the history and comparative study of religions is often a powerful hindrance when we come to meet and to listen to actual men and women of faith. The label of the particular faith or ideology in which they have been brought up or which they profess can only be a first clue to discerning their rich individuality. It is sound ethical practice to approach another person with as few presuppositions as possible, and not to label or stereotype him or her. As Frederick Denison Maurice remarked in one of the earliest books ever written about the relationship of Christianity to the other religious traditions: 'A man will not really be intelligible to you if, instead of listening to him and sympathizing with him, you determine to classify him.'[3]

This advice parallels an experience often noted by the practitioners of interreligious understanding, namely that beginning by focusing on systems rather than on individuals is inevitably to enter a blind alley. If one is determined to believe that propositions carry all the substance of a religious tradition, the doctrines of the Christian faith and the Islamic revelation will necessarily be mutually exclusive. 'Jesus Christ cannot be confessed as the Risen Lord if he was taken up from the cross before he died';[4] 'Ultimate Reality cannot be at one and the same time the impersonal Brahman and the God and Father of our Lord Jesus Christ'; 'Dialectical Materialism is incompatible with theistic belief'; and so on. Differing ideologies and religious systems tend to exclude one another. But the same is not true among human beings. We have long been aware that it is possible for people with very different beliefs to hold one another in close friendship.[5] In the words of the BCC 1981 *Guidelines*: 'What makes dialogue between us possible is our common humanity, created in the image of God. We all experience the joys and sorrows of human life, we are citizens of one country, we face the same problems, we all live in God's presence.' The right order of going, therefore, is to enable ordinary people (including ordinary theologians) to meet each other at the level of friendship. It is almost instantaneously hopeless for future interreligious activity in a given town or neighbourhood to invite a Christian minister, a rabbi, an imam and a Hindu pundit to share the same platform and to discuss religious questions. This will almost certainly be a debate, if not a dispute, rather than a dialogue. It will close doors rather than open them.

These two practical considerations have been given deep theological and philosophical grounding in the work of four pioneers of inter-religious dialogue. Martin Buber and Emmanuel Levinas, both of whom are Jewish: Raimon Panikkar, a Roman Catholic; and Wilfred Cantwell Smith, a member of the United Church of Canada.

Martin Buber and Emmanuel Levinas ✺

Much of the theory of dialogue was laid out by Martin Buber, who wrote as early as 1929: 'A time of genuine religious conversations is beginning — not those so-called but fictitious conversations in which none regarded and addressed his partner in reality, but genuine dialogues, speech from certainty to certainty, but also from one open-hearted person to another open-hearted person. Only then will genuine common life appear, not that of an identical content of faith which is alleged to be found in all religions, but that of the situation, of anguish and expectation.' These words appear in his book *Zwiesprache,* or 'Dialogue', in which Buber intended to clarify the 'dialogical principle' set out in his much better known work *I and Thou.* Even though *Zwiesprache* was not translated until 1947 (as *Between Man and Man*), it remains a pioneering theoretical work on interfaith dialogue, with its emphases on experiencing 'the other side' of a relationship that has transformed itself from the 'I–It' involved in everyday encounters to the 'I–Thou' of genuinely human encounter. Another key Jewish thinker was Emmanuel Levinas, who extended the dialogical relationship beyond the 'I–Thou' to the 'We–Thou', entailing ethical commitment to and responsibility for the other person of faith. Levinas linked this commitment to the ethical relationship with God. As he once remarked, 'There can be no "knowledge" of God separated from the relationship with human beings.'

Raimon Panikkar ✺

Raimon Panikkar's guidelines for dialogue, 'The Rules of the Game in the Religious Encounter', first appeared in 1978, and were republished in 1999.[6] They have been widely influential because Panikkar himself has been a figure of extraordinary stature in contemporary interreligious encounter. Indeed, encounter was embodied in his own being, for he was born into two of the major traditions, the Roman Catholic and the Hindu. When someone once described him as half-Spanish, half-Indian, Panikkar countered by saying that he considered himself 'fully Spanish, fully Indian'. Panikkar is reputed to be a difficult writer to understand, and probably the chief cause of this difficulty lies in his ability to think in no fewer than four and perhaps up to twelve languages. He is at home in all the religious traditions and cultures of which these languages are the vehicles. Out of this extraordinary range of experience he has written some thirty books on interreligious relations, or as he would prefer, 'intrareligious dialogue', most of which have not yet been translated into English.[7]

Panikkar's 'Rules of the Game' make several theoretical positions clear. Panikkar insists that *the Religious encounter must be a truly religious one.* Anything short of this simply will not do' (the italics are his). 'Religious' for Panikkar does not mean 'mere piety or commitment', but rather stands for the integrality of the entire person engaged in the dialogue. He sets out some of the consequences of this requirement for a genuinely religious encounter: 'It must be free from Particular Apologetics', for 'if the Christian or Buddhist approaches another religious person with the *a priori* idea of defending his own religion by all (obviously honest) means, we shall have a valuable defence of that religion and undoubtedly exciting discussion, but no religious dialogue, no encounter, much less a mutual enrichment and fecundation.' Apologetics has, he said, its proper place, but 'we must eliminate any apologetics if we want to meet a person from another religious tradition'. In dialogue we are discussing ourselves, and we are putting the whole of ourselves at the negotiating table: 'and therefore in genuine dialogue we must face the challenge of conversion'. As a corollary, Panikkar went on to say that dialogue 'must be free from General Apologetics'. By this he meant the intention to enlist the other person into a religious league against 'un-religion' or 'irreligion'. 'If to forget the first corollary would be to indicate a lack of confidence in our partner, to neglect the second point would betray a lack of confidence in the truth of religion itself, and present an indiscriminate accusation against "modern Man".' This, he said, may be understandable, but it cannot be considered to be 'a religious attitude'.

Wilfred Cantwell Smith ✠

The thinking behind many of the propositions in the World Council of Churches' 1979 *Guidelines on Dialogue* owes a great deal to the Canadian scholar Wilfred Cantwell Smith. By the late 1970s those committed to dialogue had absorbed Smith's insistence that 'religions' were not to be reified so that they became entities in themselves ('impersonal theoretical systems') that could be juxtaposed and compared. And certainly Smith's thought-provoking statement, 'Ask not what religion a person belongs to but ask rather what religion belongs to that person,'[8] lies behind the WCC's first principle. Like Buber before him, Smith affirmed that the distinctive quality of the human being was *faith* rather than a cognitive assent to a particular set of beliefs, and that therefore dialogue was from faith to faith, or in Buber's expression from 'one open-hearted person to another open-hearted person'.[9]

Smith suggested that faith should be seen 'as a characteristic quality or potentiality of human life: that propensity of man that across the centuries and across the world has given rise to and has been nurtured by a prodigious variety of religious forms, and yet has remained elusive and personal, prior to and beyond the forms'.[10] Smith was intensely aware of the difficulty of defining faith: 'Involved here is a sense of that transcendent reality to which faith has been said to be a relation, as well as the source from which it derives. The fact of its being the human awareness of and response to that reality, and the very fact of the reality's being transcendent, together explain, and even entail, the further fact of inescapable limitation of any instances of faith here on earth. How then could it be defined?' Smith could only point to specific instances: 'My own view would be that any appreciation of beauty; any striving for good; any pursuit of justice; any recognition that some things are good, some are bad, and that it matters; any feeling or practice of love; any love of what theists call "God"; all these are examples of personal, and communal, faith.'[11] Because faith is this primary constitutive human reality, we meet other persons primarily as people of faith and not primarily as Hindus and Buddhists, Muslims or Jews. Indeed it was Smith himself who taught us in *The Meaning and End of Religion* (1963) to question the unthinking use of the concept of 'a religion' or 'a faith'. We must respond by avoiding the widespread usage of the terms 'religions' and 'faiths' to indicate socio-theological communities.

Not bearing false witness ❧

'Dialogue can be welcomed as a way of obedience to the commandment of the Decalogue: "You shall not bear false witness against your neighbour,"' said the WCC *Guidelines* in 1979. We may put this positively: at least one goal of engagement in dialogue is to remove misunderstandings and misrepresentations, and to allow friendship built upon trust to emerge. The BCC 1981 *Guidelines* saw this happening, in so far as Christians were concerned, by the deliberate avoidance of misleading and hurtful terminology about other people, in the refusal to dismiss other religions as human attempts to reach God with nothing of God's grace in them, by allowing other people to define themselves in their own terms, and by accepting responsibility themselves to help other people to clear away misconceptions about what Christians themselves believe and teach. Such activities the WCC *Guidelines* say can be seen 'as a welcome way of obedience to the commandment of helping Christians not to disfigure the image of our neighbours; of other faiths and ideologies'. Both truth and love are involved here.

But the application of this guideline will never be easy. Other persons are not transparent to us, and we inevitably impose our own categories in interpreting both their words and their actions. But in situations of religious pluralism we may not throw up our hands in dismay and simply acquiesce in this state of affairs. There are rules to learn and skills to acquire that we all have to master in order to avoid blundering into 'bearing false witness'. Some of these we can acquire from the academic discipline known as religious studies; some we learn from our experience of interreligious encounter, and still others are inspired by simple common sense.

The 'Golden Rule' of interreligious hermeneutics ✠

Raimon Panikkar has suggested that the golden rule of any hermeneutic is that the interpreted thing should be able to recognize itself in the interpretation.[12] Any interpretation from outside has to coincide with an interpretation from within, i.e. with the believer's own viewpoint. For example, Westerners have characteristically called Indian *murtipujakas* 'idol worshippers', using the term 'idol' as it is commonly understood in the Judaeo-Christian-Muslim context as a 'graven image', i.e. as an 'abomination'. But an entire philosophical and religious tradition undergirds the notion of *murti* for a Hindu devotee. We have no word in English to translate *murti*. Such terms as 'image' or 'deity' are merely approximations for the shapes or forms that for Hindus mediate invisible realities to normal perception. Only by talking with a Hindu can we begin to sense what they represent for the worshipper. The imposition of biblical or Qur'anic categories on Hindu thought and practice clearly transgresses this rule. It is necessary to begin by listening to the *murtipujakas* themselves, and then, to the best of our ability, find new words to describe their experience.

But mispresentation may occur even within religious traditions that are not so far apart. Sometimes the false witness can happen within the Jewish–Christian–Muslim encounter. Let me record a characteristic Christian error, but one of my own. I had for several months been telling the story of the conversion of Sammy Davis Junior to Judaism. He is reputed to have replied to the question, 'Why Judaism rather than Christianity?' by saying, 'Because Christians talk about love, but Jews about justice.' This I had been doing in good faith, to illustrate the individualism and privatization of Christian ethics, compared with

Jewish concern for how people live together. These, it seemed to me, were the great themes of Torah, Talmud, and Halakhah. I mentioned this story to the late Rabbi Hugo Gryn. 'But, Kenneth,' he said, 'we Jews also believe in love.' I could tell that Hugo felt that I had simply been reinforcing the stereotype of legalism that Christians so often lay upon the Jews, however unintentionally, however out of the best of motives. I apologized then to him, and I apologize now to all my Jewish friends. In such matters, so full of anguish in the light of the Christian history of persecution of the Jews, Christians need constant conversation with Jewish partners to keep them straight.

Part of the problem for Christian theologians and teachers is that they are normally driven by circumstances to talk about 'the others', for the latter are rarely present in the churches or seminaries. (From time to time in the seminary where I currently teach, a member of the class is a Muslim, a Jew, or a Hindu devotee, and then the dynamic changes radically.) Normally preachers and teachers have to use the first person plural as an excluder: there is 'we' and 'us'; and beyond that boundary there is 'they' and 'them'. The 'we' form suggests always subjective, firsthand knowledge, and the 'they' form must suggest objective knowledge, knowledge of an object. But, as Wilfred Cantwell Smith pointed out, objective knowledge 'does not yield personal understanding, or the kind of knowledge on which to found friendship'. He added in this context, 'last century's missionaries, who were objective in another fashion (individually very friendly, but in their group's theoretical relation to the "other" religion, and in their writings, objectivist, alienist) were victims essentially of the same we–they fallacy . . . *mutual understanding between groups is part of the truth, in this realm; it provides a criterion, a verification principle*'.[13] One of the ethical imperatives for involvement in interreligious conversations is to enable us all (and here as so often in this book I want to use the 'we' to include all members of the human community) to find that 'mutual understanding between groups'.

The practical consequences of arranging opportunities for such encounters are highlighted in the various *Guidelines*. So the most recent guidelines from the WCC (2002) say that because 'religious traditions vary vastly in their structures and organizations, and individuals within the different religious traditions have different constraints on speaking for or in representing their respective faith communities', it is important to respect 'the integrity of religious traditions and their institutional self-understandings. This respect must also be extended to individual participants who may or may not be able to speak for his or her tradition. Clear objectives, transparency, commonly agreed criteria for the conduct of dialogues, and honest evaluations go a long way in making dialogue a fruitful activity.'

But all the practical guidelines in the world never wholly replace intuition, empathy, flair, interest in the needs of others, and the deep willingness to be friendly and to engage solely with the other for the sake of friendship.[14] John Macmurray offered a philosophical framework for such engagement in the first volume of his Gifford Lectures, *The Self as Agent* (1957), where he intended to construct and illustrate the 'form of the personal'. Macmurray argued that 'personal existence is constituted by the relation of persons' and gave us a remarkable dictum that encapsulates the motive for interreligious dialogue: 'All meaningful knowledge is for the sake of action, and all meaningful action is for the sake of friendship.'[15]

DIALOGUE MAKES IT POSSIBLE TO SHARE IN SERVICE TO THE COMMUNITY

When the WCC set out on the path of dialogue in the early 1970s one of its first ventures was to invite representatives from other faith communities to its Assembly in Nairobi in 1975.[16] They were disappointed that the question of seeking community in the contemporary world was not taken up with a greater sense of urgency. A number of hypotheses might be advanced as to why this may have been so. One may be the prevalence of a conviction about the exclusiveness of the Church. For example, the great twentieth-century theologian Karl Barth, in the very act of arguing eloquently and persuasively that the

Church is 'the community for the world', seeing and finding its own cause in that of the world, and that of other men in its own, remarked, 'Now there can be no doubt that in the discharge of its mission to them the community has in a sense to keep its distance, and even to contradict and oppose them. Without saying No it cannot really say Yes to them.'[17] Barth speaks of this withdrawal from engagement as 'well-founded and solemn', 'well-meaning and justifiable', because it proceeded from the 'profoundest commitment to the whole of humanity and each individual man'. Some kind of thinking like this underlay the widespread expressions of fear in the early days of interfaith relations that the practice of dialogue might compromise Christian convictions about Christ, undervalue the urgency of mission, and lead eventually to syncretism.[18]

But slowly and steadily the ecumenical climate has been changing, as we may see from the *Ecumenical Considerations for dialogue and relations with people of other religions* from the Office of Inter-Religious Relations of the WCC in 2002. The world has undergone dramatic changes since 1979 and the churches and the ecumenical movement have changed with them. We can point to at least three of these changes. Since 1979 we have seen rapidly increasing migration, with consequent political implications. There are many more religiously plural societies than there were a generation ago, and diversity has not always been welcomed. Second, increased contact between communities has resulted in greater knowledge and awareness of one another's religious beliefs. Although, to be sure, there are many people who continue to find this disquieting, a major response to the experience of religious pluralism has been the evolution of interfaith groups and organizations, and in the past thirty years interfaith organizations have proliferated.[19] There have been major attempts to develop common agreements on ethical values, the common responsibilities of humanity, and on shared responses to issues such as the ecological crisis, the rise of racism and the need for a more just global economic system. All people concerned with justice, peace and harmony are well aware that religious traditions cannot address these issues in isolation. They need to be in conversation with one another and to be able to draw from every one of them resources needed for the common task.

Accordingly, the *New Guidelines for Dialogue* (2002) offer cogent suggestions for renewed efforts where people of good and generous faith can work together. As we list some of the issues highlighted in the *New Guidelines,* we may note that all these topics have already surfaced in conferences and consultations around the world, and the WCC's house journal *Current Dialogue* fairly bursts with information that shows the depth of co-operation of followers of different religious paths.[20]

Good and generous faith on the part of Christians includes a concern for a sustainable creation. The melting of the polar ice caps and the rising of the sea level because of global warming threaten everyone, and all of us need to tackle this with unremitting urgency. Other problems confront global agriculture. As the *New Guidelines* say: 'In this area expanding the dialogue partners requires an increase in cooperation with indigenous peoples, farmers and those who live close to and respect the land, for sustaining the earth is not just an ecological but also a spiritual issue; a question not simply of justice but also of spirituality.'[21] Religious traditions and religious communities are also rightly or wrongly implicated in situations of violence. 'Religious communities inherit the polarizations engendered by these conflicts and are left to deal with the deep divisions, hatreds and enmities that are, in most cases, passed down from generation to generation. Therefore religious communities need to build peace with each other as well as work together for peace.' The dialogue about these things is hardly begun, and so far many interfaith meetings have been content to appeal to the so-called Golden Rule that we should treat others as we should wish to be treated ourselves.[22] But our experience so far suggests that people who are finding new depth of trust through interfaith dialogue can begin to tackle the 'non-theological and non-spiritual factors' that lie behind many of our religious divisions.[23] As Martin Forward has noted:

If humans genuinely seek peace in the world, it is important not to be sentimental and simplistic about core values, and foolish to locate agreement and even difference between religions in the wrong places. For certain, we need not only an ethic of agreement but also an ethic for coping with disagreement, where religions have wronged others.[24]

Forward gives as an example of this the oppression of the Dalit peoples by the Sanskritic tradition of Hinduism, and the centuries-old 'teaching of contempt' for the Jews by the Christian churches. These are issues of interpersonal justice. People involved in interreligious encounter are beginning to recognize that they share concerns about poverty, deprivation, exclusion and discrimination. All are forms of dehumanization that need the attention of all religious traditions. With the rapid globalization of the economic and financial markets we are as religious communities challenged to pool all our resources to counter the forces of injustice and, in so doing, become part of the transformation of the world. Here is Martin Forward again:

They must not simply admire their theoretical resources. They have to transform themselves in the contemporary world, if they are truly to be homes for the human spirit. They must learn from each other, and explore each other's deepest resources for faithful adaptation to the context of our global village.[25]

Dialogue as a medium of authentic witness

We have seen how insistent Raimon Panikkar was in his 'Rules of the Game' that 'the religious encounter must be a truly religious one': it is more than 'just a congress of philosophy', more than 'merely an ecclesiastical endeavour'.[26] Panikkar is clear, as are the WCC and BCC *Guidelines,* that one must face the challenge of conversion: 'to enter the new field of religious encounter is a challenge and a risk. The religious person enters this arena without prejudices and preconceived solutions, knowing full well that he may have to lose his life: he may also be born again.' This clear statement of the openness and vulnerability that can be expected of participants in the deepest forms of 'dialogue' is matched by other writers like for example Lesslie Newbigin: 'If it is impossible to lose one's faith as a result of an encounter with another faith, then I feel that the dialogue has been made safe from all possible risks.' Newbigin added, 'A dialogue which is safe from all possible risks is no true dialogue.'[27]

This ideal, however, should not be set out as an absolute condition, since earlier stages in interreligious encounter represented the first of the BCC principles, 'Dialogue begins when people meet each other.' People just beginning to dip their toes into the water of interreligious encounter need reassurance that the environment is in fact 'safe'. Similarly, it is certainly possible to work in a dialogical relationship with people of other religious commitments for a better human community without being challenged to this ultimate form of openness and vulnerability. So too is it possible for people utterly committed to their own faith-understandings to explain themselves to each other without anyone expecting that they should be, in Panikkar's expression, 'without prejudices and preconceived solutions'. If such was the necessary condition, many opportunities of interreligious discourse would be foreclosed, and few members, if any, of the world religious traditions could ever set out on this path.

But central ethical issues are involved in the encounter. The Indian pioneer of interfaith dialogue within the WCC circles was Stanley Samartha, whose invaluable collection of essays from the 1970s and 1980s, *Courage for Dialogue,* contains more than one reference to the reactions of people of other faiths to the new-found Christian enthusiasm for dialogue. Here is one such:

Do not think I am against dialogue . . . on the contrary, I am fully convinced that dialogue is an essential part of human life, and therefore of religious life itself . . . Yet to be frank with you, there is something that makes me uneasy in the way in which you Christians are now trying so easily to enter into official and formal dialogue with us. Have you already forgotten that what you call 'inter-faith dia-

logue' is quite a new feature in your understanding and practice of Christianity? Until a few years ago, and often still today, your relations with us were confined, either merely to the social plane, or preaching in order to convert us to your dharma . . *For all matters concerning dharma you were deadly against us, violently or stealthily according to cases.*[28]

This Hindu from North India was politely declining to take part in a dialogue instigated by Christians: the memory of past attacks and derogatory remarks was too fresh in his mind. What also perhaps he was too polite actually to express in words was the fear that others have made explicit, that in this context dialogue remains a disguised form of mission: 'You have failed to convert us by direct methods, now you will try to manipulate us by dialogue.'

Both in the older (1979) and newer (2002) versions, the WCC *Guidelines* struggle with the problem of 'integrity' in commending the way of interreligious dialogue to Christians, who like everyone else enter into such dialogue with prior commitments, in the Christian case commitment to Jesus Christ as Lord.

Their first step is to recognize that in serious dialogue participants acknowledge and make explicit these commitments. To the best of their ability they have to free themselves of 'hidden agendas' or 'concealed ideologies'. The WCC *Guidelines* have stated that Christians must come as 'partners, genuine fellow-pilgrims', yet must also speak of what we believe God to have done in Jesus Christ. The BCC *Guidelines* affirmed that 'If we are concerned with religion we cannot avoid being concerned with truth — otherwise we are playing games, and dangerous games at that,' and that 'Christians will wish to be sensitive to their partners' religious integrity and also to witness to Christ as Lord of all.' Panikkar wrote, 'If the encounter is to be authentically religious, it must be totally loyal to truth and open to reality.' Samartha expressed it like this: 'The freedom to be committed and to be open is the prerequisite of genuine dialogue.'

Once again I have approached the ethical and social issues from a viewpoint within the Christian tradition. Strictures against less worthy forms of behaviour in dialogue have been laid at the door of Christians: positive precepts and prescriptions have been couched in Christian terms and Christian language. It is reassuring, however, that these fundamental positions and commitments are susceptible to interpretation in terms of the other religious traditions of humankind, and indeed that from time to time it is possible to hear people within those traditions expounding them for their communities. Just as we Christians have to hear, mark and inwardly digest comments like those of the Hindu scholar quoted in this section, so comments made by Christians to, say, Muslims or Hindus have to be heard on their side, for Christians also sometimes find themselves 'manipulated', and not treated as 'fellow pilgrims'. Part of truth-seeking dialogue is to help one another in this process, so that all of us become as 'the disciples of Aaron, loving peace and pursuing peace', with good and generous faith loving our fellows and drawing them nearer to God.

THE WIDER IMPLICATIONS OF ENGAGEMENT
IN INTERFAITH ACTIVITY

In his 1981 book *Towards a World Theology,* Wilfred Cantwell Smith dealt with the question of why 'objective knowledge' is an obstacle to interfaith understanding. He wrote then, 'my contention is that objective knowledge in the humane realm is an inherently immoral concept. Many practitioners of this brand of knowledge are, of course, better than their theories; many are better men and women personally than individual scholars with more humane ideas. The goal of an objective scientific knowledge of man, however, is wrong. One element in this inadequacy, shall we say, is its moral wrongness.'[29] Smith's remarks are consonant with Panikkar's similar reflections on the inherent wrongness of forms of cultural superiority. One aspect of this in our global village is the predominance of 'the enslaving Western Myth, the myth of history' in which a correct (and Western) ideology will prevail throughout the world. Such a myth will lead inevitably to the 'clash of civilizations' that some contemporary thinkers are already predicting. Pannikar wrote of this 'Western Myth':

> *To assume* a priori *that a given conceptual form can serve as a framework for an encounter of cultures represents, from a philosophical point of view, an unacceptable, uncritical extrapolation. Sociologically speaking, it represents yet another vestige of a cultural colonialism that supposes that a single culture can formulate the rules of the game for an authentic encounter between cultures.*

Such issues form the wider background to the discussion of ethics in interreligious encounter. Smith and Panikkar, men of good and generous faith from the West and the East, direct our attention to some crucial philosophical and sociological imperatives. Panikkar insists that human beings are called to go beyond the 'Myth of history' and grow into a 'Myth of tolerance and communion'. Wilfred Cantwell Smith became increasingly concerned about this supreme ethical issue in his last years, focusing on the whole of humanity, that 'corporate body of which I am a member, of which all are members'. He viewed the whole human race as 'interdependent, corporately serving God by severally attending to our intertwining and mutually determinative roles'.[30] Through this interdependence he hoped that we should come finally to real and lasting collaboration and communion. There are many obstacles on the road before us. As he wrote:

> *I have no idea whether it will be practicably feasible to build together a better world; the modern world is a gloomy and unpromising place. We may fail, as Christians and others have failed in part to actualize their vision to which God has severally called us. Yet fail or succeed, surely it is clear that God's will for the twenty first century, the mission that God has trusted to us and all humanity, is some such ideal. Or at the very least, we may reach out to build friendship and mutual trust and affection between and among individual persons, whatever their background.*[31]

Panikkar's 'Myth of tolerance and communion' and Smith's concern for 'the community world-wide and history-long of humankind' point to the need of good and generous faith, on the part of not only Christians but of us all, a truly global ethic.

Is Your Heart Right with My Heart?

A Spirituality for Religious Pluralism

In the previous chapter we saw some of the results of the experience of interfaith dialogue in terms of underlying ethical principles. Inter-religious spirituality is much more speculative: indeed there are many who view such matters as interfaith worship and interreligious prayer meetings with nothing but alarm. This chapter therefore is but a ten-tative exploration of the feelings and experiences of those who have explored the spiritual dimension of religious pluralism. All prayer is by nature precarious, an act of faith, and the spirituality of the new relationships to which God calls us in our time is only just beginning to be worked out.

First, it is necessary to comment on the term 'spirituality' itself. For some Christians it has rather suspicious overtones. In the seventeenth century, for example, 'spirituality' carried a negative sense, describing a type of piety which was 'too refined, rarified, insufficiently related to earthly life'.[1] This sort of piety has a long history and indeed was present in the earliest days of Christianity. In Corinth, for example, Paul had to deal with self-nominated 'spiritual persons' (*pneumatikoi*), whose notion of the Christian life was extractionist and other-world-ly to the point of turning the life and death of Jesus into a gnostic redeemer myth.[2] Jesus came they believed as an illuminator to impart spiritual knowledge so that a few might be taken up from the dross and dirt of daily living. Those who make this same fallacious distinction between spirit as the source of all good and flesh as the source of all evil, or between this world and some another super-sensible world, are present in Christian communities today. They are people who have become, in the words of the old gibe, 'so heavenly-minded as to be of no earthly use'. Some of this suspicion seems justified in our own time as we observe billionaire entertainers and celebrities in quest of their personal spiritual satisfactions, without having any sense that their own lifestyles cannot be deemed to be 'holy' in a world where two-thirds of their fellow humans on this planet have neither decent food nor healthy drinking water.

But the common sense embedded in the Christian tradition enables us to cut through such deviations and to affirm that, in the words of Gordon Wakefield, 'mutual indwelling with God in Christ is at once the means and the end' of Christian spirituality.[3] But this means the willingness to be caught up into the mystery and meaning of the life, teaching, death and resurrection of Jesus. This kind of spirituality does not deliver us, according to Wakefield, 'from the tensions, dangers and sufferings of the world around us'. It is not an absorption into the infinite, but rather a plunging into ordinary life with all its perplexities and contradictions.

In the New Testament the claim to mystical experience is frequently transformed into love of the brother and sister, and then into service to the community. In this-world-directed behaviour, 'God is love, and those who abide in love abide in God, and God abides in them . . . Those who say, "I love God", and hate their brothers or sisters, are liars; for those who do not love a brother or sister whom they have seen, cannot love God whom they have not seen' (1 John 4.16–20). This kind of loving and serving means having the mind of Christ (Phil. 2.5). The incident of the washing of the disciples' feet in John's Gospel captures this: disciples can perform such menial acts of service to each other and to the world only in so far as they abide in Christ and he in them. 'All who obey his commandments abide in him, and he abides in them. And by this we know that he abides in us, by the Spirit that he has given us' (1 John 3.24).

This kind of love is motivated and enabled by Jesus: 'We love because he first loved us.' And Christians must remain committed to Jesus, for he is the way, the truth and the life. In Chapter 2 we saw that this way, truth and life lived out in Jesus of Nazareth is the 'exegesis' of the Word by which all things were made and who fills the universe, who became flesh and dwelt among humankind. Committed to what they know of Jesus' relationships with those who were not his own people (members of the occupying forces of the Roman empire, despised Samaritan semi-pagans, the Syro-Phoenician woman, and so on), Christians follow their Lord into loving and life-giving relationships with people beyond the boundaries of the Christian Church. They are at once committed to Jesus and open to new ways of being with people. Because of this, we shall speak first of a spirituality of commitment and openness.

But we shall also use three more categories that emerge from this pattern of loving commitment and openness. There is a spirituality which recognizes that there is 'a time for keeping silence', in which Christians may sit or kneel in loving contemplation surrounded by their friends and companions of other devotional paths. At the same time, many Christians have discovered ways in which they can empathetically enter into the spirituality of the other: we shall head this section 'passing over and coming back'. One deep note sounded in Christian spirituality is 'provisionality', the sense that God provides only as much as we need for this day's journey, and ideas that cluster here include those of 'pilgrimage' and 'poverty'. Finally, there is the idea of the paschal mystery, by which is meant the following of Jesus though Holy Week and Calvary to Easter Day. Like Thomas, they go with Jesus in order that they may die with him. Only after the passion and the death on the cross are Christians able to say 'my Lord and my God'.

COMMITMENT AND OPENNESS

There is a Wesleyan strand within the Christian tradition that carries an extraordinary openness to other traditions. It can be found in its full expression in a sermon by John Wesley (1703–1791) that he entitled 'Catholic Spirit',[4] which has nourished many of his Methodist followers in the same path, contributing both to the ecumenical movement and to new interfaith initiatives.[5]

Wesley's text for this sermon comes from one of the most unlikely sections of the Old Testament and includes two of its oddest characters, Jehu and Jehonadab. Jehonadab we know of from a reference in Jeremiah 35, where he appears as a fanatical Yahwist and the founder of an extremist sect opposed to the sedentary culture of the Canaanites. Jehu goes on from his meeting with Jehonadab to slaughter the prophets and priests of Baal. But, its context apart, the sentiments and force of the text itself have firmly impressed themselves on John Wesley's successors: It reads in the KJV: 'And when [Jehu] was departed thence, he lighted on Jehonadab the son of Rechab coming to meet him: and he saluted him, and said to him, Is thine heart right, as my heart is with thy heart? And Jehonadab answered, It is. If it be, give me thine hand' (2 Kings 10.15).

The oddity of the encounter between Jehonadab and Jehu was not lost on Wesley. He notes that it may be very possible that many good men and women may even now 'also entertain peculiar opinions; and some of them may be as singular herein as even Jehonadab was'. Wesley thought it was the inevitable consequence of the 'present weakness and shortness of human understanding' that people will be of different minds in religion as well as in everyday life. 'So it has been from the beginning of the world and so it will be "till the restitution of all things"', Wesley says. The wise will therefore recognize their own fallibility as well as the fallibility of others and they will only ask those with whom they desire to unite in love the simple question, 'Is thine heart right with my heart?'

The force of the words: 'If it be, give me thine hand' cannot mean, Wesley says, 'be of my opinion', nor 'embrace my mode of worship'. Such matters do not depend on choice. People must believe as they are fully persuaded in their own minds. Wesley addresses the other person: 'Hold you fast that which you believe is most acceptable to God and I will do the same.' To be sure, in 1749 he was addressing only Christians, but in a context of religious pluralism where people were seriously alienated from one another on account of their religious beliefs. Against a background of mutual disdain and suspicion, Wesley wanted Roman Catholics, Quakers, Presbyterians and Independents of all kinds to adopt the following attitudes: (1) 'Love me, and not only as thou lovest all mankind . . . love me as a companion in the kingdom and patience of Jesus, and a joint heir to his glory;' (2) 'Commend me to God in all thy prayers;' (3) 'Provoke me to love and good works;' and (4) 'Love me not in word only but in deed and in truth so far as in conscience thou canst (retaining thine own opinions, thine own manner of worshipping God) join with me in the work of God and let us go on hand in hand, and thus far, it is certain thou mayest go. Speak honourably wherever thou art, of the work of God by whomsoever he works and kindly of his messengers.'

> *While he is steadily fixed in his religious principles, on what he believes to be the truth as it is in Jesus; while he firmly adheres to that worship of God which he judges to be the most acceptable in His sight, and while he is united in the tenderest and closest ties to one particular congregation — his heart is enlarged towards all mankind, those he knows and those he does not; he embraces with strong and cordial affection neighbours and strangers, friends and enemies. This is catholic or universal love. And he that has this is of a catholic spirit. For love alone gives the title to this character: catholic love is a catholic spirit.*

So clear is this, despite its eighteenth-century turns of phrase, that little further comment is needed. The openness and commitment spoken of here is the reason why I return to my own Methodist roots in thinking about a spirituality for interfaith dialogue. Wesley's Sermon on the 'Catholic Spirit' provides the answer to a question once put sharply to me by a colleague: 'What is one of Mr Wesley's preachers doing in the interfaith movement?' On the evidence presented in Chapter 2, Wesley would have recognized the faith and love and hope of people of religious convictions beyond the Christian community. The universal catholic love applies to neighbours and strangers, friends and enemies across the board, Jews, Muslims, Hindus, everyone. Like Wesley, Christians can hold fast to Jesus and at the same time have their hearts enlarged toward all humankind, those they know and those they do not know. This kind of 'catholic spirit' leads to good and generous faith.

'A TIME TO KEEP SILENT'

We turn now to consider what form of Christian spirituality might be adequate to those situations where we Christians find ourselves with those who are also praying, but not through or in the name of Jesus Christ. In other words, we speak now of the vexed issue of interfaith worship. Because common prayer is so often at the heart of religious practice, when Christians make a serious attempt to get to know people of other faiths they are quickly confronted by the question, 'Can we join in with their prayers?' There is now much helpful guidance on this theme but one of the pioneering documents was the BCC booklet *Can We Pray Together?*, published in 1984. In that book, Sister Hannah of the Community of St Francis in London asked that readers meditate with her on the words of the book of Wisdom: 'For while gentle silence enveloped all things, and night in its swift course was now half gone, your all-powerful Word leapt from heaven from the royal throne' (Wisd. 18.14–15). With this text as her guide, Sister Hannah pointed to shared silence as the prayer of friendship:

> *Few of us can withstand long periods of silence in conversations with strangers or acquaintances. It is only with those we know well and trust that silence can comfortably and naturally become part of our relationship. Shared silence, when it is mutually desired, is an intimate experience and therefore not one to be entered into lightly. If we are led to share such silence with those of other religions it is likely to be a leading of the heart rather than the mind. We are bound to enter such an experience with questions and perhaps*

doubts. We shall be wanting to share what is most precious to each of us in the hope that it will lead to further truth rather than hinder it; but theology will be a second step.[6]

The common practice of meditative silence draws Eastern and Western Christians together, and both are learning that the art of contemplation can be learnt in all faith traditions.[7] For Christians the writings of John of the Cross, Francis de Sales, Père Grou, Evelyn Underhill, Staretz Silouan, R. Somerset Ward and many others all emphasize the place of silence in the inner life of the soul, silence in which we begin to ask the right questions about God, about the world and about ourselves, and to listen for the voice of God. So far the common fund of experience of shared silent prayer, unsurprisingly, has been largely contributed to by members of religious orders. Sister Hannah is herself a case in point, but we may refer also to the considerable literature now available from people like Abhishiktananda (the chosen name of the French Benedictine monk Henri Le Saux), the English Benedictine Bede Griffiths, the American Cistercian Thomas Merton, the Irish Jesuit William Johnston, the Indian Carmelite Albert Nambiaparambil, or the Sri Lankan Jesuit Aloysius Pieris.

Swami Abhishiktananda was the first to speak of the meeting between Hindus (particularly of the Advaitist tradition) and Christians in what he called the 'Cave of the Heart'. When reporting a gathering of Hindus and Christians of various denominations who met in Nagpur at Christmas-time in 1963 to read and ponder the Upanishads together, he wrote: 'Faith can only be recognised by faith, in the same way that only a *jnani* understands a *jnani*. It is only in the depth of their spiritual experience that Christians and Hindus alike are able to understand each others' sacred books, and thereby to outgrow the limitations inherent in every particular tradition.'[8] Abhishiktananda wrote that his fellow Christians should look for the treasures hidden in India's ancient scriptures and even more in that *guha* or secret place of the heart in which they were first heard:

For this guha, *from which the Upanishads welled up as from a spring of living water, is the inmost heart of every man; and it is to that inner centre that the Christian is invited to penetrate under the guidance of the Spirit, to discover in its fulness the mystery of the atman, the Self which was glimpsed there by the rishis. There in fact is the place of the ultimate encounter; there man's spirit is henceforth one with the Spirit of God, the Spirit who proceeds from the Father and is communicated by the Son, the Spirit who is that essential non-duality* advaita, *which held India's seers spellbound, and who at the same time is perfect communion, flowing from the Father's heart and shared with us by his incarnate Son. There the Spirit, drawing us into the mystery of his own indivisible unity, teaches us to say to God: 'Abba Father!'*[9]

How Henri Le Saux trod the path that led him into his reconciliation of 'the mystery that has a face' (as he calls the gospel that presents itself in the person of Jesus Christ) and at the same time 'the mystery that has no face' as it is revealed in the heart of India's rishis, need not be entered into here. Abhishiktananda has told the story of his period in the ashram of the Hindu sage Gnanananda in *Guru and Disciple*.[10] The fruits of his reflection on the meeting of advaitist Hinduism and Catholic Christianity may be found in two books, *Saccidananda: A Christian Approach to Advaitic Experience* and *The Further Shore*.[11] One of his translators, Sister Sara Grant, herself a follower of the same path, may have a last word:

Only in the cave of the heart can true dialogue between Christianity and Hinduism take place; contact at any other level can never be more than superficial and fleeting. Too often in the past Christians have given the impression that they were not even aware of the existence of this space within the secret place of the heart . . . where resides the supreme Bliss . . . and too often, perhaps, the impression was true. Now, however, the time has come for Christians and Hindus to recognize in each other the gift of the Spirit, and for that both must go silently down to the depths of their own being, to the 'place where the Glory dwelleth'.[12]

The English Benedictine monk Bede Griffiths knew both Henri Le Saux and his colleague, the Abbé Jules Monchanin, when they lived at their ashram on the banks of the river Kavery in South India. He has described how they lived there wearing the dress of the Hindu holy man, going barefoot, sleeping on a mat on a floor, and adapting themselves in all their habits of food and behaviour to Hindu customs. Those who visited the ashram, he writes, 'know how deep was the silence and the solitude, the atmosphere of peace and of the "desert" in this ashram'.[13] A similar atmosphere I am told still pervades this place and countless others where the same vision of the dialogue of silence 'in the cave of the heart' holds sway. The endless discourse of 'poor little talkative Christianity', as E. M. Forster once disparagingly called it, is giving way in many places to a rediscovery of interiority and contemplation.

The theology for all this comes only in second place, and for this we turn to the Jesuit scholar of mystical theology William Johnston, for insight into the theology of silence. He wrote in the Preface to his study *The Inner Eye of Love:* 'I am aware that for many professional theologians mysticism is a peripheral affair: an esoteric and embarrassing subject which has rightly been relegated to an obscure position in the curriculum of any self-respecting school of theology.'[14] But he argues that this cannot be allowed to remain so, and following the Roman Catholic theologian Bernard Lonergan, he believes that mysticism is at the centre of all religion and theology. This, he is convinced, is of the utmost importance for the future: 'One need be no great prophet to predict that Western theology of the next century will devote itself primarily to dialogue with the great religions of the East. And I myself believe that this dialogue will be a miserable affair if the Western religions do not rethink their theology in the light of mystical experience.'[15]

Johnston's central argument is that it is possible to distinguish in religious experience between a superstructure (which he calls 'belief') and an infrastructure (which he calls 'faith'). 'The superstructure is the outer word, the outer revelation, the word spoken in history and conditioned by culture. The infrastructure, on the other hand, is the interior word, the word spoken to the heart, the inner revelation.'[16]

This 'inner word' is a spiritual gift which at first is, so to speak, form-less. It is present in the heart prior to any outer cultural or doctri-nal formulation. So Johnston offers his own interpretation of what happens in the deep silence of shared spirituality, especially in cases where the theological expressions differ so vastly as in the case of Christianity and Buddhism. He describes that kind of silence which is almost palpable, uniting people more deeply than any words. What, he invites us to ask, is this silence which unites both Christians and Buddhists?

His answer is threefold. First, there is the existential level. 'When we sit together in silent meditation, just being, we are experiencing our true selves at the existential level, we are all doing the same thing, just being. And that gives birth to a powerful unity.' This applies to more than just Christian–Buddhist dialogue, but to all true human encounter. Just being together in the silence of friendship, for exam-ple, is itself a profound aspect of the spirituality for the new relation-ship between people of differing faith. But Johnston goes one step further. There is, he says, a practical form of that distinction between the superstructure of belief and the infrastructure of faith. 'Here we have the situation in which the eyes are turned away from words and concepts and images to remain in empty faith . . . This is the union of people who are in love without restriction or reservation and whose love has entered the cloud of unknowing. They are one at the centre of things: they are one in the great mystery which hovers over human life and towards which all religions point.'[17]

Yet neither Johnston himself nor Lonergan would want to stop there, and both suggest that the outer world of belief is important. First, there is a mediation of meaning given in the tradition. What is it that is being experienced in the silence of empty faith? For Christians it is doubtless the presence of Christ; but it is also the presence of Christ for those who have never heard of him. The distinction then may be made between the universal grace of God acting salvifically towards all human beings (1 Tim. 2.4) and the fullness of the Chris-tian meaning of that grace. Johnston quotes the words of Bernard

Lonergan: 'What distinguishes the Christian then is not God's grace, which he shares with others, but the mediation of God's grace through Jesus Christ our Lord.'[18]

The second point is that the inner gift of faith is, in itself, always imperfect and incomplete and must seek outward expression. The analogy Johnston chooses to illuminate this for us is of two people who love one another. If they both feel the same way about each other, and yet never confide their feelings to the other one, they cannot be said to be in love. 'Their very silence means that their love has not reached the point of self-surrender and self-donation.'[19] Silence, therefore, is not sufficient in itself. Far from it. The outer word is not merely incidental but has a constitutive role, both in the mutual commitment of wife with husband or friend with friend. It is in accordance with this sense that Wakefield rightly declares, 'Let heart speak to heart, but there must be an engagement of the mind which demands its own asceticism.'[20] It is to this asceticism of the mind that we now turn.

'PASSING OVER AND COMING BACK'

'Passing over' and 'coming back' are expressions borrowed from the writings of the American Roman Catholic theologian John S. Dunne, who wrote that 'passing over is a shifting of standpoint, a going over to the standpoint of another culture, another way of life, another religion. It is followed by an equal and opposite process we might call "coming back" with new insight into one's own culture, one's own way of life, one's own religion.'[21] By these words Dunne helps us to focus on the twofold nature of the spirituality of empathy and imagination that marks persons of good and generous faith when they share the aspirations of other people.

We begin with what may be two helpful analogies. First let us contemplate the rigours of learning another language. A Czech proverb says that as often as you learn a new language you become a new person. It is notable, but unsurprising, that there is no similar aphorism in the English language. The linguistic insularity of both the English (not so much the Welsh, the Scots and the Irish) and their English-speaking contemporaries in North America and Australasia goes back a long way.[22] Nonetheless, there have always been those among the British and American people who have transcended their monoglot condition, and who have discovered an expansion of mental and spiritual horizons by learning to see the world through the eyes and perceptions of people of different cultures and different worldviews. They have understood from their experience the degree to which language determines how we think and what we see. This insight is at least as old as the grandson of Jesus Ben Sirach, who committed himself to translating his grandfather's writings. This translation is known as Ecclesiasticus, and he asks for indulgence and care as we read his Greek translation. He wrote: 'For what was originally expressed in Hebrew does not have exactly the same sense when translated into another language.'[23] Because of detailed studies in the field of linguistics and semiotics we can say much more about language today. Language is made up of more than words with their meanings; these words and meanings are themselves part of much larger patterns of meaning belonging to whole cultures. In learning another language we learn another culture system, and when we begin to understand and speak another language we stand within the framework of that culture system. The pioneering sociologist Max Weber once spoke of the human being as 'a creature suspended in webs of significance that he has spun'. By this he meant that there is no generic 'human nature' as such, but only individual men and women who have been moulded as persons by their language and culture.

We are able to pass over into the experience and the worldview of other human beings only to the extent that we are willing to learn their languages. We need to know how that other person uses words by gaining some kind of insight into the way those words are used within the total framework of meaning. Missionary literature is full of stories of gross blunders that have been made through lack of attention to both language and culture. Lamin Sanneh has recently told of the missionaries' translation of Romans 3.23 in one place in Africa. Their version of 'we have all sinned and fallen short of the glory of God' failed to take any account that the language they were translating into had two forms of the first person plural pronoun: 'we' in one form was exclusive, in the other inclusive. The African hearers were intrigued to hear the missionaries say, 'We whites have sinned and come short of the glory of God', but were mildly surprised that they would come all the way to Africa to say so.[24]

Learning a language means therefore the painful discipline of struggling with grammatical structures and acquiring basic vocabulary. But it is only after such obstacles have been overcome that we can even begin to enter the linguistic world of the other. But the experience of many is that they have achieved so much that they know themselves to have crossed a frontier. They stand within a new circle of relationships and perceptions. In this there is an enormous exhilaration ('I have become another person') but there always remains a sense of opaqueness; things that do not quite make sense but that are obviously luminous to the native speaker.

Most of the features of this process are comparable to crossing religious boundaries. Since most Western Christians will never master Arabic or Urdu, Sanskrit or Hindi, Pali or Singhalese, yet have to enter into dialogue with Muslims, Hindus, Buddhists, it is important to emphasize how much there is that Christians can do to learn the inwardness of the religious outlooks of other people.

This is not done easily. There is the unavoidable 'ascesis' or self-discipline involved; there is both a 'grammar' and a 'vocabulary' to be mastered. But a moment does come when the outsider begins to think, however fleetingly, like a Hindu or a Buddhist, Muslim or Jain when he or she sees how their view of life 'makes sense'. This will not be only at an intellectual level, though often Christians might quite frequently find themselves 'almost persuaded' to become a Muslim, or a Hindu, or a Buddhist. There may come that intense moment of a realization that a whole new world is open to them, and in that instant they may respond with their whole being to this new world. As with the process of learning another language, and experiencing the exhilaration of having become a 'new person', but at the same time realizing that the outsider can never understand the world in the same way as a native speaker of that language, so too Christians despite their best efforts at empathetic understanding will recognize that the Muslim or Jewish or Hindu or Buddhist world will never be theirs. At this point they come back. Our mother tongue is the medium we use for our deepest expressions, our ultimate perceptions: in moments of ecstasy or crisis, we cry out in our own tongue. However much we pass over into the other linguistic frames of reference, ultimately we come back to that which grasped us and moulded us from the beginning of our lives. In the same way, however much Christians enter into the worship, culture, literature and community life of people of different faith they remain rooted in their own tradition.[25]

That this analogy has commended itself to others may be seen from this account of the American monk Thomas Merton, who died in an accident at an interreligious meeting in Bangkok in 1968. His biographer Monica Furlong wrote:

> *Yet even as he set out on that last journey, with so much of his inner journey completed, he knew that something had still eluded him and hoped very much that he would find it in the Asian religious communities. Some Christian observers have seemed to take offence at this, as if Merton might only be permitted to drink truth from a Christian source and as if all other springs might be contaminated, like the spring behind the hermitage. But Merton never thought or wrote of ceasing to be a Christian. Christianity was, quite simply, his language, and could not more be renounced than any native tongue; but this did not mean that other languages might not be loved and yield striking new insights in the old familiar phrases and ideas. In a number of the Buddhist and Hindu teachers Merton met in Asia, he found holiness and a deep knowledge of the realities of prayer, and he was humble enough to listen and to learn.[26]*

Another fruitful analogy that may help us to understand the spirituality required of Christians in a religiously plural world, the process of passing over and coming back, comes from the domain of literature and of literary studies. Here is one professor of literature talking about this field: 'A literary education', he says, 'has not been fully effective if literature still means to the student an array, however splendid, of distinct and independent works, however intimately known.' Great literary talents offer to the rest of us an extension of the range of possibilities, 'a means of attaining, and a standard of judging, a discovery of self'.[27]

The English poet John Keats termed part of that literary talent 'negative capability'. By this Keats meant the ability of a writer (he had Shakespeare particularly in mind) to be in 'uncertainties, mysteries, doubts, without any irritable reaching after fact and reason'.[28] He wrote elsewhere: 'let us not therefore go hurrying about and collecting honey, bee-like buzzing here and there impatiently for a knowledge of what is to be aimed at; but let us open our leaves like a flower and be passive and receptive'.[29] Keats's own ability in this area was significant. He spoke of the way in which other people would impose their personalities on him to the extent that he often felt that he had to leave a room lest he be annihilated. He tells us that 'if a sparrow come before my window I take part in its existence and pick about the gravel', and elsewhere he tells us that 'I lay awake last night listening to the rain with a sense of being drowned and rotted like a grain of wheat.'[30] Another poet, W. H. Auden, also spoke of this extraordinary openness and passivity of creative writers in a simple verse, 'Whatever their personal faith/All poets, as such, /Are polytheists.'[31] Auden means that the poetic imagination is capable of taking in all kinds of other ideals and aspirations and hopes, things that are to be loved and worshipped. Both Auden and Keats are far from suggesting that the poet as such is a cipher. The 'negative capability' is part of a total, strong integrity of mind and spirit. The gift possessed by the poet or the dramatist is to unite the perceptions of their openness and receptivity within a single controlling vision.

Many of the Christian pioneers of interreligious relationships have demonstrated 'negative capability', this ability to live with uncertainties, mysteries, doubts, without an irritable reaching after fact and reason, alongside a single controlling vision of Jesus and their commitment to him. Just one illustration of this form of spirituality is found in the life of Roger Hooker (1934–99), who spent 13 years in the service of the Church Missionary Society in Varanasi, North India.[32] Hooker spoke of the need to

> submit ourselves to the patient and humble discipline of listening to others, of being content to spend time with them because God loves them infinitely more than we do. It is only in this context that we can discover how strange and incomprehensible other people find our language, our customs and our beliefs. And it is only when we have made that humiliating, painful and very necessary discovery that we learn that communication is not an automatic process that happens by itself, but an art which has to be learnt, and it is precisely our friends of other faiths who are our teachers in it.[33]

This was Hooker's rebuke to any Christians who are over-active and aggressive in their relationships with people of other faith. Many are too impatient, unimaginative, and 'bee-like, buzzing here and there'.[34] Speaking in the context of evangelical missionary work, he says: 'Our evangelism is still far too often limited to traditional stereotyped language. We do not stop to ask ourselves what effect our words really have on those who hear them or why so many do not think what we say is worth hearing anyway. A narrow and self-justifying concentration on "results" produces an impatience which betrays the very love we seek to proclaim. A Hindu friend once remarked to me: "In the past the missionaries did not want to spend time with someone like me, they went where they thought their efforts would be more fruitful."'[35]

Much of the process of passing over and coming back in religion is dependent upon the processes whereby Christians or others 'distance' themselves from their own ingrained set of attitudes in order to gain a sympathetic or empathetic understanding of others' religious ways. We all have learned from students of religion, or comparative religionists, about 'bracketing' our own beliefs so that we hold our own convictions 'in abeyance': as though we did not have them. With such methods Christians can venture into the enormous complexity of other religious worlds without too much prejudice or bias. But having said this, it is always important to remember that the study of religion, or 'comparative religion', exists in its own right, and is never merely ancillary to the Christian theological task, however much people in dialogue have been helped by scientific analysis of the religious world.[36]

But in the last two decades another rather special development has been taking place in this area. This has come to be called 'comparative theology' (never to be confused with 'comparative religion'). Associated with such names as Francis X. Clooney, John Keenan, Leo Lefebure, Aloysius Pieris and James L. Fredericks,[37] this shift of perspective asks what might happen if, when doing theology in a religiously plural context, Christians did not begin by trying to find traces of the Logos everywhere, or imposing any other kind of theological matrix into which the 'other' religion must be located. Suppose for a moment that they were to try to hear what is being said in the sacred books and the teachings of other faith traditions. Suppose they were to put ideas like 'fulfilment' on one side and allow other traditions to speak in their own right as bearers of their own truth and insight. How could such insight and truth influence the understanding of Christian faith? This would be to do 'comparative theology'.

Paul Knitter offers an illuminating analogy to help in the understanding of this particular process of passing over and coming back. Comparative theology, he says, is not just an 'added room' built on to the big house of Christian theology, like a side annexe in addition to the existing rooms of biblical, historical and systematic theology. Rather:

> *'Comparative theology' or 'dialogue' with other religious view points is to become a way of living in all the rooms. In a way, the other religious traditions become our room mates as we explore the different levels of the Christian house. We are constantly talking to them as we try to talk to ourselves and to the texts and witnesses of our*

own tradition. Comparative theology, therefore takes with demand-
ing seriousness the insight and claims . . . about conversation with
others being a necessary stepping stone to the truth.[38]

The American Jesuit Francis X. Clooney is one of these pioneers of 'comparative theology'. He has said that he and his colleagues insist on asking 'questions about the truth of their own and other communities' knowledge of God'. Unwilling ever to reduce their own tradition's faith-claims to mere information requiring no personal response, comparative theologians likewise refuse to reduce other traditions' faith-claims to mere safe information. 'Knowledge', says Clooney, 'if taken seriously challenges the lives of the knowers.'[39] So comparative theology is not a form of religious studies, in the sense of a search for accurate understanding of the meanings of other religions, but is engaged in a fully truth-seeking Christian theology.

Clooney himself spent years in India and Nepal going deeply into Indian texts; Keenan, Lefebure and Fredericks have likewise immersed themselves in the Buddhist scriptures; Aloysius Pieris represents the growing number of Asian theologians who 'pass over and come back' on a daily basis from the religious worlds that surround them. What they may do for us is to report on their findings. In 'coming back' from the house of their friends where they have felt thoroughly at home, they are laden with exciting truths and insights, even with new ways of reading the Bible and traditional Christian writings. Of course this inevitably creates tension. As Fredericks puts it: 'The comparative theologian is a believer in the crisis of understanding fomented by the intrusive presence of the Other. This means that the comparative theologian operates within a tension defined by (1) vulnerability to the transformative power of the Other and (2) loyalty to the Christian tradition.'[40] Space forbids us here to go into what comparative theology has already learnt from the 'intrusive presence of the Other':[41] our concern now is more with the depth of the spirituality that lies behind the kind of 'passing over and coming back' represented in this developing movement. As they go ever more deeply into other texts and traditions, comparative theologians form profound friendships with the men and women who live out of their teachings. Indeed they would claim that in their experience it is impossible to appreciate the qualities of the religious texts without coming to know and appreciate and love those who follow the paths set out in those texts.[42]

PROVISIONALITY, PILGRIMAGE, AND POVERTY

When forms of spirituality become ends in themselves they fail to serve God's ultimate purposes for God's world. In Jesus Christ Christians believe that God has revealed the heart of the relationship that each human being is to have to every other man or woman as well as to God. Christian relations with those who cannot or do not believe as Christians do are exactly those that Christians should have with each other. God stands in the same relationship to all human beings: therefore these relationships themselves are part of the commonwealth of reconciliation symbolized in the vision of the City of God in Revelation 21.22, as we saw in Chapter 1.

But this is an eschatological vision: the Church on earth always lives with the realities of provisionality and uncertainty. The central prayer of the Church is for a Kingdom that has not yet come, and not for a Jesus who is our exclusive possession in the here and now. The Lord's Prayer is remarkable in that Jesus appears to have deflected the demand of the disciples for a prayer that would be for their own private use (this is the force of their request in Luke 11.1: 'Lord teach us to pray as John taught his disciples'). The Lord's Prayer is not that of an exclusive group, nor does its content support the idea of extractionist salvation in which individual souls are removed from this world. The words that Jesus taught the Christian community ask for a kingdom to come on earth, when God's will shall be done here as in heaven. As part of the coming of that new world, the Church prays that it may be given strength for its pilgrimage ('our daily bread') and that it may already be the community of the future, a community of mutual forgiveness ('forgive us our sins as we forgive one another'). All this will lead to what Jewish tradition looks forward to as 'the mended creation'.[43]

Any community that prays such a prayer is indelibly marked by the future, and not by the past. The consequences of this for our inter-faith spirituality are fourfold. First, we affirm that Christian spiritual-ity belongs to a people on the way, *in via,* for which the best image is that of pilgrimage. Here in the present world we have no abiding city, much less a fortress to guard us from the world's assaults. Second, and as a consequence, the Christian's spiritual life depends on just enough bread for the day's journey. The people of the Exodus wanderings had to learn to trust in such a daily provision (Exod. 16), and so too Chris-tian spirituality is a spirituality of radical dependence on God. Third, this experience of dependence upon God leads Christians to affirm their condition of spiritual poverty of which the monk or nun, Eastern or Western, is the symbol. Christians hold onto all things lightly. And fourth, to use Wakefield's words once more, Christian spirituality is not an absorption into the infinite, but rather 'a being caught up into the paschal mystery'.[44] For Christians there is no bypass around the tensions, dangers and sufferings of this world. Yet all these are made luminous by the cross and resurrection. We speak very briefly of these four marks of Christian spirituality as marks of good and generous faith in our religiously plural situation.

PILGRIMAGE

One key image in the BCC *Guidelines,* titled *Relations with People of Other Faiths,* is that of the Christian as a 'fellow-pilgrim' with all other religious people who are seeking a new future. This image was derived from the WCC *Guidelines,* which had said: 'We feel able with integ-rity to assure our partners in dialogue that we come not as manipula-tors but as genuine fellow-pilgrims, to speak with them of what we believe God to have done in Jesus Christ.' It was a happy metaphor, for it reminds Christians that they are Abrahamic people, still looking for 'a city that has foundations, whose architect and builder is God' (Heb. 11.10). They are not to be a settled community, living on the traditions of the past, but rather to be those who realize that 'here we have no abiding city'. The image of the quest or sacred journey is nearly universal in the religious traditions of the world, and for Christians it is decisive. The Christian community has as one of its profoundest symbols the image of the *Parousia* or coming of Christ at the end of history, to which the clause 'thy kingdom come' points. So there are no road maps for the Christian journey in this religiously plural world, only the guarantee of a 'journey through unfamiliar territory'. Those committed to God's future will have to learn to accept the stance of vulnerability which dialogue brings. In good and generous faith alongside people who are Jewish or Muslim, Buddhist or Sikh, Christians will offer their witness as fellow-pilgrims.

To be vulnerable in this way is hardly comfortable or congenial. Like other people, Christians would prefer to live in gated communities within well-walled cities. Pilgrims, on the other hand, set out from their places of security in quest of the holy place: a city or a kingdom which lies somewhere over the rainbow, beyond the furthest horizon. They set out, knowing that there will be perils, dangers, vicissitudes all along the way.

One of the by-products of such a pilgrimage is self-knowledge. As the BCC *Guidelines* put it: 'Pilgrims learn truths about themselves and their fellow pilgrims when they travel on the road together, sharing its rigours, its difficulties and dangers. They come to understand their common humanity.' As Christians travel alongside their partners in dialogue they learn that they share the same fears, the same sorrows, the same anxieties. From this experience there arises the sharing of such resources as we may have: 'Pilgrims have gifts and strengths that they may share with others, and their fellows have gifts and strengths to share with them.' The BCC *Guidelines* then suggest that it is in this context that authentic witness to the dialogue partner would find its proper place. 'Through dialogue in commitment to our own faith, we are able to point fellow-pilgrims to where we have found Bread and Water, Rest and Healing.'

PROVISIONALITY AND PILGRIMAGE

The fourth petition of the Lord's Prayer, 'Give us today our daily bread', is instructive. The two versions that we have in the Gospel records (Matt. 6.11ff. and Luke 11.3ff.) raise two major questions of interpretation. One of these turns on the form of the verb, 'Give'. Is this to be translated, following Matthew, 'Give us once and for all', or should it be, following Luke, 'Keep on giving us'? In the one case the appropriate time expression will be 'this day' (as in Matt., *sēmeron*) and in the second case, 'each day' (as in Luke, to *kath' hēmeran*). The second difficulty lies in the interpretation of the adjective applied to 'bread', ordinarily translated 'daily' (*epiousios*). Raymond Brown has written about the persistent problem of translating this word: 'In the third century the word puzzled Origen, who could find no example of it in other Greek writers. Seventeen centuries later we are not much better off.'[45] The only real help here is in etymology, and Brown's detailed discussion leads him to the conclusion that this petition should be understood not so much as a petition requesting that the daily needs of the Christian community be satisfied, as in Luke, but rather as an eschatological reference, pointing to God's new future. The Bread Christians are asking for is the Bread of Tomorrow (Heb. *lehem mahar*), the food of the Messianic Banquet, when peace shall come upon the whole earth. But on its way to that great festal day, the Church still needs its provisions for the journey. To understand this, there is the powerful imagery provided by Exodus 16. 'The LORD said to Moses, "I am going to rain bread from heaven for you, and each day the people shall go out and gather enough for that day. In that way I will test them, whether they will follow my instruction or not"' (Exod. 16.4). But, as the Exodus story goes on to tell us, the people were not content with this provisionality. Instead of gathering a sufficiency for one single day, they wanted to ensure that they would have an adequate supply for the future. The result of this was that the manna 'bred worms and became foul' (Exod. 16.20). As a pilgrim people we are entitled to ask from God some of tomorrow's bread today, sufficient to get us through, and no more.

All this is of course figurative. If Christians choose Matthew's, rather than Luke's, interpretation of the fourth petition, they will think rather of the sustenance of heart and mind (John 6.27; 6.47ff.). We may apply it to the kind of theology and spirituality we need to sustain us in the religiously plural world: it will be given to us as we proceed in faith. 'Those who have already begun the journey into such unfamiliar territory have reminded us that theology is always provisional. It is out of experience in dialogue with our tradition, under the power of the Holy Spirit, that our theology flows. We are given to the Spirit, who is with us and who goes before us.' [46] These words, written by one of the Church of England's pioneers in interfaith dialogue, are a kindly but firm warning that we may not have either a theology or a spirituality which is clad in armour. The pilgrim moves towards the new age neither in an armoured Humvee nor with the logistical back-up of a mobile supermarket. Jesus did not say, 'Blessed are those who are rich in spirit', any more than he said, 'Those who seek to save their souls will save them.'

POVERTY

On the contrary, Jesus affirmed both the blessedness of the poor who were materially poor (Luke 6.20), and the blessedness of the poor in spirit (Matt. 5.3), which may, or may not, be the same thing. There is no need for Christians to decide on which interpretation they need to follow, for people of other faith traditions have already done that for us. Since the thought of the Sri Lankan Jesuit Aloysius Pieris has already been used in the chapter, let me describe an experience of my own in Fr Pieris's home on the outskirts of Colombo. I discovered there a Buddhist monk, working at the invitation of Fr Pieris on a wall sculpture of Jesus in the act of washing the disciples' feet. Now in Theravada Buddhist cultures it is quite a familiar event that a disciple should wash the feet of a monk; but hardly that a monk should wash the feet of a disciple, and all the shock and scandal of that action had been brought out in the sculpture in the faces of St Peter and of the disciples standing with him. Fr Pieris told me of the many exchanges he had had with the monk while he was working on portraying this incident. One day he had said to Fr Pieris: 'If you Christians had looked like this' (and he then pointed to the kneeling Jesus), 'we Buddhists would not have turned to Marxism.' The panoply of wealth and power of Western Christianity, and its individual representatives, some of whom have the temerity to call themselves 'born-again' Christians, impress the monks and nuns of the East very little.

From the fourth century onwards, the Christian protest against Christendom mainly has taken the form of monasticism, Thomas Merton's chosen vocation. Merton's last recorded talk was on 'Marxism and Monastic Perspectives', filmed by an Italian television company in Bangkok. His biographer describes it: 'What interested him, Merton said in his lecture, was the man who took up a critical attitude towards the world and its structures, whether monk or Marxist . . . Such a one believes that "the claims of the world are fraudulent". Both monk and Marxist want a world open to change: "the world refusal of the monk is in view of his desire for change."'[47]

Pieris weaves the insight of Merton's spirituality into his own perception of the way in which Christians in Asia relate to the monastic traditions of Hinduism and Buddhism. He has remarked that if the Church really wishes to enter into dialogue with Asia, it will be necessary for it to learn from its own monks the language of interiority, which is equally that of Asian monastic tradition, as well as the language of *agapē*, love, which is the only language the poor of Asia can understand.[48] The first of these languages speaks about a spiritual illumination which leads to an inward liberation from the instinct to acquire ever more things, and the second calls for an emancipation on the social level from all the structures of oppression, which are created by that same instinct to possess.

Such people are able to defuse the tensions within the Christian churches set amid the grinding poverty of Asia when they proclaim the gospel 'to our people in our own languages'. For the gospel of Jesus Christ is the new covenant into which God and the poor have entered against Mammon, their common enemy. 'When that happens', says

Pieris, 'liberation and inculturation will no longer be two things, but one in Asia.'

Pieris was dealing with the situation of the south-east Asian countries, but what he wrote has its implications for the way Christians are in interfaith dialogue in the West as well. Men and women have always been drawn to find ways of living together in common testimony to other, more transcendent, realities than the conventional wisdoms in their own societies. Now, with the coming of a consciously pluralistic religious world, it seems that the same Spirit is acting to bring these Buddhist and Hindu monastic forms into close association with Christian monasticism. Monks and nuns from these three traditions are now meeting in new and remarkable ways. We may surmise that the statement: 'Dialogue becomes the medium of authentic witness' will find its most complete fruition in the realm denoted by 'spirituality'. When we move beyond intellectual discussion to mutual endorsement, mutual support, mutual testimony in shared life and shared prayer, new things are born in us.

THE PASCHAL MYSTERY

The attitude of the pilgrim, the vulnerability of those who have left aside the old securities, the trust that there will be provision adequate for one day at a time, the commitment to a new poverty of spirit for the sake of the oppressed, make sense only in the light of the pattern of death and resurrection which we call the paschal mystery. Jesus reigns from the cross. In his obedience even unto death on the cross we have seen into the heart of God. Because of this obedience God has highly exalted him (Phil. 2.11). But Thomas's words form the counterpoint. 'Let us', he said, 'also go, that we may die with him.' We will see the marks of the nails, for dialogue is an element of the cross we are called to bear. Christian spirituality cannot be an avoidance of the tensions or dangers of 'the world of action'. But the living out of the paschal mystery means that there is also the release of creativity, openness, joy in the power of the resurrection. So we go on, in Wesley's words:

'rooted in the faith once delivered to the saints and grounded in love, in true catholic love,' until we are 'swallowed up in love for ever and ever!' In Wilfred Cantwell Smith's words there will come 'the end of religion, in the classical sense'. It will have reached 'its purpose and goal, that to which it points and may lead, namely God. Contrariwise, in the sense that once He appears vividly before us, in His depth and love and unrelenting truth, all else dissolves; or at the least religious paraphernalia drop back into their due and mundane place, and the concept "religion" is brought to an end.'[49]

At that point God will be 'all in all' to everyone (1 Cor. 15.28). In that day Christians will join with all those who have come 'from east and west' to sit at table with Abraham, Isaac and Jacob in the kingdom of Heaven (Matt. 8.11). So much at least is the expectation of those with good and generous faith.

5

To Bear an Authentic Witness

A Missiology for Religious Pluralism

Some exponents of the need for interreligious dialogue have forcibly argued that the words 'mission' and 'evangelism' need to be dropped from Christian vocabulary. Many others see mission and evangelism in contrast to the way of dialogue, so that Christians have to make a choice either to be evangelists or to be followers of the way of dialogue, or have to be evangelists one day and 'dialogicians' the next.[1] Others again have suggested mission may continue in the humanitarian fields of health, education and the like, but should not aim at converting adherents of the so-called higher religions where God's saving grace is already at work.[2] The argument of this chapter is that none of these positions is correct. I want to affirm first that dialogue is the most appropriate form of mission and evangelism in today's world, and second that good and generous faith on the part of Christians necessarily commits them to sharing their belief in the message of Jesus Christ in ways that affirm the spiritual awareness and religious commitment of their neighbours, that is dialogically.

Mission is what all human beings owe to
one another

But first we need to rescue the words mission and evangelism from the clouds that hang over them. The first of these clouds is the long association of mission with imperialism and colonialism. In the West, Christians are only just now beginning to rid themselves of the sense that civilization is in their hands and that they alone can bring light to benighted souls.[3] From the early nineteenth century, apologists for empire were also advocates of missions. As examples I offer William Huskisson in 1828, 'In every quarter of the globe we have planted the seeds of freedom, civilization and Christianity,' and Earl Grey in 1853, who said that the British crown 'assists in diffusing amongst millions of the human race, the blessings of Christianity and civilization'.[4] In the United States many voices in the nineteenth century lauded 'Anglo-Saxonism', speaking of the divine mission of the English-speaking peoples in particular to Christianize the world. So Lyman Abbott affirmed, 'It is the function of the Anglo-Saxon race to confer these gifts of civilization, through law, commerce, and education of the uncivilized people of the world.'[5] Samuel Harris, an Episcopal bishop of the same period, asserted of the USA that 'the consistency of the divine purpose in establishing our evangelical civilization is signally illustrated by the fact that it was primarily confided to the keeping of the Anglo-Saxon race', who were thereby committed, in the words of a New York Methodist minister, 'to conquer the world for Christ by dispossessing feeble races, and assimilating and moulding others'.[6]

With very good reason missionary activity has been judged by many to have been both the expression of a distasteful sense of cultural superiority, profoundly racist in its implications and the either conscious or unconscious tool of immoral economic and political exploitation.[7]

One set of responses to this blanket charge comes from Asian and African theologians, often the victims of cultural superiority and economic and political exploitation. In *The Common Task: A Theology of the Christian Mission*, Thomas Thangaraj defends his use of the word 'mission' autobiographically:

I come from a small village in South India called Nazareth. Around the beginning of the nineteenth century the people of my village welcomed Anglican missionaries into their midst, listened to the proclamation of the Gospel of Jesus Christ by those missionaries and accepted the Christian faith in large numbers. Such a mass conversion led to the renaming of their village as Nazareth. Though one may rightly criticize the modern missionary movement for its imperialism and for its subjection and disfigurement of particular cultures in many parts of the world, the word 'mission' for my people in Nazareth, South India, meant liberation, the flourishing of their human potential, and a regaining of their dignity and pride. These were people who belonged to the lower rungs of the India caste ladder, and for them 'mission' meant freedom from oppression and ignorance.[8]

This description, Thangaraj suggests, would not be limited to the people of Nazareth and is true to a large extent of the wider society of India. 'The word "mission"', he says, 'has stood for service, compassion and liberation. That is why Hindus in the city of Madurai do not find it problematic in any way to name their hospitals Hindu Mission Hospital and Meenakshi Mission Hospital.'[9] With this in mind Thangaraj says he can use the word 'mission' without being controlled by what he calls the post-Christian sense of guilt about the missionary enterprise so prevalent in the churches in the West.

Similarly Lamin Sanneh, who was born in the Gambia and now teaches at Yale, has recently published a sparkling book of questions and answers entitled *Whose Religion is Christianity? The Gospel beyond the West,* in which he celebrates the astonishing changes in the shape of the world Christian community. In Africa in 1900, under colonial rule there were 8.7 million Christians, that is about 9 per cent of its total population. Most of these were Copts in Egypt and Ethiopian Orthodox. Muslims outnumbered Christians by a ratio of four to one. By 1962 when Africa was slipping out of the control of the colonial powers, Britain, France, Belgium, Portugal and others, there were about 60 million Christians and about 145 million Muslims. Ten years later there were probably 120 million Christians. In 1995 the figure had jumped to just under 330 million, and in the latest year for which we have figures, 2002, to 350 million. Sanneh says the projection now is for 600 million Christians. This is simply astonishing, but the point to be made here is that by contrast with the West, and with Islam, this kind of Christianity has no reason for bad conscience about mission:

> *There have been no ecclesiastical courts condemning unbelievers, heretics and witches to death; no bloody battles of doctrine and polity; no territorial aggrandizement by churches; no jihads against infidels, no fatwas against women; no amputations, lynching, ostracism, penalties, or public condemnation of doctrinal differences or dissent.*[10]

Sanneh interprets this remarkable growth as the result of the discovery of Christianity by the indigenous communities of Africa in the light of their own experiences, rather than through their conversion by Europeans to a set of alien cultural norms. As a consequence the vast African Christian community is completely unaffected by the bad conscience of the West about mission and evangelism.

MISSION AS THE COMMON TASK OF ALL PEOPLE

Mission has in recent years become a public word: vast transnational international corporations work out their 'mission statements' with great care, as do national governments and a multitude of other organizations from universities to social service agencies. Thanagaraj claims this public usage for the mission of the Church, and insists that several consequences follow. (1) The use of the term mission puts Christians in a context that is much broader and more complex than was ever conceived by those who were committed to evangelism toward conversions and the growth of the Church. (2) It compels us to do our theology in public and in the 'open market place of ideas and concepts'. (3) It has serious methodological consequences for constructing a theology of mission. Thangaraj's own suggestions have at their centre the idea of 'conversation' as both a methodological and an epistemological category.

He borrows the work of the philosopher Hans-Georg Gadamer: 'the first condition of the art of conversation is to ensure that the other person is with us' ('dialogue begins when people meet each other', as we indicated earlier). Gadamer was primarily concerned about the interpretation of texts, and argued that readers had to move beyond the 'historical horizon' with which any text presents them. Thangaraj sees this as immediately relevant to the missionary Christians in the world. 'Therefore,' he writes, 'in choosing conversation as our method we attempt to go beyond the "historical horizon" that our talk concerning mission has presented us with so far.'

Gadamer also affirmed that conversation is a source of transformative knowledge, that is, it has epistemological dimensions. He wrote, 'to reach an understanding with our partner in dialogue is not merely a matter of total self-expression and a successful assertion of one's point of view, but a transformation into a communion, in which we do not remain what we were'.[11] In the light of Gadamer's propositions Thangaraj asks, 'If this is what we mean by conversation, how shall we begin the conversation on mission, so that it will include people of other religious and ideological persuasions, continue and sustain an ongoing dialogue, and result in novel understandings of mission?'[12] His innovative suggestion is that we adopt an approach he calls the *missio humanitatis,* the mission of humanity. By this he means the mission human beings owe one another and for the sake of each other, the very reason for their life in the world. Everywhere men and women are in fact engaged in conversations that cross religious and ideological divisions: when they meet for example in parent–teacher associations, in town or village meetings, in local and national legislative sessions and so on. One striking instance he gives from his experience in India, when a profound interreligious meeting has taken place when people of different faith have come together. Under Thangaraj's leadership this encounter did not begin with a theological or devotional theme but with the Constitution of India. This document all participants acknowledged as authoritative for their political life and therefore they were all included within the circle of discussion. From that starting point conversation easily and naturally moved to the contribution of religious traditions to their life together. In this process Thangaraj sees three communalities: responsibility, solidarity and mutuality. We cannot go into the details of how he works this out here, but we may take from him a fruitful set of insights into the possibilities of a missiology for religious pluralism. Christians may take their place alongside men and women who have their own conceptions of mission. All become missionaries in a relationship of mutuality. There are no longer the 'missioners' and the 'missioned'. All people are able to be witnesses to their faith and tradition.

DAVID BOSCH AND MISSION IN BOLD HUMILITY

Perhaps the most significant Western missiologist of the last generation was the Afrikaaner David Bosch of the University of South Africa. He died in 1992, waiting for an ambulance to arrive after a car crash. Just before his too early death he published his great work, *Transforming Mission: Paradigm Shifts in the Theology of Mission,* in 1991. Towards the end of this work he wrote of the issues that newly confront the Church, under the general heading 'Mission as Witness to People of Other Living Faiths', and reflected on the new ground that has yet to be broken 'since we are totally unprepared for facing the challenge before us'. He indicated in the same place that he shared all the concerns expressed by my then colleague Christopher Lamb and myself that 'the theology of religions (and indeed the entire area of missiology)' is 'either virtually unknown in theological institutions or relegated to the position of an unimportant subsection of pastoral theology'.[13] 'More than has ever been the case since Constantine's victory over Maxentius at the Milvian Bridge in ad 312,' he wrote 'Christian theology is a theology of dialogue . . . One-way, monological travel is out, as is militancy of any form.'[14]

After reviewing quite briefly development in the theology of religion up to 1990, and especially after citing the two statements of the1989

San Antonio Conference of the WCC in 1989, 'We cannot point to any other way of salvation than Jesus; at the same time we cannot set limits to the saving power of God,' Bosch noted that the San Antonio Statement acknowledges that these words have to be held in tension, as it says: 'We appreciate this tension and do not attempt to resolve it.'[15] Bosch then made this remarkable statement:

> *Such language boils down to an admission that we do not have the answers and are prepared to live within the frameworks of penultimate knowledge, that we regard our involvement in mission and dialogue as an adventure, are prepared to take risks, and are anticipating surprises as the Spirit guides us into fuller understanding. This is not an opting for agnosticism, but for humility. It is however a bold humility — or a humble boldness. We know in part, but we do know. And we believe that the faith we profess is both true and just, and should be proclaimed. We do this, however, not as judges or lawyers, but as witnesses; not as soldiers but as envoys of peace; not as high pressure sales persons, but as ambassadors of the Servant Lord.*[16]

Bosch spoke like this in good faith but also in generous faith, referring elsewhere to the decision of the heart to accept the existence of other religious traditions 'not grudgingly but willingly'; to expect that God has preceded us and therefore to see other men and women as 'recipients of the same mercy, sharing in the same mystery'.[17]

THE CHANGING SHAPE OF CHRISTIAN MISSION AND THE GREAT COMMISSION[18]

The story of the risen Jesus' commissioning eleven of his disciples to go and disciple the nations in Matthew 28 has served as a foundation document for Protestant Christian mission only since the end of the eighteenth century, when William Carey wrote his *Enquiry into the Obligation of Christians to Use Means for the Conversion of the Hea-*

thens. Somewhat to our surprise there was little sense of an obligation to either mission or evangelism before then, and certainly very little use was made of Matthew 28.16–20.[19] Many of the Reformers had taught that this commandment was specifically laid upon the apostles and that its force had died out with them.[20] For many others in the ultra-Calvinist wing of the Reformation any attempt to make converts by evangelistic preaching savoured somewhat of impious presumption.[21] This is the force behind Carey's title. He himself had been admonished for missionary zeal: 'Sit down young man, when God wants to convert the heathen, He'll do it without your help or mine.'[22] The Particular Baptists, Carey's denomination, adhered strictly to the Westminster Confession, and Carey had to choose his arguments carefully. In his Enquiry written for his fellow Baptists his first chapter is entitled 'An Enquiry whether the Commission given by our Lord to his Disciples be not still binding on us?'[23] Since 1792, Matthew 28.16–20 has been the central text for those concerned with Christian mission, repeatedly quoted (but more often misquoted) in support of aggressive evangelistic activity. Like John 14.6 it functions in the minds of many Christians to prevent their serious engagement with the theological problem of religious diversity. And like John 14.6 it demands much closer inspection. As a result of going deeply into the text, again as in the case of John 14.6, Christians may find positive and helpful guidance about living with good and generous faith even as they engage in mission and evangelism.

Much of this rereading of the 'Great Commission' arises as a result of exciting work done in recent years by biblical scholars. There is now an increasing consensus among them that these words form a summary of the entire Gospel of Matthew, in which all Matthew's central concerns are present. Consequently it is incorrect to lift these four verses out of their context and to give them a life of their own. Still worse would it be to conflate them with other similar sounding verses from other Gospels; this is the most common source of the regular misquotation of the 'Great Commission'.[24] As Bosch made it clear, 'Matthew 28.16–20 has to be interpreted *against the background of*

Matthew's Gospel as a whole and unless we keep this in mind we shall fail to understand it' (emphasis his).[25]

The first theme to focus upon in the Gospel is Matthew's extraordinary interweaving of Jewish particularism with a profound concern for the people of the world. On one side we have Jesus' saying, 'I was sent only to the lost sheep of the house of Israel' (15.24), and his instruction earlier that his disciples are to 'go nowhere among the Gentiles, and enter no town of the Samaritans' (10.5); but at the same time no Gospel writer more emphasizes the presence of non-Jewish people in the events of Jesus' life. This begins with Jesus' ancestry when four non-Israelite women, Tamar, Rahab, Ruth, and the wife of Uriah, are specified. It continues in the story of the visit of the Eastern magi at Jesus' birth; incidents in Jesus' ministry like his encounter with the centurion in Matthew 8, with the Canaanite woman in chapter 15; Jesus' statement in the eschatological discourse in 24.14 that the gospel will be preached in the whole world (*en hole tē oikoumenē*) to all the nations (*pasin tois ethnesin*); and the reaction of the centurion and his gentile soldiers at Jesus' crucifixion, who exclaim, 'Truly this man was God's Son' (27.54). Significant also are such matters as the identification of Galilee as Galilee of the gentiles (*Galilaia tōn ethnōn*, 4.14–16); the record of Jesus' activity in Syria; and the reference to Jesus' disciples as salt of the earth and light of the world. Some of these themes reappear in Matthew 28.16–20.

So we come to look closely at the 'Great Commission'. First we observe its setting: the place of encounter is an unknown mountain in Galilee. In contrast with Luke and John the moment of supreme revelation is far away from any one people's holy temple or holy city. Because the mountain is not specified, it represents anywhere, at any time. Because the resurrection takes place in Galilee 'of the gentiles', the non-Jewish world may become as privileged a place of faith as the Holy Land and the Holy City.

In the story of the meeting with the risen Christ we see too that Matthew refuses to privilege the disciples as extraordinary men of faith, for the Greek clause *hoi de edistasan* probably means, not 'but some doubted' as in the NRSV, but that they *all* doubted. This faithfully represents Matthew's understanding of discipleship, which is always a matter of 'little faith' (see 14.31 and 16.8). 'Faith is by its nature not the same as cocksureness, but incorporates doubts within itself even in the act of worship.'[26] Matthew is suggesting that what happened in the resurrection event does not make Christians into superlative heroes whether of faith or deeds: they remain as ordinary people among ordinary people with the same limited horizons.

In the 'Great Commission' story Jesus is presented as wholly different from the one who preached and taught in Galilee and Judaea, with his limitations of stamina and knowledge. After the resurrection he is portrayed as the bearer of all authority 'in heaven and on earth'.[27] He will accompany his disciples to the close of the age. It is this one who is the 'Great Commissioner', in whom Christians are invited to put their trust.

In the context of religious diversity, it is necessary to pay the closest attention to what Jesus is represented as commanding. First there is an apparently small point but one which may have great significance. The Greek structure of 'Go therefore and make disciples' (NRSV) is not an imperative plus an imperative, but rather a participle and then an imperative: *'going,* make disciples' (*poreuthentes mathēteusate*). 'Go' is not stressed, the aorist participle simply qualifies and reinforces the action of the main verb.[28] All the emphasis therefore falls on the Greek imperative *mathēteusate*. This is the imperative form of *mathēteuein*, a word used infrequently in the New Testament, best translated simply as 'to disciple' (cf. Matt. 13.52; 27.57; and Acts 14.21). In each of these cases *mathēteuein* is a transitive verb, and never stands alone without an object. In 28.18 the object of the verb is 'all the nations' (*panta ta ethnē*). Translations that make this task sound like gathering individual converts are simply misleading, however consonant they may be with the all-pervasive individualism of the Western mind. There is certainly a problem of interpretation here, for we can only speculate what an *ethnos*, or 'nation', might be; it will be for sure nothing like the nation-states that most Westerners have belonged to for the last three or four hundred years. One guess at its meaning comes from contemporary missiology, where the term 'people groups' describes people in their corporative social and cultural relationships. This may be the best approximation. The importance for Matthew of the 'nations' as a corporate concept is nowhere made more clear than in his final parable, the summation of his teaching, in 25.31–46, which should properly be called 'the parable of the sheep nations and the goat nations': we say Matthew, but the idea of course goes back to Jesus. In any case the point is that Jesus is not telling us to make converts on a one-by-one basis.[29] It is more fruitful to reflect on what a discipled nation might look like.

Next we may ask, 'What is the content of this discipling?' Here we have the most striking part of the Great Commission: the nations are to be baptized 'in the name of the Father and of the Son and of the Holy Spirit' (a problem to which we shall return) and are to be taught to keep all that Jesus has commanded (the Greek words here are *tērein, entellesthai,* which along with *mathēteuein* are Rabbinic terms, each one characteristic of Matthew's portrayal of Jesus as Rabbi). Matthew has already made it clear that, for Jesus, doing the will of his Father is more important than calling him 'Lord, Lord' (7.21ff.). The first Gospel is full of concepts like God's will (*thelema*), justice (*dikaiosunē*), commandments (*entolai*), the sovereign rule of heaven (*basileia tou ouranou*), together with such injunctions as to be perfect (*esesthe teleioi*), and to bear fruit (*karpous poiein*), as well as the verbs found in Matthew 28.20: to teach (*didaskein*), and to keep (*tērein*). Bosch calls this vocabulary 'extremely sober'. This, he says, is 'no gospel that may distance itself in an enthusiasm of the Spirit from the earthly Jesus'.[30]

Some consequences, highly relevant to Christian existence in the midst of religious pluralism, follow from this examination of the commission of Jesus. First, it offers no privileged status for Christians. In the midst of other seekers after the truth in other religions, they are as other men and women. They have to offer their witness 'in bold humility'. For many this was already a reality in their own experience, for they had found themselves to be fallible and 'of little faith'. They had also become aware that they have not always found the right words to express their faith. Such Christians may be reassured by the Great Commission that all they can do is to bear their testimony tentatively and prayerfully, hoping that the Holy Spirit will take their inadequate stumblings and stammerings and use them for a greater purpose. To such Christians, Matthew's suggestion that the resurrection event did not generate perfect faith offers considerable comfort and reassurance. There are other Christians, however, who need perhaps to reflect on their over-confidence, which leads them to appear arrogant and bombastic to people of other faith traditions. Cocksureness is not a pleasing quality in interfaith dialogue situations.

Second, the mandate of Jesus does not indicate that every moment must be dedicated to 'converting' the other person; this is not a proper notion of what evangelism is. Were that to be so we may doubt whether Christians would ever have any conversation partners, because a conversionist attitude destroys basic human relationships like friendship and trust. 'Evangelists' of this kind seem to feel it imperative to watch for opportunities to lead conversations in directions they desire. Often this leads them to use, consciously or unconsciously, psychologically coercive techniques, and Christian history is replete with woeful diversions into the use of the methods that Lamin Sanneh described earlier. The way of dialogue intentionally repudiates 'conversionism', and the WCC *Guidelines on Dialogue* in 1979 said that 'we feel able with integrity to assure our partners in dialogue that we come not as manipulators but as genuine fellow-pilgrims, to speak with them what we believe God to have done in Jesus Christ who has gone before us, but whom we seek to meet anew in dialogue'. There is a corollary to this. Cocksure evangelists are incapable of learning from the people they are addressing, as though all truth already resided with them.

Third, although in Christian history, particularly in the eighteenth and nineteenth centuries, the imperative 'Go' was decisive in getting European and North American Christians organized for missionary activity in Africa, Asia and the Pacific, it has to be questioned whether this remains an adequate understanding of the 'Great Commission' text for three reasons. First, such interpretation makes the commission of Jesus sound too arduous and too demanding, requiring specific action and movement. Second, it would then by implication appear to limit the task of discipling to some rather special people known as missionaries or evangelists; that is, those men and women who have been or are in a position to leave home and to make long journeys to different countries. Third, it has led ordinary church members to feel that they are exempt from the discipling process simply because they have no choice but to remain in one place. But upon reflection the 'Great Commission' suggests a rather different approach. Matthew is always aware that at the foot of any mountain the crowds are waiting with their problems and demands (Matt. 8.1ff.; 17.14ff.). The disciples have no choice but to come down from the top of the mountain and rejoin the rest of humanity. When they got down, and 'on their way' so to speak, they were to 'disciple the nations'. Michael Green described this process in the early Church as 'gossiping the gospel', done by ordinary men and women pursuing their everyday tasks in homes and market places.[31] In the context of religious diversity in the twenty-first century, Christian men and women constantly interact with faithful people of other faith traditions. For them interfaith dialogue is no set-piece carried out at a high intellectual level, but takes place in innumerable and varied settings where they can 'gossip the gospel'.

Fourth, the words 'discipling the nations' must be taken seriously (they cannot mean, let us say again, 'make converts from among the nations' or 'out of the nations'). One important clue in Matthew's Gospel is in 13.52, 'Therefore every scribe who has been trained [better "discipled", *mathēteutheis*] for the kingdom of heaven is like the master of a household who brings out of his treasure what is new and what is old.' This, it has often been suggested, may be a 'cameo self-portrait' of Matthew himself or of the members of the circles from which the first Gospel emerged. The 'scribe' here is a Jew who has pondered over a long period on the difference that the light of the events surrounding Jesus has made on his faith and beliefs. Certainly 'what is old' is still valid for Matthew: he records Jesus as saying, 'Do not think that

I have come to abolish the law and the prophets; I have come not to abolish but to fulfil' (5.17). Becoming 'discipled' involved a long process of thinking and reflection. In our religiously plural world Christians ought to be able to recognize that men and women of other faith obediences will need also the same space for their reflection on what Jesus could mean for them. Missiologies based on 'instantaneous' conversion will continue disastrously to fail to enable people newly attracted to Christian faith to 'bring out of their treasure things old and new'.

In this context (there are many others) we are suggesting that one interpretation of 'nation' (*ethnos*) is a 'people-group' that lives out of a distinctive faith tradition, Muslim, Hindu, Buddhist, Confucian, and so on.[32] If this is the case, 'discipling the nations' implies the need for serious and sustained work by Christian scholars and theologians to find ways of speaking about their faith to men and women nurtured in quite other traditions, profoundly different philosophical and cultural traditions. But this kind of deep and intense exploration is not the task of people 'gossiping the gospel'. It is a particular vocation, requiring assiduous study and constant interaction with men and women who live within a particular faith tradition. There is some light to be shed on this process from within the New Testament, in an incident briefly recorded for us in the Acts of the Apostles.

PAUL AT EPHESUS, ACTS 19.8–10

Let us set this passage out in the NRSV translation:

> *8 He entered the synagogue and for three months spoke out boldly, and argued persuasively about the kingdom of God. 9 When some stubbornly refused to believe and spoke evil of the Way before the congregation, he left them, taking the disciples with him, and argued daily in the lecture hall of Tyrannus. 10 This continued for two years, so that all the residents of Asia, both Jews and Greeks, heard the word of the Lord.*

This incident has not caught the attention of the academic commentators who normally pass quickly over the three months that Paul spent in the synagogue and the two years in which he was engaged in regular conversation in the hall of Tyrannus. One may surmise that the reason for this is that few New Testament scholars have real or deep experience of trying to express the Christian faith in terms that might be intelligible to people with different religious backgrounds.[33]

Very striking in this passage is the NRSV translators' use of the word 'argued'. Behind this term are two Greek verbs, *dialegomai* and *dialogizomai*. They mean 'to reason', 'to contend'. 'Argued persuasively' in verse 8 is a rendering of *dialegomenos kai peithōn*: and *dialegomenos* in verse 9 is also translated as 'argued'.[34] But surely 'arguing' in contemporary English has the slightly unpleasant undertone of contention and disagreement.[35] I suggest for the reasons that follow that in both cases 'dialoguing and persuading' and 'dialoguing' would much better help us to understand what Paul was doing. In both contexts, in both the synagogue and the lecture hall of Tyrannus, the means of sharing the gospel was 'dialogue', not 'argument'.

Then, just as striking, in the period of time involved in this incident, Paul was virtually stationary for considerably more than two years. He was not hastening from place to place 'lest souls pass into eternity and the torment of hell-fire without even hearing of Jesus Christ'.[36] His missionary motive was clearly something other than that: there is a clue to it in this passage to which we shall return in a moment. For the time being let us again contemplate the time-span: Paul was prepared to spend at least two years and three months in the activity described as 'reasoning and persuading', that is, in a programme of dialogue.

Where did all this activity take place? First, in the synagogue. Too much stress has in time past been laid upon words spoken in the heat of the controversy at Pisidian Antioch. At that time Paul is recorded as having said to the Jews: 'Since you reject [the word of God] and judge yourselves to be unworthy of eternal life, we are now turning to the Gentiles' (Acts 13.46). Paul's concern for and commitment to his own people never wavered, as we see later in Acts 23.6 and 24.14ff. From the first of these verses we see that not only did he refuse to think of himself as a former Jew, but that he positively remained a Pharisee, and proudly so, the 'son of Pharisees'.[37] There was not, could not have been, a clean break between his ancestral faith and his discovery of Christ, but even so, Paul deliberately put himself under the Law (see 1 Cor. 9.20) and observed all the synagogue customs in order to find ways of interpreting the gospel to Jews. He remained there sabbath by sabbath until he was forced by other Jews to leave.

Only when his enemies spoke evil of the Way did he withdraw to a second location in Ephesus: the 'lecture hall [or school, *scholē*] of Tyrannus' (19.9). Various guesses have been made as to what this 'school' was. These range from its being an actual 'school' in which Tyrannus was the pedagogue ('tyrant' might be an appropriate school-boy nickname for their schoolmaster); to a kind of shop front where consultations were available in land measurement (geometry) or pharmacology; to a guild-house meeting place for those who plied the philosophers' trade in Ephesus. A later scribe, more conversant with the habits of Mediterranean seaboard cities than most of us, had no difficulty in suggesting that the time in which Paul used the 'school' were 'from the fifth hour to the tenth', that is eleven in the morning to four in the afternoon, precisely when the 'school' was closed for siesta time. Despite the heat and humidity of a Mediterranean summer, Luke tells us that Paul was able to attract a steady following for his daily conversations (*kath hēmeran dialegomenos*).

By borrowing or renting Tyrannus' place Paul had moved into the physical environment of Greek philosophy, and by extension into the thought-world of Stoicism and Epicureanism. Here, we can speculate, was the opportunity that Paul had been waiting for since he left the Areopagus in Athens, where there had been a company of people who wanted to hear some more about Christian faith (Acts 17.32 and above, p. 33).

THE SUBJECT MATTER OF PAUL'S DIALOGUE IN EPHESUS

At this point we may ask if Luke the historian gives us any clues as to the basic subject matter of the dialoguing. There are two of these, one from the synagogue situation and the other from the school of Tyrannus. In the synagogue the conversations turn, says Luke, on the meaning of the kingdom of God. Clearly this was not in the first instance the offering of a set of proof-texts showing that Jesus is the Messiah, though this may well have been an element of the discussion. By so clearly stating the subject as the 'kingdom of God', Luke was indicating that the sabbath day conversations were about the shape of God's kingly rule in the earth, for which the synagogue was already praying in its liturgy in the first century ce: 'Magnified and sanctified be his great name in the world which he has created according to his will. May he establish his kingdom during your life and during your days, and during the life of the house of Israel, even speedily and at a near time.'[38]

Against this background almost impossible questions arose for a teacher who wanted to say that this prayer had been answered. How is it possible to say that the Messiah has come when sickness and death are still part of the everyday experience of humankind? How is the suffering and impotence manifested in Jesus' death on the cross to be related to the rule of God? That Paul felt the force of these questions is apparent in his letters written during this period of his career. Thus in 2 Corinthians 13.9, for example, he speaks of God's power being made perfect in weakness.

The second clue is embedded in the apparent Lucan exaggeration in 19.10. 'All the residents of Asia, both Jews and Greeks, heard the word of the Lord.' Either Luke was engaging in unwarranted hyperbole or he had something else in mind, for 'All the residents of Asia' simply did not hear, in a literal or physical sense; Asia Minor was to be the scene of much missionary activity in the second, third and fourth centuries. Luke had no doubt another purpose in using this expression. He was implying that as a result of the constant discussions

with Greek intellectuals in the school of Tyrannus, and of the daily
encounters with Greek philosophical concepts and their underlying
thought-patterns; as a result of seeing the various gleams of understanding in the systems and doctrines propounded by the Stoic, Platonic and Epicurean philosophers, the early Church had put itself in
a position to 'tell the story properly' to the mind of Asia: perhaps the
precise use of the word 'Greeks' (*hellēnas*), rather than gentiles (*ethnē*),
in 19.10 is an indication of this.

As a result of the daily intellectual struggles for understanding, in
the hours-long discussions, month in and month out, with Greek philosophical and theological concepts, Paul brought all the resources of
his disciplined mind to engaging their underlying thought-patterns.[39]
How could what he had glimpsed of Christ be expressed in words
which resonated with the systems and doctrines which were held by
those who frequented the school of Tyrannus? Could such Hellenistic
concepts as *eikon, prōtotokos, archē, plērōma, theotēs,* be used as the
medium for christological statements? In Paul's own letters from this
period, some of them from Ephesus, we can see Stoic or Platonic or
even Epicurean thought forms being used to express the meaning of
Jesus Christ. The idea of the *plērōma* conception that forms the basis
for the christological statement in Colossians 2.9: 'in him the whole
fullness of deity [*plērōma tēs theotētos*] dwells bodily', and the ecclesi-
ological statement in Ephesians 1.23 about church, 'which is his body,
the fullness of him who fills all in all' (*to plērōma tou ta panta en pasin
plēroumenou*) may originate here. In Paul's letters as well as the other
writings of the New Testament we can see how soon Christianity took
over concepts from the Hellenist thought world in order to explain
the mystery of Christ.[40] Incidentally it is worth just remarking that
this literature has associations with Ephesus, the city of 'dialogue'.[41]
Luke no doubt believes that here is the part for the whole — a kind of
'first-fruitage' of all this — now all Asia could really hear the gospel in
a language addressed to its mind as well as to its heart. Were we Christians more generally to take this model seriously, we would be far more
concerned than we often appear to be to find ways of expressing our

faith so that Muslims or Marxists, Hindus or Humanists could really be said to have 'heard the word of God'. For most people of other faith traditions the gospel story just has not yet been properly told.

Dialogue and other aspects of Paul's work

There is still more to be said about Paul at Ephesus, for it would be highly misleading to suggest that 'dialogue' was the only form of mission in which he was engaged. Actually there were at least three other forms. One was a kind of ecumenical or intra-faith dialogue with some disciples or followers of Jesus who 'knew only the baptism of John' (see the well-known story of Acts 19.1–7). Another form of mission was the frontal attack on spurious and false religion — what we probably would call a 'new religious movement' with Jewish syncretistic elements, practising exorcism and magic arts (see Acts 19.13–19). The human world of religion is always ambiguous, indeed is often open to invasion by demonic forces. Dialogue is not the appropriate stance when confronted by the kind of people represented by the seven sons of Sceva, then or now. The third kind of mission is what we might call the 'unmasking' of an ideology. The one prevalent in Ephesus was connected with the cult of the goddess Artemis, 'Diana of the Ephesians'. In an almost Marxist sense, the worship of Artemis both buttresses and is buttressed by the economics of big business. This surely is how we must read the story of Demetrius and the silversmiths (Acts 19.23–41).

So we may state that dialogue with people of other faiths and ideologies is misunderstood if it is presented as the only way of mission or if it is represented as being complacent and tolerant in the face of evil ideology. But with the example of Paul before us we may equally conclude that evangelism is distorted if it is presented as happening only by monologue, by one-way proclamation, or by slick propaganda. Paul at Ephesus shows us that the way of dialogue is a way of patience, sometimes frustrating, always time-consuming. It shows us, too, that the way of dialogue means meeting the other person on his or her own terms and really attending to what they say, believe, feel. We also see that it is a way of seeking to share persuasively the best of our own conviction, to share that which has most persuasively laid hold of our own minds and hearts. It was a way that plainly made many friends for Paul in Ephesus: what a significant comment is in Acts 19.31: 'some of the Asiarchs also, who were friends [*philoi*] of his'.[42] For some Christians it may seem a little surprising that Paul had friends who were leaders of the cult of the Roman emperor and the Roman gods.

Paul is the best one to sum it all up. In a letter he wrote during this period in Corinth he bears his own testimony to his way of dialogue: 'To the Jews I became as a Jew, in order to win Jews . . . to those outside the law I became as one outside the law . . . To the weak, I became weak . . . I have become all things to all people, so that I might by any means save some. I do it all for the sake of the gospel, so that I may share in its blessings' (1 Cor. 9.20–3).

Paul speaks in his own terms of what we today would call empathy and identification and of a deep loving concern for the other. In the last words, 'that I may share in its blessings', there is what has been called 'the purest missionary motive of all'.[43] Christians share in dialogue about Jesus and the kingdom because they themselves want to discover more of the riches of the gospel.[44]

DIALOGUE IN THE HISTORY OF THE CHRISTIAN MISSION

In the centuries that followed very little remained of a sense that the gospel had to be gossiped. Other forces took their place. When he became the first Christian emperor, Constantine wanted one standard form of Christian belief throughout his empire and imposed it by coercive means. Early medieval kings became converted to Christianity and ordered all their subjects to be baptized. The dross of mass baptisms, crusades against Muslims, forcible conversions of Jews, edicts against heretics, the inquisition, all followed. Then came the period of colonialism with the equally disagreeable compulsory Christianization of subject races. But the great tradition of 'reasoning and persuading' was never wholly lost. Even the period of 'grand Christianity' in the high Middle Ages could produce figures like Ramon Lull and Francis of Assisi.

By the sixteenth century there were other factors at work leading to the rediscovery of dialogical methods in missionary work. Andrew Walls has suggested that we look at the different circumstances of the Spanish and Portuguese seaborne empires. 'The Spanish presence was concentrated in America and the Philippines. The Portuguese presence stretched like a thread along the coasts of Africa, along the Persian gulf and across the Indian Ocean, into South India and Sri Lanka and the coasts and islands of Southeast Asia and offshore China and on to Japan — not to mention Brazil.'[45] With only limited resources and confronted by resistant Islam, Hinduism and Buddhism, the Portuguese-type missionary necessarily became a person of dialogue and persuasion, exemplified in such figures as Robert de Nobili and Giuseppe Beschi. As Walls remarks: 'In this strange way, interfaith dialogue was born of frustrated colonialism. Putting it another way: in the mercy of God, the king of Portugal never had enough servants to go out into the highways and byways and compel them to come in.'[46] I want now to point to some of the most striking figures in the missionary movement of the last three centuries who lived in good and generous faith, and who demonstrated that the most appropriate means of telling the good news is dialogue. Certainly these are some of the most effective people in the history of the Church. I nominate a Lutheran pietist of the early eighteenth century; a late-eighteenth-century Anglican evangelical; a mid-nineteenth-century English Congregationalist; a great Dutch missiologist of the twentieth century; and a Canadian missionary and scholar of comparative religion who died just as the twenty-first century was beginning.[47]

BARTHOLOMAEUS ZIEGENBALG: THE PASSIONATE STUDENT OF HINDUISM

The first Protestant missionary in India was Bartholomaeus Ziegenbalg (1683–1719).[48] He arrived in Tranquebar on 19 July 1706 and immediately set out on a path of unremitting labour that led to his early death at the age of 35. His achievements focused on the study of Tamil language and culture. He prepared dictionaries, published a Tamil grammar, and collected Tamil manuscripts. Firmly set against the westernization of Indian Christians, Ziegenbalg was assiduous in teaching Tamil schoolchildren their own language and customs. To do this he set out on a self-appointed task of understanding Hinduism from within. Unfortunately, some might say, his informants were not Hindu scholars and pundits but rather the ordinary citizens of Tranquebar. A recent study offers this view about Ziegenbalg's achievement:

> *For it turns out that his ignorance of the historical element of Hinduism, his less than perfect understanding of the abstract and philosophical nature of Hindu reformers and sages are matched by an unparalleled knowledge of the populist gods and forms of worship, his very detailed observation of Hindu rituals, a thorough familiarity with legends associated with various gods and their fasts and festivals, and accurate descriptions of phenomena that are of very great ethnological interest: the* tilaks *and other caste marks of various sects, the special prayers used by them, the musical instruments in use at the time, or the arrangement of folk deities around a major god in a temple complex.*[49]

Equipped with such a mass of information, and speaking Tamil fluently, Ziegenbalg turned to what Brijraj Singh calls, perhaps anachronistically but accurately enough, 'interfaith dialogue'. Though he was not aware of it, Ziegenbalg was entering into India's living tradition of interfaith colloquies or dialogues, a pattern that had been set by the great Mughul emperor Akbar (1556–1605). To be sure, Ziegenbalg's motives included a desire to defeat Hinduism and Islam by showing up their errors, but he himself was not of a polemical spirit. Furthermore he was quite without the taint of racism or imperialism that was often manifested in other eighteenth-century pioneers of the study of Indian language and customs.[50] On the contrary Ziegenbalg believed 'in a genuine spiritual conversion' which could only be gained through a process of 'reading, learning, meditation, thought and prayer'.[51] His profound Lutheran pietism led him to emphasize the importance of books: in his attempts to build up a library for the people, in his starting a printing press, and in his educational work and establishment of schools. His work in dialogue was characterized by a profound respect for the intellectual achievements of Tamil people whom, he said, God has liberally blessed 'with Strength of Thought and Readiness of apprehending the various Aspects of and mutual Relations of all Sublunary Things'. Elsewhere he praised their skill in debate and argument, affirming that talking with them had led him into a 'deeper consideration of many subjects, and in both theology and philosophy learned much of which neither I nor other students had thought before'.[52] As a result throughout his writings Ziegenbalg faithfully recorded all opposing views: 'His greatness lay in his willingness to listen to other points of view instead of trying to suppress them. In his pages the voices of his Hindu adversaries are often heard, and they are heard in argument, in dissent, and in a refusal to accept or be convinced.'[53]

This concern with winning arguments fairly was not, however, conducive to church growth. It has been estimated that at the time of his death in 1719 Ziegenbalg left behind him only 250 new Christians, a fact which was gleefully seized upon by the advocates of more forceful methods of making converts. Coercive mission was far from the mind of the first Protestant missionary to India.

HENRY MARTYN: THE MAN WHO LOVED MUSLIMS

Henry Martyn (1781–1812) is our next example of dialogical evangelism. Henry Martyn died at the age of 31 and we are left to speculate what might have been if both he and Ziegenbalg had reached the height of their powers, and had been able to guide missionaries in India and Persia for a longer period.[54] Strictly speaking Martyn, a brilliant Cambridge linguist and mathematician, was never a missionary. He served as a chaplain with the East India Company, and was posted to Dinapore and Cawnpore. In both places his refusal to regard Indians as inferior and his respect for Indian culture annoyed and alienated his fellow-English. He annoyed the British General at Dinapore by suggesting that Indians were not fools and that 'ingenuity and clear reasoning were not confined to England and Europe'.[55] But the climate of India caused severe and rapid deterioration in his health (he was a victim of tuberculosis) and he began a long overland journey home. He purposely travelled through Shiraz, where he wanted to present his Persian translation of the New Testament to the Shah of Persia.

During Martyn's lonely vigil in Shiraz — 'A Year among the Doctors', Constance Padwick calls it — there were significant moments of sharing the good news of Jesus that happened among the Sufi community. Martyn recorded in his Journal: 'I am sometimes led on by the Persians to tell them all I know of the recesses of the sanctuary, and these are the things that interest them.'[56] But eventually he attracted the attention of the more strictly orthodox and was lured into controversy with the Mullah Mirza Ibrahim and other members of the scholarly class. These debates were later published as *Controversial Tracts on Christianity and Mohammedanism* (1824) and have left perhaps an impression that Martyn was an ardent polemicist. In fact Martyn confided to his Journal that, while a debate might 'entice a spirit of enquiry', he did not overvalue 'much stress upon clear argument: the work of God is seldom wrought in this way'. Constance Padwick offers a firm corrective of the suggestion that polemics and controversy were part of Martyn's character in a little-noticed appendix to her biographical study. The report she reproduces there contains a reminiscence by the Revd C. F. Oakley, speaking in London in 1864. Oakley told of a long journey across French Algeria to meet a 'chief of considerable power':

> *I found all the hospitality which an Arab chief could give . . . He caused a large box to be opened before my eyes. From this box he took out a very singular collection of Arabic manuscripts and books. At last he came to a book in Persian, the sight of which in the great desert quite surprised me; it seemed like finding a Russian book in the Scotch Highlands. I said, 'How came this book here? Can you read it?' 'No.' 'Then why do you keep it with all this care?' (It was wrapped in folds of silk.)*

The answer concerned the chief's father who in 1812 had undertaken the *hajj* and had gone from Mecca to Persia, afterwards visiting Shiraz. There he heard of an Englishman who had come to that city. He had visited him, and had been 'received by him with kindness'. During the time they both remained in Shiraz they often talked about many things connected with religion, and 'the Englishman spoke particularly to my father concerning Sidi 'Isa (Jesus Christ), and my father heard him gladly. After a time the Englishman went away, and among the books he used to read was the one I have here.' For the sake of his English friend the chief's father had brought that book home with him when he returned to the Sahara. As he lay dying the old man had told his son that 'if there ever come to the Sahara an Englishman declaring that he is the servant of Jesus Christ' he was to be treated as a brother. This 'for the sake of that Englishman who was a brother to me while I was at Shiraz in Persia'.[57]

THOMAS EBENEZER SLATER: THE FIRST THEORETICIAN OF MISSION AS DIALOGUE

The freshness of their breaking new ground has meant that the stories of Ziegenbalg and Martyn needed telling rather more fully than those that now follow. Thomas Ebenezer Slater (1840–1912) had the benefit of many decades of London Missionary Society work in India and elsewhere behind him when he began publishing works which might have been seminal on the theory of mission and the Christian understanding of Hinduism.[58] His first major work, *The Philosophy of Modern Missions: A Present Day Plea* (1882) showed the profound influence of the Anglican theologian F. D. Maurice, especially his *The Religions of the World* (1846). Quoting Maurice indirectly, Slater wrote that missions revealed 'Christ as the organic Root and Head of the Human family; the representative of the race, in who every tribe is interested, and towards whom every soul stands in vital relation.' Missions, Slater continued, pointed 'to Him as the light of the world, as the fountain of all the truth and goodness, that gleamed out in the

ancient world, as the fulfiller of all pre-Christian hopes and aspirations, as the central truth that reconciles the systems of men'.[59]

As early as 1882 Slater had affirmed that 'All other religions await
for their fulfilment in Christianity.' Though the fulfilment theory is
often attributed to J. N. Farquhar and his *The Crown of Hinduism*
(1913), its beginnings are in Slater. The fulfilment idea was to dominate missionary understanding of other religions at least until 1938,
and does so still in some circles.[60] Slater believed that this was the
most philosophic of the grounds 'on which the claims of mission could
be based'.[61] Slater's own long career in India began with teaching, but
later centred upon extensive work with college graduates, where he
had already formulated this principle in addressing them: 'The aspect
in which I would set Christianity before you is not an aspect of antago-
nism but consummation.' In this spirit he wrote many books about
Hindu thought, culminating in his most influential work *The Higher Hinduism in Relation to Christianity* (1902). In this book Slater's
theme is that the 'revelation of the Gospel will be in complete accord
with the best sentiments of her [sc. India's] best minds, the true reali-
sation of the visions of her seers, the real fulfilment of the longings
of her sages' (emphasis his).[62] We may note in passing that revelation
here is a concept located in the future. The last words of *The Higher
Hinduism* are, 'We shall never gain the non-Christian world until we
treat its religions with justice, courtesy and love.'[63]

HENDRIK KRAEMER: THE MISSIONARY AS THE
LOCUS OF DIALOGUE

By 1910 the missionaries who responded to Commission Four of the
World Missionary Conference in Edinburgh had come to much the
same point of view, summed up by the commission chairman David
Cairns as 'the generous recognition of all that is true and good' in other
religious traditions. Their task could only be carried out if they treated
the religions of other men and women with profound respect: for them
this would be done by showing how all their best thought pointed to

Christ and thus 'fulfilled' them. The outstanding Dutch missionary and missionary thinker Hendrik Kraemer (1888–1965) was radically to challenge this position at the International Missionary Council's conference in Tambaram, just outside Madras in 1938.[64] The proposals of the book he wrote specially for this gathering, *The Christian Message in a Non-Christian World*, make it one of the most influential works about the Christian mission ever written.[65] Commissioned as a book on the 'evangelistic approach to the non-Christian religions', Kraemer's work grew into a complex and profound theological statement. He made a distinction between 'biblical realism' and all other forms of religious experience, emphasizing a profound discontinuity between human religion and Christian revelation. For Kraemer there were no 'points of contact' in the other religious traditions upon which missionaries could build and thus 'fulfil' the longings of Hinduism or Buddhism.[66]

Yet, despite his reputation for making harsh decisions about the status of other religious traditions,[67] Kraemer endorses sharing religious experience as 'valid and very valuable' on page 298 of *The Christian Message in a Non-Christian World,* and shows himself fully aware of why Christian missionaries should take such an approach. He refers to a 'haunting dread of all superiority feeling' and to 'the delicate and justified desire to have real human contact' which should be 'on the footing of spiritual give and take'. Kraemer also refers to an understandable aversion from 'dogmatic' religion and speaks of a 'too one-sided stress on preaching'. This he says is often in reality 'mere annoying interference'. Equally valid is the path of social service which he sees as a noble insistence to demonstrate in practice that being a Christian means a new quality of life:

> All these elements co-operated in making the emphasis on the sharing of religious experience and social service intelligible and partly justified. Every good missionary who knows something of the apostolic and prophetic temperament of Biblical realism knows about sharing religious experience and even loves it; likewise he sees the necessity of social service and will be devoted to it.[68]

We may well see these remarks as autobiographical. Kraemer had a multitude of Indonesian friends and remained a guide and counsellor to them long after he left Indonesia in 1937. Embedded in his approach to Muslims was his instance on 'direct personal contact' where the Muslim was 'treated not as a non-Christian but as a fellow man with the same fundamental needs, aspirations and frustrations', and 'whose religious experience and insight are as worthwhile as the missionary's because he is a living human being'. To be sure there is no question of 'fulfilment' here, nor any hope of finding 'fragments' of truths upon which to build a new doctrinal superstructure. The teachings of Islam 'simply belong to another plane of religious apprehension'. The missionary accordingly has to continue with 'unwearying perseverance' to explain what the elements in Islam, which have been borrowed from historical Christianity, according to biblical realism, really mean.[69]

Kraemer therefore is adamant about the need for 'faith, hope and love' in the hearts of those who wish to share their Christian faith with the Muslim world. Any missionary, he said, who has fallen 'a victim to the attitude of fear or disgust or hatred of Islam, does better to go home and never come back'.[70]

In these and many other ways, Kraemer was advocating an attitude of dialogue, with its attendant attributes of deep interest in the other person, its repudiation of interest in 'systems' and in winning arguments, its desire for the deepest well-being of the other. These are essential ingredients when there comes an opportunity to bear authentic witness. 'Witness has to be conceived as real ministry and ministry as real witness.' In witness to people of different faith commitments the central issue is the attitude of the missionary. After a long chapter in which Kraemer has shown the inadequacy of the so-called 'points-of-contact' approach, suddenly he stands his argument on its head and insists that there is in fact a 'point of contact':

This point of contact is the disposition and attitude of the missionary. It seems rather upsetting to make the missionary the point of contact. Nevertheless it is true, as practice teaches. The strategic and absolutely dominant in this whole important problem . . . is the missionary worker himself. *Such is the golden rule, or if one prefers, the iron will in this matter. The way to live up to this rule is to have an untiring and genuine interest in the religion, the ideas, the sentiments, the institutions – in short, in the whole range of the life of the people among whom he works, for Christ's sake and for the sake of those people. (emphasis his)*[71]

Kraemer continued that only 'a genuine and continuous interest' created real points of contact. This is because people know 'intuitively whether their actual being is the object of human interest and love'. They know if they are the 'objects of interest only for the reasons of intellectual curiosity or for purposes of conversion'. Humane natural contact is the 'indispensable condition of all religious meeting'.

WILFRED CANTWELL SMITH: THE THEORIST
OF WORLD COMMUNITY

Our last witness to the good and generous faith on the part of the missionary is Wilfred Cantwell Smith (1916–2000). His career ranged from educational missionary work in Lahore in the early 1940s to professorships of Comparative Religion in McGill, Dalhousie and Harvard Universities.[72] For the last half of the twentieth century he was an interpreter both of the significance of religion in human life and of the importance of interreligious encounter and he has some claim to be the most quoted of all the scholars referred to by contemporary practitioners of dialogue. His experience of the ordinary people of the Muslim world in north-west India (along with their many Hindu and Sikh neighbours) in the 1940s suggested to him that what human beings had in common was the quality of faith. To illustrate this proposition he has told a story of climbing in the Himalayas where he came across a fruit seller, 'a humble and poor and loveable old man with a stack of oranges that he was selling by weight'. For scales, Smith tells us, he had a rough and ready balance.

> *He put oranges in one pan and weighed them with some rocks that he had there, a middle sized one and two smallish ones the three of which made up one sir (two pounds). He was too poor to own metal weights stamped and standard. That the three stones actually weighed a sir was an unverified presumption, though I personally believe that they did. I watched him for a while, as he made occasional sales to passers-by; and afterward fell into conversation with him. He was far from any possibility of having his dealings checked; and there was no external measure of his honesty, which I found was sustained rather by a verse from the Qur'an which runs, 'Lo, he over all things is watching.'*[73]

To this humble Muslim the Qur'an had become the word of God, and his response was for Smith, quite simply, faith. This kind of faith, says Smith, is a universal quality. Human beings everywhere, he contends, have always lived out of, or from 'faith', losing it only when they have been ultimately overtaken by what can be called nihilism or existential despair. Consequently 'any appreciation of beauty; any striving for good; any pursuit of justice; any recognition that some things are good, some are bad, and that it matters; any feeling or practice of love; any love of what theists call "God"; all these are examples of personal, and communal, faith'. Because all human beings work within this common dimension of faith, human discourse about religion is not only possible, it is essential. It takes place at human levels of mutual personal disclosures. Certainly there are the doctrines, the ethics, rituals, of the world religious traditions, but these serve to undergird and build up faith. They are, in his language, the 'mundane cause' of faith. At the same time the response of men and women within these traditions is normally a response to 'transcendence', as those traditions bear their own testimony to the 'divine' and to the 'beyond'.[74]

Christians therefore have to take seriously both the faith and the tradition of other women and men, and that demands a profound change in their understanding of evangelism. For Smith this also has to become dialogical, because, he says, 'I have been blessed by being able also to listen, for instance, to "the good news" that Buddhists and the others manifestly have to share.' Smith equally affirms the task of evangelism. The Church may not abandon or by-pass 'the matter of talking with persons outside the church on the deepest spiritual and human and eternal matters'.[75] Mission remains, for him, 'the endeavour (and the delight) to share in God's unfinished work among men that He began in Bethlehem. It is simply the business of the church to do God's will as Christ has made this known and possible.' He continued:

> *The mission of the Church is God's mission to mankind that He has entrusted to us. Few of us Christians know much abut God's mission in the Islamic venture; God's mission to India, and nowadays . . . to the world, through the Hindu complex; God's mission to East Asia, and nowadays to the world in the Buddhist movement. Few Christians have any appreciation of God's mighty mission to the world in the post Biblical Jewish community. But we can learn. Especially our youth are learning it. Only as we see God's activity in other movements shall we serve Him well in and through our own.*

Smith frequently offers his own pointers to enable Christians to move forward in their 'always-slowly-changing conception of mission'. Smith wrote for example a major programmatic statement entitled 'Participation: The Changing Christian Role in Other Cultures'.[76] Since mission now had to involve a sense of concern and responsibility for the spiritual life of all humankind, 'participation' becomes the key concept. The role of the missionary was now to act as an agent in bringing into reality a worldwide community. 'The missionary assignment', he insisted, 'for the next phase in human history is to take the leadership in this participation.' Such a vocation would have immediate consequences for the self-image of missionaries. They should become people who feel 'that Christianity has caught a certain vision of God, has seen an aspect of ultimate truth, which is to be communicated to the general search for God and truth in which people of other communities are also engaged'. In their new guise missionaries will become persons committed to the way of dialogue, or in Smith's own preferred terminology, 'colloquy'. The idea of colloquy indeed stands at the heart of Smith's controlling vision of a single world community, in which human beings talk in non-exclusive language about us all in the twenty-first century, and maybe even move towards a world theology.[77]

Although these six thinkers are very different, they have in common one central and profound insight. Bartholomaeus Ziegenbalg's extraordinary willingness to listen to and record different points of view; Henry Martyn's modelling of friendship and empathy; T. E. Slater's insistence upon an interpretation of the religion of other men and women that turned upon justice, courtesy and love; Hendrik Kraemer's insistence upon patience and genuine interest in other people including their religion and their whole range of life; and Wilfred Cantwell Smith's insistence that the evangelist must become a participant in other people's cultures albeit as one with great good news to share; these all testify to good and generous missionary activity. By sitting where other people sit, by engaging them in conversation, behaving with courtesy and friendship, by offering gentle information and reasonable arguments, more is accomplished for the sharing of the good news of Jesus than by coercive and crusading tactics of other forms of proclamation and preaching.

The telling of these stories not only counts as excellent advice to all who are concerned with the mission of the Church in the twenty-first century, but must surely reassure any who feel in bad conscience that 'dialogue' is a betrayal of our missionary ancestors. On the contrary, their good and generous faith is an inspiration to those who follow them.

A MISSIOLOGY FOR THE TWENTY-FIRST CENTURY

We may sum up our findings. Christians, particularly in the Western churches, need to find a new self-confidence for their mission, and they may use Thomas Thangaraj's phrase *missio humanitatis*. It is not only perfectly proper for them to bear witness to their Christian faith among people of other faith; it is imperative that they do; otherwise they are not contributing anything to the conversation. Indeed if they are silent or diffident this will be profoundly disappointing to their partners, who characteristically expect Christians to be as genuine and as committed as they themselves are. Because there is a conversation, Christians must expect to hear the witness of people of different faith and, as Wilfred Cantwell Smith said, to be blessed by being able also to listen to the good news that they have to share. This is the way Christians become fellow-pilgrims and not 'manipulators'. We saw far-reaching examples of this process in the last chapter: the increasing number of 'comparative theologians' who become participants in the truth of other traditions and begin to recast the shape of Christian faith.

Such is mission in bold humility, and it makes friends across the faith-barriers. As I draw to a close I would like to repeat some words I wrote in 1986 about my *Towards a New Relationship*. I said then:

> *I write as a believing Christian first of all to my fellow believers. But I know full well that men and women of other convictions will be looking over our shoulders to see what is being said or implied about them. Scores and scores of them will be my personal friends: Jews, Muslims, Hindus, Buddhists, Sikhs, Baha'is, followers of new religious movements as well as some who would not call themselves religious at all. I hope two things will come to them as they read. First of all, that they may see one Christian wrestling with an issue that confronts all people everywhere in every tradition. As I wonder how I am to remain faithful to Christ and yet make sense of the faith of other people, so, for example, a devout Hindu or Muslim must also have a conceptual framework which makes sense of the faith of those who are not Muslims or Hindus, Jews or Buddhists. They, too, in the words of Wilfred Cantwell Smith, must aspire to a statement of God and his diverse involvements with humankind. Second, I hope that they will see, particularly in the last two chapters, the universal implications of what I am saying, though this be couched in Christian terms. For though I write of ethical issues in inter-faith*

relations as they now confront Christians, what is said there about the pattern of relationships ('the four principles of dialogue') applies across the board. What is said about the possibilities as well as the perils of praying together applies to us all.[78]

Twenty years later, such men and women remain my friends, joined by I guess many hundreds more, all around the world. I still find myself welcomed to their inner counsels, to participate in their own attempts to draw up guidelines for dialogue, invited to their celebrations, even asked to address their worshipping congregations. Often I am asked for the reasons for the hope and the faith that is in me, and to the best of my ability and trusting in God, I try to answer with 'gentleness and reverence' (see 1 Peter 3.15–16).[79]

Mission in the midst of religious pluralism is action in good and generous faith for the sake of friendship: friendship among the peoples to be sure, but also and ultimately in relation to the God who was revealed in Jesus Christ and wills that all of us shall be his friends.

Appendix 1

Ambivalent Theology and Ambivalent Policy: the World Council of Churches and Interfaith Dialogue 1938–1999

Future historians will need help in unravelling the mystery of the World Council of Churches' ambivalence toward interfaith dialogue over the past five decades. Those of us who participated in the various twists and turns of WCC theology and policy no doubt stand too close to the events of the seventies, eighties and nineties to present an objective and finely nuanced account of these vicissitudes. But the very complexity of the issues would seem to demand as many personal and subjective accounts as possible, lest significant dimensions of the debate and the decision-making processes be missed or underestimated by those looking back on this period. What is offered now is the view of one participant in the Working Group of the Sub-unit on Dialogue with People of Living Faiths and Ideologies (DFI), later the Dialogue Sub-unit, from the late 1970s until its demise in 1991. I have two additional perspectives. The first is that of my experience as the Secretary for Relations with People of Other Faiths of the British Council of Churches (BCC) from 1978 to 1988, when we were faced with exactly the same issues as the WCC. The second is that of a historian. I have for many years been studying the ways in which many missionaries and theologians have sought to reach a just and courteous appraisal of the religious traditions of humankind, replacing as it were the dark entails of their inherited negatives.[1] Perhaps this second perspective will serve to offer a sense of the long-term historical forces at work in more recent years.

So we turn to the approach of the WCC to the theological understanding of other religious traditions and its stance concerning mission, witness, dialogue and co-operation with people of these traditions. In both its theology and its policy it has operated, I believe, with two diverse sets of values, the one quite negative and exclusive, the other open to dialogue and co-operation. This ambivalence has manifested itself, I suggest, in seven ways within the WCC's history over the past fifty or more years. These patterns I will set out now and then discuss in detail. I have formulated each of these in the negative mode, but of course each of them implies much positive achievement as well, to which I shall point in my commentary.

1 The slowness in setting up a sub-unit for interfaith dialogue. This took place only in 1971, 33 years after the founding of the WCC, and ten years after the accession of the International Missionary Council to the WCC.

2 The 14-year gap between *Nostra Aetate* in 1965 and the *Guidelines for Dialogue with People of Living Faiths and Ideologies* issued by the WCC Central Committee in 1979.

3 The hostility to interfaith dialogue displayed at the Nairobi Assembly of the WCC in 1975, which echoed almost to the letter the rigorism of the Tambaram Assembly of 1938.

4 The grudging negotiations on the floor of the Assembly at Vancouver (1983), which finally led to a formulation which denies the presence of God in other religious traditions.

5 The effective marginalization in the years following Vancouver of the Dialogue Sub-unit within Programme Unit Two, which precluded its full participation in the CWME San Antonio Conference, 1989.

6 The loss almost without trace in WCC thinking of the Baar Declaration on 'Religious Plurality: Theological Perspectives and Affirmations' since 1990.

7 The virtual abandonment in 1991 of the theological achievements
   and trajectories undertaken by the Dialogue Sub-unit.

At various points these seven marks of ambiguity overlap with each
other, but it will be convenient if I deal with them one by one.

1   THE SLOWNESS IN SETTING UP A SUB-UNIT FOR INTERFAITH DIALOGUE

Historians have had no hesitation in suggesting that the greatest
impetus in the twentieth century toward the reunion of the fragment-
ed Church of Jesus Christ was the great World Missionary Conference in Edinburgh, 1910. The spirit of unity which animated so many
participants in this Conference overflowed into a generous desire to
recognize the best in the other religious traditions of the world. The
Scots theologian David Cairns, who had been charged with the chair-
manship of Commission Four on *The Missionary Message in Relation
to the Non-Christian Religions,* was able to speak accurately of the
'practically universal testimony' that the attitude of the Christian missionary community toward other religion traditions 'should be one of
true understanding and, as far as possible, of sympathy'.[2] Cairns fully
acknowledged that there were elements in other traditions which 'lie
outside the possibility of sympathy' and that in some forms of religion
the evil was appalling. But nothing, he suggested, was more remarkable in the whole of the evidence presented to his Commission than
the 'agreement that the true method' of assessing other forms of faith
and belief 'is that of knowledge and charity'. Other religions had 'nobler
elements' and some of them in their 'higher forms' plainly manifested
'the working of the Spirit of God'.[3]

At the first Conference in Jerusalem in 1928 of the International
Missionary Council (hereafter IMC), set up as a result of the great
Edinburgh conference, the theme of the Christian message in the
world of many faiths was equally high on the agenda. Many participants thought that the most serious and appropriate response to the

challenges of secularism and communism should be that religious
groupings take counsel together and present some kind of united
witness to the transcendence of God. To be sure, members of this
Conference did call upon 'followers of non-Christian religions to join
with us in the study of Jesus Christ as He stands before us in the
Scriptures, His place in the life of the world and His power to sat-
isfy the human heart . . .'. But they went on to ask of those same
followers of other religions that they should both 'hold fast to faith
in the unseen and eternal in face of the growing materialism of the
world' and 'to co-operate with us against all the evils of secularism'.
We should notice also affirmations in the Jerusalem document about
the 'sense of the Majesty of God' of the Muslims, the 'deep sympathy
for the world's sorrow and unselfish search for the way of escape' of
the Buddhists, the 'desire for ultimate reality conceived as spiritual'
of the Hindus and the belief in 'the moral order of the universe and
the consequent insistence on moral conduct' of the Confucians.[4]
Such affirmations might well have served the IMC as a platform from
which to pioneer interfaith dialogue, had this term been known at that
time.[5]

Even the next IMC Conference (at the Madras Christian College,
Tambaram, India, December 1938), despite its reputation to the contrary, had its implicit warrants for interfaith dialogue. To be sure, in
the intervening ten years (which saw the rise to power of National
Socialism in Germany and the entrenchment of Marxist Leninism in
Russia), some Christian thinkers had become more inclined to believe
that other religions were potentially the allies of anti-Christian movements, rather than intrinsically forces for good. But the South Indian theologian O. J. Jathanna has vigorously protested against using
'Jerusalem' as a short-hand term for the positive and 'Tambaram' as an
equally short-hand term for the negative view of other religions. 'This',
he writes, 'is a grave over-simplification of the issue. In both meetings differences of opinion remained.'[6] He notes that the leadership
of both meetings was essentially the same, and that therefore they
should be seen hermeneutically as mutually correcting one another.

He sees no reason therefore for jumping to a conclusion that Tambaram ruled out the possibility of interreligious dialogue. On the contrary it formulated one great principle which would be fundamental to the earliest attempts by the WCC at interfaith dialogue in the late 1960s and 1970s. This lay in Tambaram's focusing upon the direness of the human situation, the break-down of community, and the urgent need for sources of renewal and new life. Thus there is the striking affirmation of Recommendation Four: 'The Church is called to the Encouragement of Co-operative Relations Between its Members and Those of Other Faiths in all Good Social and Community Movements'. That is surely a mandate for interfaith dialogue. But the comment on this recommendation is even more striking. 'This does not mean the dilution of the Christian message, nor a compromise in Christian morals. It does mean *living with and for our neighbours,* and expressing in service our ultimate loyalty to Christ. Christians should *share in all the healthy aspirations* of the non-Christians around them and *co-operate with them* in all good works, and in combating the evils which cripple the life of man.'[7]

There is also in the Tambaram 'Findings' an implicit theological undergirding for dialogue in their concern for religious truth, and not just for better human relationships. Here we begin to touch upon the ambiguity that has marked the IMC and WCC approach to interfaith dialogue these last sixty years. Jathanna suggests that without Tambaram and its 'emphasis on taking seriously *religious truth* and the objective revelation of God, the whole enterprise of dialogue would become superfluous and in the end meaningless'.[8]

> *In terms of theology alone one can clearly discern the influence of Tambaram in the present day dialogue: its explicit or implicit dialectical understanding of the religious situation of man and mankind; its pragmatic and socio-ethical point of view; its Christo-centric basis; its stress on the place of the Bible; its emphasis on man rather than religious systems; and its concept of the new creation, involving conversion and regeneration.*[9]

This is well said, but it leaves us with even more of a problem. Why were both the IMC and later the WCC so reluctant to engage in interfaith dialogue if its rationale is as impeccable as this? For an answer we turn to assessments critical of the legacy of Tambaram from two other South Asian theologians, both of whom have served as Directors of the WCC dialogical programme, Stanley Samartha and Wesley Ariarajah. Samartha, speaking out of his personal struggle to make sense of the slowness of the WCC to inaugurate its dialogue programme, has described the 'conceptual framework' of Tambaram as a 'missiological prison'.[10] He sees this imprisonment as caused by the radical dichotomy that runs through Tambaram and its aftermath, namely the 'either/or' of the 'Christian' and the 'non-Christian' world.

This 'either/or' is nowhere more manifest than in the title of the Tambaram conference theme book by Hendrik Kraemer, *The Christian Message in a Non-Christian World*.[11] Commissioned by an 'Ad Interim Committee' of the IMC in 1936 as a work on the 'evangelistic approach to the Non-Christian religions', Kraemer's book grew into a major theological statement, complex and profound, and despite its reputation, often generous and dialogical. Take for example his endorsement of 'sharing religious experience' and 'social service' as methods of approach and accurate expressions of the Christian mind. Kraemer suggests why missionaries were taking these routes in 1938:

> *There is a haunting dread of all superiority feeling; the delicate and justified desire to have real human contact on the footing of spiritual give and take; the partly intelligible aversion from 'dogmatic' religion and many forms of too one-sided stress on preaching, which is in reality mere annoying interference. Another reason is the noble insistence to demonstrate in practice that being a Christian means a new quality of life . . . All these elements have co-operated in making the emphasis on the sharing of religious experience and social service intelligible and partly justified. Every good missionary who knows something of the apostolic and prophetic temperament of biblical realism knows*

> *about sharing religious experience and even loves it; likewise he sees*
> *the necessity of social service and will be devoted to it.*[12]

Yet in many respects Kraemer's influence was quite other than he intended. It is not hard to see why. The very next words that follow this fine statement of openness and sharing are negative: 'To raise these methods of approach and expression of the Christian mind to the status of essential motive and purpose is a different matter. When to this is added the rejection of its apostolic and prophetic inspirations we have fundamentally speaking, nothing else than the suicide of missions . . .'.[13] I fear that it was rhetoric of this kind which lingered in the minds of most readers of *The Christian Message in a Non-Christian World.*

Moreover there are many passages about Islam and Hinduism in Kraemer's book which are truly negative and quite ungenerous. Both Samartha and Ariarajah castigate Kraemer for what they see as these ill-advised comments. Kraemer wrote that 'Islam was a great syncretistic body', that it was a 'superficial religion', 'a religion which has almost no questions and almost no answers', which nevertheless has given rise to 'an enormous amount of stubborn, ingenious theological thinking'.[14] Elsewhere he referred to its 'iron rigidity', 'to its 'fanaticism', to its 'bitter and stubborn resistance' to any efforts that involve any change of religion or a 'break in group solidarity'.[15] Samartha tells of his visit to the Algerian minister for religious affairs who had listed a whole string of such quotations which he had culled from *The Christian Message.* The minister suggested, sardonically I suspect, that Christians could only expect dialogue with Muslims on the basis of respect.[16]

Kraemer's views on Hinduism were equally unnuanced. Hinduism was 'essentially a polyphonic expression of the primitive apprehension of existence and a continuation of religion among tribal peoples.'[17] The *bhakti* versions of Hinduism, he thought, are 'exclusively individualistic and essentially eudaimonistic'.[18] Hinduism 'is not really interested in religious truth but in the endless possibilities of religious realization and expression'.[19] Devoid of any truly transcendental understanding of God, the Hindu world, in Kraemer's view, is naturalistic and monistic. Such judgements make one's spirit feel heavy and oppressed, so different as they are in tone from the Report of Commission Four in Edinburgh, 1910. Sadly such judgements became the staple of later writers. Thus a less generous view of Tambaram than that set out by Professor Jathanna was formed: this view allows the word 'Tambaram' to become short-hand for 'discontinuity' and 'negativity' in the theology of religion.

Like Stanley Samartha, Wesley Ariarajah highlights the undialogical aspects of Tambaram. Speaking of Edinburgh and Jerusalem as well, Ariarajah has written that 'it was only Tambaram that had actually worked out a theologically argued position on other religions and their theological "status" in regard to the gospel'.[20] Kraemer's conclusion that the gospel was discontinuous with every other religious tradition prevailed among the leaders of the IMC. Ariarajah also affirms a strong 'Tambaram position' as having emerged. Religious diversity had in its view 'to be fought and overcome'.[21] Renewed efforts to evangelize the world had to be made. As the 'Findings and Recommendations' of Tambaram insist:

> *We believe that Christ is the Way, the Truth and the Life for all, that He alone is adequate for the world's need. Therefore we want to bear witness to Him in all the world. There are many non-Christian religions that claim the allegiance of multitudes. We see and readily recognise that in them are to be found values of deep religious experiences and great moral achievements. Yet we are bold enough to call men out from them to the feet of Christ.*[22]

To this vision the leaders of the IMC, and (after 1961 when the IMC merged with the WCC) of the Division on World Mission and Evangelism of the WCC, were to devote themselves unreservedly. They uttered the same kind of judgements about Hinduism and Islam as Kraemer had offered.

But we cannot leave it there. Tambaram's 'Findings and Recommendations' themselves remain ambiguous. Even in these central sentences of the 'Findings' just quoted, the 'deep religious experiences' and 'great moral achievements' in other faiths were recognized in a more generous way than Nairobi or Vancouver managed. The 'Findings' also acknowledged that not all missionary thinkers (either present in Madras or corresponding from around the world) were happy with the Kraemerian analysis. A significant sentence lurking within the same document reads: 'As to whether the non-Christian religions as total systems of thought and life may be regarded as in some sense or to some degree manifesting God's revelation, Christians are not agreed.'[23] Such ambiguities are at once prescient of and pregnant with the discussion which would eventually be taken up in the sixties and the seventies.

But in the meantime the question of how to understand other religions was off the theological agenda of the IMC. It was not to reappear until 1968. It was equally missing from the agenda of the theological circles within the founding member churches (which were mainly European and North American) of the newly formed WCC. From a Eurocentric point of view the reason for this is obvious. The Second World War and the massive upheavals within Europe during and after that war demanded the total theological energy of European church people. The WCC came to birth in 1948 in the wreckage of the old Europe symbolized by the ruins and craters in Amsterdam itself. The wreckage of the old Christendom dominated the whole Assembly, as witness the title of the Assembly Report, *Man's Disorder and God's Design*. The prophetic voices at Amsterdam were of those of European stalwarts like Karl Barth, Emil Brunner, Paul Maury, Jacques Ellul, aided and abetted by such North American figures as Paul Tillich, Walter Horton, John C. Bennett and the Niebuhr brothers. Their influence pervades each of the four official Conference reports, which in turn become monuments to the contextualized European/North American theology of this period.[24]

Of the four Commissions at the Assembly, the one most closely concerned with the theology of mission was entitled 'The Church's Witness to God's Design'. We may note that Hendrik Kraemer was the President of this Commission. Within its programme we find Lesslie Newbigin giving a keynote address on 'The Duty and Authority of the Church to Preach the Gospel'. Of the 17 members of the Commission only three came from Asia: Paul Devanandan, D. T. Niles and Vi Fang Wu of Nanking. Except for a few published articles about evangelistic processes among Hindus, traditional people and Jews (the fundamental questioning of the mission to the Jewish people had not yet taken place), little attention was paid to the religious life of the world beyond European and North American boundaries. There was, however, this passing remark in the Report: 'The religions of Asia are being challenged and profoundly modified. In the period of transition, the minds of millions are more than usual open to the Gospel,' and then a reference to the tendency in new nations to 'press an ancient religion into service as the foundation for a politically homogenous state'.[25] Just a faint trace of ambiguity was allowed to creep in, and dialogue with other religious traditions might just have been on the agenda.

The International Missionary Council, during this period, offered no contradiction to the general stance of the WCC simply because prominent figures in WCC circles were also the designated leaders of the IMC (as for example Lesslie Newbigin). The IMC was clear that the world of living faiths was to be addressed by the word of God, which should be proclaimed with 'authority', and consequently without any dialogical option. The IMC Conferences in Whitby, Ontario, in 1947, and in Willingen, Germany, in 1952, hardly touched upon the world's religious multifariousness, being rather more struck by Christian multifariousness and the pressing need for church unity.[26]

But somewhere out there was the sense of the religiously plural world. There were warning voices at Willingen which were bothered in 1952 about 'religious relativism' and 'syncretism'. The men and women at Willingen and, two years later, at the second WCC Assembly at Evanston in 1954 knew that the world was not giving up on the ancient religions. In fact the older traditions were renewing themselves, as newly independent nations sought after cultural cohesiveness and relevant moral imperatives. Thus Asian thinkers like M. M. Thomas, D. T. Niles and P. D. Devanandan began to speak to newly receptive audiences. Three years after Willingen and one year after Evanston, this new awareness led the IMC and the WCC (through its Department of Studies) to plan for a joint study programme entitled 'The Word of God and the Living Faiths of Men'. The English Baptist Victor Hayward became its secretary.

Almost immediately this programme became the forum in which it was possible to conceive that the Tambaram debate could be reopened. Now there were highly articulate participants in this programme from Asia for whom the 'Christian world/non-Christian world' dichotomy made no sense, even if it had to many (not all) Europeans and North Americans in 1938 and 1948. Equally there were far-sighted Europeans who had worldwide experience of the new movement of interfaith dialogue who supported these fresh and vigorous Asian voices. One such was Dr Dirk C. Mulder. He tells of being present at a 'Word of God and the Living Faiths of Men' study conference in Broumana, Lebanon, in 1966:

> During that conference some of us urged Dr. Hayward to start thinking about the possibility of the WCC starting a department on interreligious relations in imitation of the Vatican [sc. the 'Secretariatus pro non-Christianis.'] . . . 'Why could not the WCC follow this example?' But Victor Hayward was adamant in his refusal. Interreligious dialogue was such a sensitive topic among member churches of the WCC that there was no possibility of support for such a proposal.[27]

At Hayward's back were Willem Visser t'Hooft, General Secretary of the WCC and author in 1963 of *No Other Name: The Choice between Syncretism and Christian Universalism* and Lesslie Newbigin, General

Secretary of the IMC and then the DWME, and author in 1961 of *A Faith for This One World,* and in 1969 of *The Finality of Christ.* These titles suggest their dominant concerns, an intense animus against any kind of syncretistic challenge to the purity of Christian orthodoxy and a conviction that somehow soon the world would become a community of Christian faith. But in 1966 significant changes were on the way which Hayward could not have foreseen. The first of these changes reflected the personal quotient. The two foremost guardians of the Tambaram tradition were soon to step down from their leadership positions. Visser t'Hooft gave way to the American Presbyterian ecumenist Eugene Carson Blake, and Lesslie Newbigin gave way to Philip Potter, a Methodist from Dominica.

But less personal factors also made for a change of atmosphere at the WCC Fourth Assembly in Uppsala in 1968. These ranged from the assassination of Martin Luther King in April that year (just four months before he was due to have addressed the Assembly) through to the action of Buddhist monks in Vietnam, which particularly drew attention to 'liberative forces' in other religions. Politically the Middle East was in turmoil after the Arab–Israeli War of 1967 and the late sixties saw also the full fruition of the struggles of nations in Africa and Asia to attain independence. New nation-building needed, in every case, the rediscovery of identities based on their own languages, customs, cultures and, of course, religious traditions. Ecumenically this was the era of Vatican II and especially of *Nostra Aetate.*

The Uppsala Assembly was thus being prepared to move out of the Tambaram and Amsterdam mentality. At the Assembly itself its Section II on 'The Renewal of Mission' observed that

> *The meeting with men of other faiths or of no faith must lead to dialogue. A Christian's dialogue with another implies neither a denial of the uniqueness of Christ, nor any loss of his own commitment to Christ, but rather that a genuinely Christian approach to others must be human, personal, relevant and humble.*[28]

This is the first time 'dialogue' as a technical term appears in WCC official talk. In the following year at the meeting of the WCC Central Committee in Canterbury there came the decision which would lead to the formation of the DFI in 1971. The 1969 resolution indicates that the Central Committee 'welcomes the increased emphasis on dialogue with men of other faiths', asking for further study about the relation of mission and dialogue, and finally approving plans for 'an ecumenical consultation on dialogue with men of other faiths' in Beirut. This desire for 'further study about the relation of mission and dialogue' becomes entangled with the next of our 'signs of ambiguity', namely the 14-year gap between *Nostra Aetate* and the *Guidelines for Dialogue with People of Living Faiths and Ideologies*.

2 THE 14-YEAR GAP BETWEEN NOSTRA AETATE AND THE GUIDELINES FOR DIALOGUE WITH PEOPLE OF LIVING FAITHS AND IDEOLOGIES

What the Central Committee was searching for in the second element of this resolution was a set of Guidelines following the pattern of *Nostra Aetate*. But a somewhat wearisome sequence of events, meetings, controversies and publications had to be endured before another Central Committee meeting could receive the highly effective 1979 document *Guidelines for Dialogue with People of Living Faiths and Ideologies*. Ambiguity marked every step of the way.

The first step was to hold the Beirut meeting (actually in Ajaltoun in 1970). This was the first time that people of four different faiths met together under the auspices of the WCC. The WCC was no longer talking about dialogue but practising it, at least through its representatives. Though 'a dialogue of the few on the behalf of the many', as one participant put it, Ajaltoun was of immense importance because it signalled 'possibilities'. For the Christian participants its findings formed the raw material for the famous 'Zurich aide-memoire' worked out by a group of 23 theologians, Roman Catholic, Orthodox and Protestant.[29]

Samartha has described the Zurich discussions as the 'breaking of the Tambaram log jam', because the dominant assumption was no longer how to replace other religions by Christianity. It had developed into the question 'How to relate the living faith of Christians to the living faiths of people in a pluralistic world?' Samartha rightly notes that 'this question is more theological than missiological'. The findings of Ajaltoun and the general tone of the Zurich meeting gained wider publicity through the 'book of the conference', *Living Faiths and the Ecumenical Movement* (1971), and for the first time in many years the WCC community had the question of the theology of religion firmly in its sights.

The next meeting of the Central Committee (in Addis Ababa, 1971) was able therefore to set up a 'Sub-unit on Dialogue with People of Living Faiths' within the Programme Unit of Faith and Witness. As an afterthought it added 'and Ideologies' to the title, making it the 'DFI' Sub-unit. This was a new departure for the WCC and was to be the counterpart of many study centres, ashrams and universities around the globe, whose work and insights it frequently laid under tribute. Dialogue was in vogue and relating to other people of faith now urgent.

The meeting at Ajaltoun was followed by a Christian–Muslim consultation in Broumana, also in the Lebanon, and by another multi-lateral conversation in Colombo in 1975.[30] This new spirit affected even the CWME conferences of the period, and a Buddhist scholar addressed a plenary session of the Bangkok conference in 1972 (it would have been unthinkable to have invited a Hindu scholar to speak at Tambaram in 1938).

Those who shared in the DFI dialogue programme began to articulate the insights and conceptions which were to shape the answers to the request for further study of the relation of mission and dialogue. A passage written by Stanley Samartha in this period conveys the consensus which was beginning to emerge:

We are at a time when dialogue is inevitable, urgent and full of opportunity. It is inevitable because everywhere in the world Chris-

*tians are now living in a pluralistic society. It is urgent because all
men are under common pressure in the search for justice, peace and
a hopeful future and all are faced with the challenge to live together
as human beings.*[31]

The ecumenical consensus of those taking part felt good: dialogue
takes place in community and its subject matter is the search for justice and peace. And Christians could not achieve these goals without
help from their neighbours of other faith traditions.

Or could they? The consensus was about to receive a severe jolt.

3   THE HOSTILITY TO INTERFAITH DIALOGUE DISPLAYED AT THE NAIROBI ASSEMBLY OF THE WCC IN 1975, WHICH ECHOED ALMOST TO THE LETTER THE RIGORISM OF THE TAMBARAM ASSEMBLY OF 1938

The DFI Sub-unit was challenged to the very core of its being by
events at the Fifth Assembly in Nairobi. In one sense DFI brought
this challenge upon itself. Had it simply gone about its business on
the periphery of the WCC it would not have attracted any attention.
But the DFI believed profoundly that Christians were not free to talk
about God among themselves, as though the non-Christian world
was too pagan and too God-forsaken to be either interested or able to
understand what Christians were about. This conviction had caused
the DFI to press the Central Committee to invite five guests from
other faith communities to be non-participating guests in the Fifth
Assembly. Five were duly invited, from the Jewish, Muslim, Hindu,
Buddhist and Sikh communities.

Perhaps even then their presence would have escaped notice if the
Sikh participant, Dr Gopal Singh, had not asked permission to speak
to the whole Assembly on behalf of all five guests. He was refused
this permission. 'There was a murmur of resentment led by a few
people who insisted that a "non-Christian" could not be allowed to
address a *Christian* assembly.'[32] In a subsequent debate on the Report

of Section Three this resentment resurfaced. A church leader from Norway, a country not normally noted for its deep and wide experience of diversity of ethnicity or religion, alleged that the report of Section Three would be understood as 'spiritual compromise', and other voices referred to syncretism, the finality of Christ and the betrayal of mission. The German missiologist Hans Margull, the moderator of the Sub-unit at the time, feared that the Assembly would put an end to interreligious dialogue.[33]

But here the WCC ambiguity came once more into play. Section Three brought back its report with a preamble touching on all the points raised by the traditionalist voices. One clause from the preamble gives (in its overemphasized denials) a clear idea of where the shibboleths of many members of the WCC were seen to lie: 'We are opposed to any form of syncretism, incipient, nascent or developed, if we mean by syncretism conscious or unconscious human attempt to create a new religion composed of elements taken from the different religions.' In the debate that followed this the voices of experts in religious pluralism Russell Chandran of India and Lynn de Silva of Sri Lanka prevailed. The latter touched the concerns of many when he stressed that dialogue was a safeguard against syncretism rather than a means of temptation: 'in dialogue we get to know one another's faith in depth'.[34] Both he and Chandran stressed the Asian realities of the world Christian community. 'Dialogue', said de Silva, 'was essential for us to discover the Asian face of Jesus Christ, and for the church to be set free from institutional self-interest and play the role of a servant in building community.'[35]

Once again the positive aspirations of the ecumenical movement triumphed, and the Dialogue work was mandated to continue. The urgency now was to take a new step forward, and to make the DFI Consultation scheduled for Chiang Mai in April 1977 as constructive and seminal as possible. The Central Committee asked the Chiang Mai consultation to clarify the nature and purpose of the great theme we saw emerging before Nairobi, namely that of 'Dialogue in Community'.

Guidelines on dialogue ▪

The people at Chiang Mai worked with considerable passion to achieve a remarkably precise statement: *Dialogue in Community* (1978). This attracted more attention than had any other document from the DFI, and in less than a year 20,000 copies were in circulation. One issue of the WCC Journal *Risk* (4,000 copies) was devoted to Chiang Mai under the title *Inside Out: A Style for Dialogue,* and all the papers and Bible studies were published in *Faith in the Midst of Faith* (1978). There were many articles and reviews in the church newspapers of the world. As a result Stanley Samartha could report 'widespread satisfaction' in the churches and a sense that Chiang Mai had provided a sound basis 'on which dialogue can move forward as a common adventure of the churches in a pluralist world'.[36] Indeed so satisfactory was this document in providing an 'ethics of community relationships' that clearly the statement could be made the foundation for the long-hoped-for WCC *Guidelines on Dialogue.* So it transpired. The DFI Working Group meeting in Trinidad, in May 1978, prepared a document for the Central Committee consisting of the two theological-ethical statements arising from Chiang Mai, On Community and On Dialogue together with some 42 specific guidelines. These were unanimously adopted, without amendment, at the Kingston, Jamaica, meeting of the Central Committee in August 1979. Perhaps there is no clearer statement of the WCC at its most generous and affirmative than the words of the last paragraphs of the *Guidelines*:

> *To enter into dialogue requires an opening of the mind and heart to others. It is an undertaking which requires risk as well as a deep sense of vocation. It is impossible without sensitivity to the richly varied life of humankind. This opening, this risk taking, this vocation, this sensitivity are at the heart of the ecumenical movement and in the deepest current of the life of the churches. It is therefore with a commitment to the importance of dialogue to the member churches of the WCC that the Central Committee offers this statement and these Guidelines to the churches.[37]*

These words mark one of the less ambiguous moments of the WCC, and have inspired much fruitful encounter ever since between people of different faith commitments.

4 THE GRUDGING NEGOTIATIONS AT VANCOUVER (1983), WHICH EVENTUALLY FOUND A FORM OF WORDS TO DENY THE PRESENCE OF GOD IN OTHER RELIGIOUS TRADITIONS

The weaknesses of the *Guidelines* were apparent to many from their first publication.[38] They lay in the deliberate eschewing of any kind of theological statement about the status before God of men and women of other faiths, and, particularly, in the painfully weak statement about 'syncretism'. Stanley Samartha said even before they were published that the section on syncretism was 'timid', 'pre-Nairobi' and 'represented no kind of breakthrough'.[39] In fact the most penetrative questions remained unanswered. As formulated by the Trinidad Working Group meeting they were:

> *What is the relationship between the universal creative/redemptive activity of God towards all humankind and the particular creative/ redemptive activity of God in the history of Israel and in the person and work of Jesus Christ?*

> *Are Christians to speak of God's work in the lives of all men and women only in tentative terms of hope that they may experience something of Him, or more positively in terms of God's self-disclosure to people of living faiths and ideologies and in the struggle of human life?*[40]

To be sure, the terms of the second question show the direction in which the DFI thought that the answer must be given. Other documents emanating from the WCC at this period affirmed God's self-disclosure as well as the importance of interfaith dialogue. Notable among these was the CWME-inspired *Ecumenical Statement on Mission and Evangelism* (adopted by the Central Committee in 1982), which was clear that 'The Spirit of God is constantly at work in ways which pass human understanding and in places that to us are least expected. In entering into a relationship of dialogue with others, therefore, Christians seek to discern the unsearchable riches of God and the ways he deals with humanity' (para. 42).

It was the more disappointing therefore that the Vancouver Assembly in 1983 became a battleground again and the older exclusivist position was reasserted. A suggestion to the Assembly that it put in its final Report the words

> *While affirming the uniqueness of the birth, life, death, and resurrection of Jesus to which we bear witness, we recognize God's creative work in the religious experience of people of other faiths.*

became the point at which the 'Tambaram' tradition reasserted itself. Many delegates felt they could not give assent to the idea that God was at work beyond where Christ was named. After a heated debate in a physically steamy atmosphere (it was August on the west coast of North America), and after trying a dozen or so alternative proposals, the Assembly settled for this watered-down version:

> *While affirming the uniqueness of the birth, life, death, and resurrection of Jesus to which we bear witness, we recognize God's creative work in the seeking for religious truth among people of other faiths.*[41]

To be sure, there was a raft of positive proposals about interfaith dialogue in paragraphs 40–49 of the Vancouver Report, and the presence of guests from other faith communities was especially highlighted in the words: 'We value their contribution, and their presence has raised questions about the special nature of the witness Christians bring to the world community.' But there was no word of encouragement to any who thought that it might be part of the mission of the WCC to encourage learning from people of other living faith commitments. Instead the Vancouver Assembly contented itself with the anodyne suggestion that 'in the next seven years we anticipate further reflection on the nature of witness and dialogue which will encourage the life of the Christian community in many different parts of the world'.[42]

5 THE MARGINALIZATION OF THE DIALOGUE SUB-UNIT WITHIN PROGRAMME UNIT TWO

When the Programme Unit on Faith and Witness (known as Unit One) was set up in Addis Ababa in 1971, the three partners of the DFI within that Unit were the Commission on Faith and Order, the Sub-unit on Church and Society, and the Commission on World Mission and Evangelism.

Despite the immensely good personal relationships which existed among the staffs and commission or working-group members there was always a sense of a great distance between the concerns of each of the others and those of the DFI. As a member of the Dialogue Sub-unit working group I personally found this immensely frustrating. I remember for example how excited I was at the proposal that the four commissions and sub-units should meet together in Potsdam in the summer of 1986. Even the physical activity of travelling in the same planes and cars as members of the other sub-units seemed to say that bridges were being built. But despite worshipping, eating and even partying together we still met in separate rooms in different buildings. There was little or no co-operation between the sub-units in terms of our programmes and projects. I have my own memory of being deputed to ask the Faith and Order Commission to find us a place on their agenda, if only as 'any other business', so that we could engage their theological skills to address the question of 'My Neighbour's Faith and Mine'.[43] Though treated with great courtesy by the Moderator and his colleagues I was left in no doubt that they were too busy with the 'reception' of the formidable *Baptism, Eucharist and Ministry* (BEM) Statement in the churches to be able to give any attention to our questions.[44]

At the same Potsdam meeting we made strong approaches to the CWME commissioners suggesting that we should inaugurate a programme of Bible studies together, since it was apparent that differences in biblical exegesis often divided those committed to dialogue and those committed to evangelism. In fact both Wesley Ariarajah and I were deeply committed to reflecting on the Christian scriptures, he having published *The Bible and People of Other Faiths* in 1985, and I having just published *Towards a New Relationship: Christians and People of Other Faith* in 1986, with its three chapters of biblical exegesis, just a month or two before the Potsdam meeting. A few members of the CWME, staff and commissioners, discussed this proposal with members of the working group, but as an idea it trickled into the dust, nothing ever happened. Thirteen years later I still regard the task of biblical exegesis as crucial for all parties engaged in either dialogue or mission, and affirm that the explication of the Christian faith in the context of religious plurality is as much the responsibiliity of Faith and Order, as it is of the specialists in interfaith dialogue.

Wesley Ariarajah has his own view why these and similar ideas from the Dialogue side never came to fruition at least as far as the CWME was concerned:

> *In spite of the sustained interaction and communication between the CWME and the sub-unit on dialogue, and despite the fact that both emphases have their origin within the discussions within the IMC it was evident that these two foci within the WCC were building upon two distinct theological emphases and sets of theological assumptions about the significance of other faiths. No effort was made to reconcile these assumptions; nor were they easily reconcilable.*[45]

Yet always optimistic and diplomatic, Ariarajah had high hopes for the outcome of next major CWME Conference, which took place in San Antonio, Texas, in May 1989. He noted this as the first time since 1938 that the relationship with people of other faiths had been on the agenda of a Mission conference. 'Even though "witness among people of other faiths" was only one of four sub-sections of Section One on "Turning to the Living God," the report, if correctly interpreted and followed up can put the neglected back on to the World Mission agenda.'[46] But I, less optimistic and diplomatic, merely note that 'witness among people of other faiths' was only a fraction of a fraction, and that the Dialogue Sub-unit staff were not expected to make a great contribution.

Furthermore, external pressures were being brought to bear on San Antonio. The April 1989 issue of *The International Bulletin of Missionary Research* discussed the issues likely to be raised at San Antonio. Among its contributors was Lesslie Newbigin, who referred disparagingly in his lead article to the 'contemporary output of the interfaith industry'. He asked delegates (each of whom received a copy of this issue) to the Conference to remind themselves of Nairobi and Vancouver in this way:

> *The WCC has been asked at two general assemblies, to accept statements that seemed to call into question the uniqueness, decisiveness, and centrality of Jesus Christ. It has resisted. If in the pull of the strong current, it should agree to go with the present tide, it would become an irrelevance to the spiritual struggles that lie ahead of us. I pray and believe that it will not.*[47]

Despite such a ringing call to commence hostilities (and heated discussions on mission and dialogue did in fact take place in San Antonio), the final statement of Section One: 'Turning to the Living God' represents a positive approach to people of other religious traditions.[48] Quoting from the 1982 document *Mission and Evangelism* that 'The Spirit of God is constantly at work in ways that pass human understanding', the San Antonio Statement goes on to declare boldly that we cannot 'set limits to the saving power of God', that 'witness does not preclude dialogue but invites it', and that 'dialogue does not preclude witness but extends and deepens it'. Dialogue was affirmed as having specific value: 'dialogue has its own place and integrity and is neither opposed to nor incompatible with witness or proclamation'.

But in the end of the day San Antonio had to be content with ambiguity (here in the guise of paradox):

We are well aware that these convictions [sc. 'Salvation is offered to the whole creation through Jesus Christ' and 'Our mission to witness to Jesus Christ can never be given up'] and the ministry of witness stand in tension with what we have affirmed about God being present in and at work in people of other faiths; we appreciate this tension, and do not attempt to resolve it.

Ambivalence yet again.

6   THE LOSS ALMOST WITHOUT TRACE IN LATER WCC THINKING OF THE JANUARY 1990 BAAR DECLARATION *Religious Plurality: Theological Perspectives and Affirmations* [49]

At its meeting in July 1984 the Central Committee authorized a 'long term programme on the significance of the People of Other Living Faiths and their Faith Convictions with local involvement and an eventual conference'.[50] Staff member Allan Brockway reflected at the time that this was a change of gear for the WCC.[51] 'Hitherto dialogue had been explicated both for member churches and for world consumption as anything but an inter-*religious* encounter. Dialogue had been seen as neither affecting the Churches' usual patterns of missionary activity nor as having any consequences for their traditional theologies. But now it was seen that interreligious dialogue might indeed be inter-*religious*. The WCC had moved to the stage where it could recognize that "we Christians may actually have something to learn from other faiths that will *change* our Christianity".'[52] So the positive aspect of the ambivalence of the WCC is nowhere more clearly to be seen than in this new programme. With the blessing of the Central Committee the newly renamed Dialogue Sub-unit programme was going to ask, in effect, 'What have we to learn from our neighbours which will in some way change our self-understanding?' The Dialogue Sub-unit went to work with a will, holding many meetings of leading ecumenical theologians and eventually producing a well-wrought booklet entitled *My Neighbour's Faith and Mine*. This was to be translated into

16 languages and to be used all around the world.

After letting the programme run for six years, the Dialogue Unit gathered a group of specialist theologians to evaluate the responses. Under the moderatorship of Diana Eck of Harvard, scholars in the field of the theology of religion (including the Orthodox Metropolitan Georges Khodr, Archbishop Anastasios Yannoulatos, Georges Bebis, Tarek Mitri and Alexandru Stan; Roman Catholics Bishop Pietro Rossano, Michael Fitzgerald, Jacques Dupuis and Paul Knitter; Methodists Robert Neville, Itumeleng Mosala, Peter K. H. Lee and myself; the United Church of Canada theologian David Lochhead; Lutherans Bishop Björn Fjärstedt and Françoise Smyth-Florentin, as well as Judo Perwowidagdo of Indonesia, Otavio Velmo from Brazil, Joyce Tsabedze from Swaziland and Yasuo C. Furuya of Japan) worked for five days to produce a 'Statement on Religious Plurality: Theological Perspectives and Affirmations.' Most of these are well-published scholars and theologians of religion, rather than (as is so often the case within the ecumenical movement) essentially amateurs coming afresh to the problematics of this immensely difficult area. The WCC had, somewhat absent-mindedly perhaps, actually asked the opinions of those who knew something about the subject.

The process of the Baar meeting has been described by Paul Knitter in an article in *Current Dialogue,* entitled 'A New Pentecost? A Pneumatological Theology of Religions'.[53] Knitter highlights the breakthrough which occurred as the group began to focus on a new understanding of the Holy Spirit in relation to world religious traditions. As a result the crucial paragraphs in the document read like this:

We see the plurality of religious traditions as both the result of the manifold ways in which God has related to peoples and nations as well as a manifestation of the richness and diversity of humankind. We affirm that God has been with them in their seeking and finding, that where there is truth and wisdom in their teachings, and love and holiness in their living, this like any wisdom, insight, knowl-

edge, love and holiness that is found among us is the gift of the Holy
Spirit. (II, para. 4)

We are clear, therefore, that a positive answer must be given to the
question raised in the Guidelines on Dialogue (1979) 'is it right and
helpful to understand the work of God outside the Church in terms
of the Holy Spirit' (para. 23). We affirm unequivocally that God the
Holy Spirit has been at work in the life and traditions of peoples of
living faiths.

Further we affirm that it is within the realm of the Holy Spirit that
we may be able to interpret the truth and goodness of other reli-
gions and distinguish 'the things that differ' so that our 'love may
abound more and more, with knowledge and all discernment.' (Phil.
1.9–10)

We also affirm that the Holy Spirit, the Interpreter of Christ and of
our own Scriptures (John 14.26) will lead us to understand afresh
the deposit of the faith already given to us, and into fresh and unex-
pected discovery of new wisdom and insight, as we learn more from
our neighbours of other faiths. (IV, paras. 2, 3 and 4)

The signatories to this Declaration, which goes so far beyond San
Antonio, intended their work to have direct relevance to the Seventh
Assembly in Canberra in the following year. Indeed the Assembly's
theme 'Come Holy Spirit, Renew the Whole Creation' had been in
their minds from the beginning. It is therefore poignant to read again
Paul Knitter's commentary on the Baar Declaration, where he affirms
that new beginnings of understanding of the Holy Spirit in relation to
the world religions had been achieved. 'Our hope is', he writes, 'that
those beginnings at Baar will continue to stir at Canberra.'[54] Sadly
this was not to be so. In view of the serious controversy which erupted
when Professor Chung Hyun Kyung from Korea forcefully presented
'the Holy Spirit's political economy of life' (she used images from the

Korean conception of Han and the Mahayana Buddhist goddess of compassion *Kwan In*)[55] it is deeply regrettable that no attention was paid to the Baar Declaration by the four thousand or so Christians gathered in Canberra. Furthermore I find no reference to the Baar Declaration in the Minutes of the Central Committee Meetings since 1991. It is almost as though it had never been.

Or is this the case? Again we are faced with ambiguity, for the Declaration, so long out of sight, reappears in the magnificent anthology entitled *The Ecumenical Movement* edited by Michael Kinnamon and Brian E. Cope.[56] To be sure, this is not an official document of the WCC, and the editors intentionally have selected material from many other sources than the official documents of the WCC itself. But astutely and wisely they have recognized that the whole ecumenical movement has been transformed by recognition of religious pluralism, and that the older controversies are on their way to being transcended.

7   THE VIRTUAL ABANDONMENT IN 1991 OF THE THEO-LOGICAL ACHIEVEMENTS AND TRAJECTORIES UNDERTAKEN BY THE DIALOGUE SUB-UNIT

The 43rd meeting of the Central Committee, September 1991, set out to reorganize the way in which the officers of the WCC went about their tasks. To be sure, there were excellent reasons for undertaking such a 'programmatic' reorganization. Since 1971 the four Units had accumulated to themselves no less than 16 sub-units, each with their own staff, financial support system and a Commission or Working Group to help them. This situation was deemed to be on the one hand unwieldy and expensive, and on the other the cause of why the WCC could not 'present a focused and integrated vision' of its purposes and achievements. Accordingly all sub-units were abolished, and their work put within four new Units: (1) Unity and Renewal; (2) Mission, Education and Witness; (3) Justice, Peace and Creation; and (4) Sharing and Solidarity. A group of 'Offices' within the General Secretariat were created to deal with outside relationships and communications. One of these was the Office of Interfaith Relations which would continue with programmes of dialogues, seminars and workshops. Reflection on the theological significance of other religions was made the responsibility of the Unit on Mission, Education and Witness. The Unit on Unity and Renewal was mandated to give attention to theological work on the Church and the Jewish People. In this way the work of the Dialogue Sub-unit was divided into three parts, though it was expected that a high degree of interaction and co-operation would take place among staff members.

In principle much of the thinking which lay behind this reorganization is welcome and reassuring. The Mission, Education and Witness Unit is the right place to have to take seriously the issues related to theology of religion or religions. Faith and Order specialists must address the status of the Jewish people within the economy of God (little work has been done there since the Meeting of Faith and Order in Bristol in 1967[57]). Yes, it was right, too, to recognize that interfaith issues now permeate all departments of WCC life, from relief and rehabilitation work on into education and environmental issues. Yes, it was wholly correct to set up an Office within the General Secretariat that could, for example, facilitate the rebuilding of Christian–Muslim relationships after the Gulf War debacle or share in the resolution of the Christian–Muslim conflicts in Nigeria or Bosnia or Lebanon.

And yet there had to be misgivings about this approach. As early as 1992, Professor Dirk C. Mulder, moderator of the DFI Sub-unit from 1975 to 1983, expressed his concern lest the concern for the theology of religion get overshadowed. In particular he posed four questions: 'Was it a good idea to separate interreligious relations and theological reflection by placing them within two different offices? Can we expect that the new Unit on Mission, Education and Witness will seriously pursue the issue of the theological significance of other religions? Can the reflection on the relation with the Jews be limited to their significance for Christian theology? Will there still be a place for multilateral dialogue?'[58]

Mulder's doubts about the Mission, Education and Witness Unit sprang from a justifiable concern lest gospel and culture issues, long espoused in the former CWME and made a major theme since Canberra, remain a device for avoiding the theological issues. Stanley Samartha more than once pointed to the danger here: 'By probing into the essence and expressions of culture, the *theological* challenge of *religions* is avoided in a proliferation of studies in culture.'[59] There is some evidence that this is what has transpired. Some magnificent work has been done in local and regional contexts, as witness a fine series of Gospel and Cultures pamphlets in the years 1995–7. But to the deep disappointment of many the 'CWME Conference on the Gospel in Diverse Cultures' held in Bahia, Salvador, Brazil, 1996, found nothing new to say about the religious component which lies at the heart of culture and broadly speaking took refuge in the 'paradox' formulated by the San Antonio conference. As a Conference it was still at sea over the tension between witness and dialogue, as we can see from the last sentence of its three Acts of Commitment: 'We shall continue to explore the implications of the inter-relationship between our commitment to witness to Christ and our determinations to dialogue with people of other faiths and culture.' On this evidence it would seem that no theological advance can be made from within the circles most committed to mission and evangelism.

We can note, too, that Mulder's fourth fear lest multilateral dialogue has become a thing of the past seems to have been realized. No multilateral dialogues have taken place under the auspices of the WCC in these recent years.

Yet ambivalence remains even to the present moment. In his overview of the WCC's work in the 1997 Risk Book, *To Be the Church: Challenges and Hopes for a New Millennium,* Dr Konrad Raiser, the WCC's current General Secretary, affirms 'the fading dream of Christian hegemony' and 'the growing challenge to acknowledge cultural and religious plurality' as 'enduring features of human society'.[60] 'Like all religions today,' he writes, 'Christianity is challenged to reassess its long standing exclusivist claims and to contribute to building a new culture which includes and sustains plurality.'[61]

Within the General Secretariat, and clearly with the blessing of the General Secretary himself, the Office on Interreligious Relations has done a magnificent job in holding the theological question before the ecumenical community. The eminently readable journal *Current Dialogue* has appeared regularly with forceful articles containing much serious theological reflection (not least in the Christian understanding of Judaism) as well as its reports on bilateral, sometimes trilateral dialogues on practical questions in regional contexts. It bears witness within the heart of the WCC to the central perception that 'interfaith dialogue' has, in Wesley Ariarajah's words, 'shaken deeply the theological and religious consciousness of the ecumenical movement'.[62]

Accordingly the Office on Interreligious Dialogue is planning a Consultation (to take place in Geneva in April 1999) on the 'theology of religious plurality', with vigorous participation from sociologists, liturgists, artists and scholars from other faith communities, as well as from Christian theologians of religion. We hope that a forceful statement may arise from this meeting which will take us beyond the old arguments about mission and dialogue and the time-honoured assertions of traditional Christology, and so lead the ecumenical movement churches into a confident and hopeful new millennium, in which they can gladly affirm the presence of God in all the world. If this is the case perhaps the WCC may put an end to the ambiguities which have beset it from the beginning.

[In fact several consultations took place, leading to a final meeting at Chateau Bossey, Geneva, in October 2004. The findings of this Consultation, 'Religious Plurality and Christian Self-Understanding', are printed as Appendix 2 on pp. 207]

APPENDIX 2

THE BOSSEY DECLARATION: RELIGIOUS PLURALITY AND CHRISTIAN SELF-UNDERSTANDING

PREAMBLE

'The earth is the Lord's and all that is in it, the world, and those who live in it' (Ps. 24.1).

'For from the rising of the sun to its setting my name is great among the nations, and in every place incense is offered to my name, and a pure offering; for my name is great among the nations, says the Lord of hosts' (Mal. 1.11).

'Then Peter began to speak to them: I truly understand that God shows no partiality, but in every nation anyone who fears him and does what is right is acceptable to him' (Acts 10.34–5).

1. What do the experiences of the psalmist, the prophet, and Peter mean for us today? What does it mean to affirm our faith in Jesus Christ joyfully, and yet seek to discern God's presence and activity in the world? How do we understand such affirmations in a religiously plural world?

I. THE CHALLENGE OF PLURALITY

2. Today Christians in almost all parts of the world live in religiously plural societies. Persistent plurality and its impact on their daily lives are forcing them to seek new and adequate ways of understanding and relating to peoples of other religious traditions. The rise of religious extremism and militancy in many situations has accentuated the importance of interreligious relations. Religious identities, loyalties, and sentiments have become important components in so many international and inter-ethnic conflicts that some say that the 'politics of ideology', which played a crucial role in the twentieth century, has been replaced in our day by the 'politics of identity'.

3. All religious communities are being reshaped by new encounters and relationships. Globalization of political, economic, and even religious life brings new pressures on communities that have been in geographical or social isolation. There is greater awareness of the interdependence of human life, and of the need to collaborate across religious barriers in dealing with the pressing problems of the world. All religious traditions, therefore, are challenged to contribute to the emergence of a global community that would live in mutual respect and peace. At stake is the credibility of religious traditions as forces that can bring justice, peace, and healing to a broken world.

4. Most religious traditions, however, have their own history of compromise with political power and privilege and of complicity in violence that has marred human history. Christianity, for instance, has been, on the one hand, a force that brought the message of God's unconditional love for and acceptance of all people. On the other hand, its history, sadly, is also marked by persecutions, crusades, insensitivity to indigenous cultures, and complicity with imperial and colonial designs. In fact, such ambiguity and compromise with power and privilege is part of the history of all religious traditions, cautioning us against a romantic attitude towards them. Further, most religious traditions exhibit enormous internal diversity attended by painful divisions and disputes.

5. Today these internal disputes have to be seen in the light of the need to promote mutual understanding and peace among the religions. Given the context of increased polarization of communities, the prevalent climate of fear, and the culture of violence that has gripped our world, the mission of bringing healing and wholeness to the fractured human community is the greatest challenge that faces the religious traditions in our day.

The changing context of the Christian faith

6. The global religious situation is also in flux. In some parts of the Western world, the institutional expressions of Christianity are in decline. New forms of religious commitment emerge as people increasingly separate personal faith from institutional belonging. The search for authentic spirituality in the context of a secular way of life presents new challenges to the churches. Further, peoples of other traditions, like Hindus, Muslims, Buddhists, Sikhs, etc., who have increasingly moved into these areas, as minorities, often experience the need to be in dialogue with the majority community. This challenges Christians to be able to articulate their faith in ways that are meaningful both to them and their neighbours; dialogue presupposes both faith commitment and the capacity to articulate it in word and deed.

7. At the same time, Christianity, especially in its evangelical and Pentecostal manifestations, is growing rapidly in some regions of the world. In some of the other regions, Christianity is undergoing radical changes as Christians embrace new and vibrant forms of church life and enter into new relationships with indigenous cultures. While Christianity appears to be on the decline in some parts of the world, it has become a dynamic force in others.

8. These changes require us to be more attentive than before to our relationship with other religious communities. They challenge us to acknowledge 'others' in their differences, to welcome strangers even if their 'strangeness' sometimes threatens us, and to seek reconciliation even with those who have declared themselves our enemies. In other words, we are being challenged to develop a spiritual climate and a theological approach that contributes to creative and positive relationships among the religious traditions of the world.

9. The cultural and doctrinal differences among religious traditions, however, have always made interreligious dialogue difficult. This is now aggravated by the tensions and animosities generated by global conflicts and mutual suspicions and fears. Further, the impression that Christians have turned to dialogue as a new tool for their mission, and the controversies over 'conversion' and 'religious freedom' have not abated. Therefore dialogue, reconciliation, and peace building across the religious divides have become urgent, and yet they are never achieved through isolated events or programmes. They involve a long and difficult process sustained by faith, courage, and hope.

The pastoral and faith dimensions of the question

10. There is a pastoral need to equip Christians to live in a religiously plural world. Many Christians seek ways to be committed to their own faith and yet to be open to the others. Some use spiritual disciplines from other religious traditions to deepen their Christian faith and prayer life. Still others find in other religious traditions an additional spiritual home and speak of the possibility of 'double belonging'. Many Christians ask for guidance to deal with interfaith marriages, the call to pray with others, and the need to deal with militancy and extremism. Others seek for guidance as they work together with neighbours of other religious traditions on issues of justice and peace. Religious plurality and its implications now affect our day-to-day lives.

11. As Christians we seek to build a new relationship with other religious traditions because we believe it to be intrinsic to the gospel message and inherent to our mission as co-workers with God in healing the world. Therefore the mystery of God's relationship to all God's people, and the many ways in which peoples have responded to this mystery, invite us to explore more fully the reality of other religious traditions and our own identity as Christians in a religiously plural world.

II. Religious traditions as spiritual journeys

The Christian journey

12. It is common to speak of religious traditions being 'spiritual journeys'. Christianity's spiritual journey has enriched and shaped its development into a religious tradition. It emerged initially in a predominantly Jewish-Hellenistic culture. Christians have had the experience of being 'strangers', and of being persecuted minorities struggling to define themselves in the midst of dominant religious and cultural forces. And as Christianity grew into a world religion, it has become internally diversified, transformed by the many cultures with which it came into contact.

13. In the East, the Orthodox churches have throughout their history been involved in a complex process of cultural engagement and discernment, maintaining and transmitting the Orthodox faith through integration of select cultural aspects over the centuries. On the other hand, the Orthodox churches have also struggled to resist the temptation towards syncretism. In the West, having become the religious tradition of a powerful empire, Christianity has at times been a persecuting majority. It also became the 'host' culture, shaping European civilization in many positive ways. At the same time it has had a troubled history in its relationship with Judaism, Islam and indigenous traditions.

14. The Reformation transformed the face of Western Christianity, introducing Protestantism with its proliferation of confessions and denominations, while the Enlightenment brought about a cultural revolution with the emergence of modernity, secularization, individualism, and the separation of church and state. Missionary expansions into Asia, Africa, Latin America and other parts of the world raised questions about the indigenization and inculturation of the gospel. The encounter between the rich spiritual heritage of the Asian religions and the African Traditional Religions resulted in the emergence of theological traditions based on the cultural and religious heritages of these regions. The rise of charismatic and Pentecostal churches in all parts of the world has added yet a new dimension to Christianity.

15. In short, the 'spiritual journey' of Christianity has made it a very complex worldwide religious tradition. As Christianity seeks to live among cultures, religions, and philosophic traditions and attempts to respond to the present and future challenges, it will continue to be transformed. It is in this context, of a Christianity that has been and is changing, that we need a theological response to plurality.

Religions, identities and cultures

16. Other religious traditions have also lived through similar challenges in their development. There is no one expression of Judaism, Islam, Hinduism, or Buddhism, etc. As these religions journeyed out of their lands of origin they too have been shaped by the encounters with the cultures they moved into, transforming and being transformed by them. Most of the major religious traditions today have had the experience of being cultural 'hosts' to other religious traditions, and of being 'hosted' by cultures shaped by religious traditions other than their own. This means that the identities of religious communities and of individuals within them are never static, but fluid and dynamic. No religion is totally unaffected by its interaction with other religious traditions. Increasingly it has become rather misleading even to talk of 'religions' as such, and of 'Judaism', 'Christianity', 'Islam', 'Hinduism', 'Buddhism', etc., as if they were static, undifferentiated wholes.

17. These realities raise several spiritual and theological issues. What is the relationship between 'religion' and 'culture'? What is the nature of the influence they have on one another? What theological sense can we make of religious plurality? What resources within our own tradition can help us deal with these questions? We have the rich heritage of the modern ecumenical movement's struggle with these questions to help us in our exploration.

III. Continuing an ongoing exploration

The ecumenical journey

18. From the very beginnings of the Church, Christians have believed that the message of God's love witnessed to in Christ needs to be shared with others. It is in the course of sharing this message, especially in Asia and Africa, that the modern ecumenical movement had to face the question of God's presence among people of other traditions. Is God's revelation present in other religions and cultures? Is the Christian revelation in 'continuity' with the religious life of others, or is it 'discontinuous', bringing in a whole new dimension of knowledge of God? These were difficult questions and Christians remain divided over the issue.

19. The *dialogue programme* of the World Council of Churches (WCC) has emphasized the importance of respecting the reality of other religious traditions and affirming their distinctiveness and identity. It has also brought into focus the need to collaborate with others in the search for a just and peaceful world. There is also greater awareness of how our ways of speaking about our and other religious traditions can lead to confrontations and conflicts. On the one hand, religious traditions make universal truth claims. On the other hand, these claims by implication may be in conflict with the truth claims of others. These realizations, and actual experiences of relationships between peoples of different traditions in local situations, opened the way for Christians to speak of our relationship with others in terms of 'dialogue'. Yet, there are many questions awaiting further exploration. What does it mean to be in dialogue when the communities concerned are in conflict? How does one deal with the perceived conflict between conversion and religious freedom? How do we deal with the deep differences among faith communities over the relationship of religious traditions to ethnicity, cultural practices, and the state?

20. Within the discussions in the Commission on World Mission and Evangelism (CWME) of the WCC the exploration of the nature of the missionary mandate and its implications in a world of diverse religions, cultures and ideologies have drawn on the concept of *missio Dei,* God's own salvific mission in the world, even preceding human witness, in which we are in Christ called to participate. Several issues of CWME's agenda interact with the present study on religious plurality: What is the relation between co-operation with people of other religious traditions (for justice and peace), involvement in interreligious dialogue, and the evangelistic mandate of the Church? What are the consequences of the intrinsic relation between cultures and religions for the inculturation approach in mission? What are the implications for interfaith relations if mission focuses, as the 2005 Conference on World Mission and Evangelism suggests, on building healing and reconciling communities?

21. The WCC's Plenary Commission on Faith and Order, meeting for the first time in a Muslim-majority country (in Kuala Lumpur, Malaysia, 2004) spoke of the 'journey of faith' as one inspired by the vision of 'receiving one another'. The Commission asked: How do the churches pursue the goal of visible Christian unity within today's increasingly multi-religious context? How can the search for visible unity among the churches be an effective sign for reconciliation in society as a whole? To what extent are questions of ethnic and national identity affected by religious identities, and vice versa? The Commission also explored broader questions arising in multi-religious contexts: What are the challenges which Christians face in seeking an authentic Christian theology that is 'hospitable' to others? What are the limits to diversity? Are there valid signs of salvation beyond the Church? How do insights from other traditions contribute to our understanding of what it means to be human?

22. It is significant that all three programmatic streams of the WCC converge in dealing with questions that are relevant for a theology of religions. In fact, attempts have been made in recent conferences to deal with, and formulate, positions that take the discussions forward.

Recent developments

23. In its search for consensus among Christians about God's saving presence in the religious life of our neighbours, the world mission conference in San Antonio (1989) summed up the position that the WCC has been able to affirm: 'We cannot point to any other way of salvation than Jesus Christ; at the same time we cannot set limits to the saving power of God.' Recognizing the tension between such a statement and the affirmation of God's presence and work in the life of peoples of other faith traditions, the San Antonio report said that, 'we appreciate this tension, and do not attempt to resolve it'.

The question following the conference was whether the ecumenical movement should remain with these modest words as an expression of theological humility, or whether it should deal with that tension in finding new and creative formulations in a theology of religions.

24. In an attempt to go beyond San Antonio, a WCC consultation on theology of religions in Baar, Switzerland (1990) produced an important statement, drawing out the implications of the Christian belief that God is active as creator and sustainer in the religious life of all peoples: 'This conviction that God as creator of all is present and active in the plurality of religions makes it inconceivable to us that God's saving activity could be confined to any one continent, cultural type, or group of people. A refusal to take seriously the many and diverse religious testimonies to be found among the nations and peoples of the whole world amounts to disowning the biblical testimony to God as creator of all things and Father of humankind.'

25. Hence, developments in Mission and Evangelism, Faith and Order, and the Dialogue streams of the WCC encourage us to reopen the question of the theology of religions today. Such an enquiry has become an urgent theological and pastoral necessity. The theme of the 9th WCC assembly, 'God in Your Grace, Transform the World', also calls for such an exploration.

IV. TOWARDS A THEOLOGY OF RELIGIONS

26. What would a theology of religions look like today? Many theologies of religions have been proposed. The many streams of thinking within the scriptures make our task challenging. While recognizing the diversity of the scriptural witness, we choose the theme of 'hospitality' as a hermeneutical key and an entry point for our discussion.

Celebrating the hospitality of a gracious God

27. Our theological understanding of religious plurality begins with our faith in the one God who created all things, the living God present and active in all creation from the beginning. The Bible testifies to God as God of all nations and peoples, whose love and compassion includes all humankind. We see in the covenant with Noah a covenant with all creation that has never been broken. We see God's wisdom and justice extending to the ends of the earth, as God guides the nations through their traditions of wisdom and understanding. God's glory penetrates the whole of creation. The Hebrew Bible witnesses to the universal saving presence of God throughout human history through the Word or Wisdom and the Spirit.

28. In the New Testament, the incarnation of the Word of God is spoken of by St Paul in terms of hospitality and of a life turned toward the 'other'. Paul proclaims, in doxological language, that 'though he (Christ) was in the form of God he did not regard equality with God as something to be exploited, but emptied himself, taking the form of a slave, being born in human likeness. And being found in human form he humbled himself and became obedient to the point of death – even death on a cross' (Phil. 2.6–8). The self-emptying of Christ, and his readiness to assume our humanity, is at the heart of the confession of our faith. The mystery of the incarnation is God's deepest identification with our human condition, showing the unconditional grace of God that accepted humankind in its otherness and estrangement. Paul's hymn moves on to celebrate the risen Christ: 'Therefore God has highly exalted him, and given him the name that is above every name' (Phil. 2.9). This has led Christians to confess Jesus Christ as the one in whom the entire human family has been united to God in an irrevocable bond and covenant.

29. This grace of God shown in Jesus Christ calls us to an attitude of hospitality in our relationship to others. Paul prefaces the hymn by saying, 'Let the same mind be in you that was in Christ Jesus' (Phil. 2.5). Our hospitality involves self-emptying, and in receiving others in unconditional love we participate in the pattern of God's redeeming love. Indeed our hospitality is not limited to those in our own community; the gospel commands us to love even our enemies and to call for blessings upon them (Matt. 5.43–8; Rom. 12.14). As Christians, therefore, we need to search for the right balance between our identity in Christ and our openness to others in kenotic love that comes out of that very identity.

30. In his public ministry, Jesus not only healed people who were part of his own tradition but also responded to the great faith of the Canaanite woman and the Roman centurion (Matt. 15.21–8; 8.5–11). Jesus chose a 'stranger', the Samaritan, to demonstrate the fulfilling of the commandment to love one's neighbour through compassion and hospitality. Since the Gospels present Jesus' encounter with those of other faiths as incidental, and not as part of his main ministry, these stories do not provide us with the necessary information to draw clear conclusions regarding any theology of religions. But they do present Jesus as one whose hospitality extended to all who were in need of love and acceptance. Matthew's narrative of Jesus' parable of the last judgement goes further to identify openness to the victims of society, hospitality to strangers and acceptance of the other as unexpected ways of being in communion with the risen Christ (25.31–46).

31. It is significant that while Jesus extended hospitality to those at the margins of society he himself had to face rejection and was often in need of hospitality. Jesus' acceptance of the peoples at the margins, as well as his own experience of rejection has provided the inspiration for those who show solidarity in our day with the poor, the despised, and the rejected. Thus the biblical understanding of hospitality goes well beyond the popular notion of extending help and showing generosity toward others. The Bible speaks of hospitality primarily as a radical openness to others based on the affirmation of the dignity of all. We draw our inspiration both from Jesus' example and his command that we love our neighbours.

32. The Holy Spirit helps us to live out Christ's openness to others. The person of the Holy Spirit moved and still moves over the face of the earth to create, nurture and sustain, to challenge, renew and transform. We confess that the activity of the Spirit passes beyond our definitions, descriptions, and limitations in the manner of the wind that 'blows where it wills' (John 3.8). Our hope and expectancy are rooted in our belief that the 'economy' of the Spirit relates to the whole creation. We discern the Spirit of God moving in ways that we cannot predict. We see the nurturing power of the Holy Spirit working within, inspiring human beings in their universal longing for, and seeking after, truth, peace and justice (Rom. 8.18–27). 'Love, joy, peace, patience, kindness, goodness, faithfulness, gentleness, self-control', wherever they are found, are the fruit of the Spirit (Gal. 5.22–3; cf. Rom. 14.17).

33. We believe that this encompassing work of the Holy Spirit is also present in the life and traditions of peoples of living faith. People have at all times and in all places responded to the presence and activity of God among them, and have given their witness to their encounters with the living God. In this testimony they speak both of seeking and of having found wholeness, or enlightenment, or divine guidance, or rest, or liberation. This is the context in which we as Christians testify to the salvation we have experienced through Christ. This ministry of witness among our neighbours of other faiths must presuppose an 'affirmation of what God has done and is doing among them' (CWME San Antonio 1989).

34. We see the plurality of religious traditions as both the result of the manifold ways in which God has related to peoples and nations as well as a manifestation of the richness and diversity of human response to God's gracious gifts. It is our Christian faith in God which challenges us to take seriously the whole realm of religious plurality, always using the gift of discernment. Seeking to develop new and greater understandings of 'the wisdom, love and power which God has given to men (and women) of other faiths' (New Delhi Report, 1961), we must affirm our 'openness to the possibility that the God we know in Jesus Christ may encounter us also in the lives of our neighbours of other faiths' (CWME San Antonio 1989). We also believe that the Holy Spirit, the Spirit of Truth, will lead us to understand anew the deposit of the faith already given to us, and into fresh and unforeseen insight into the divine mystery, as we learn more from our neighbours of other faiths.

35. Thus, it is our faith in the Trinitarian God, God who is diversity in unity, God who creates, brings wholeness, and nurtures and nourishes all life, which helps us in our hospitality of openness to all. We have been the recipients of God's generous hospitality of love. We cannot do otherwise.

V.   THE CALL TO HOSPITALITY

36. How should Christians respond in light of the generosity and graciousness of God? 'Do not neglect to show hospitality to strangers, for by doing that some have entertained angels without knowing it' (Heb. 13.2). In today's context the 'stranger' includes not only the people unknown to us, the poor and the exploited, but also those who are ethnically, culturally and religiously 'others' to us. The word 'stranger' in the scriptures does not intend to objectify the 'other' but recognizes that there are people who are indeed 'strangers' to us in their culture, religion, race and other kinds of diversities that are part of the human community. Our willingness to accept others in their 'otherness' is the hallmark of true hospitality. Through our openness to the 'other' we may encounter God in new ways. Hospitality, thus, is both the fulfilment of the commandment to 'love our neighbours as ourselves' and an opportunity to discover God anew.

37. Hospitality also pertains to how we treat each other within the Christian family; sometimes we are as much strangers to each other as we are to those outside our community. Because of the changing world context, especially increased mobility and population movements, sometimes we are the 'hosts' to others, and at other times we become the 'guests' receiving the hospitality of others; sometimes we receive 'strangers' and at other times we become the 'strangers' in the midst of others. Indeed we may need to move to an understanding of hospitality as 'mutual openness' that transcends the distinctions of 'hosts' and 'guests'.

38. Hospitality is not just an easy or simple way of relating to others. It is often not only an opportunity but also a risk. In situations of political or religious tension acts of hospitality may require great courage, especially when extended to those who deeply disagree with us or even consider us as their enemy. Further, dialogue is very difficult when there are inequalities between parties, distorted power relations, or hidden agendas. One may also at times feel obliged to question the deeply held beliefs of the very people whom one has offered hospitality to or received hospitality from, and to have one's own beliefs be challenged in return.

The power of mutual transformation

39. Christians have not only learned to coexist with people of other religious traditions, but have also been transformed by their encounters. We have discovered unknown aspects of God's presence in the world, and uncovered neglected elements of our own Christian traditions. We have also become more conscious of the many passages in the Bible that call us to be more responsive to others.

40. Practical hospitality and a welcoming attitude to strangers create the space for mutual transformation and even reconciliation. Such reciprocity is exemplified in the story of the meeting between Abraham, the father of faith, and Melchizedek, the non-Israelite king of Salem (Gen. 14). Abraham received the blessing of Melchizedek, who is described as a priest of 'God Most High'. The story suggests that through this encounter Abraham's understanding of the nature of the deity who had led him and his family from Ur and Haran was renewed and expanded.

41. Mutual transformation is also seen in Luke's narrative of the encounter between Peter and Cornelius in the Acts of the Apostles. The Holy Spirit accomplished a transformation in Peter's self-understanding through his vision and subsequent interaction with Cornelius. This led him to confess that, 'God shows no partiality, but in every nation anyone who fears him and does what is right is acceptable to him' (10.34–5). In this case, Cornelius the 'stranger' becomes an instrument of Peter's transformation, even as Peter becomes an instrument of transformation of Cornelius and his household. While this story is not primarily about interfaith relations, it sheds light on how God can lead us beyond the confines of our self-understanding in encounter with others.

42. So one can draw consequences from these examples, and from such rich experiences in daily life, for a vision of mutual hospitality among peoples of different religious traditions. From the Christian perspective, this has much to do with our ministry of reconciliation. It presupposes both our witness to the 'other' about God in Christ and our openness to allow God to speak to us through the 'other'. Mission, when understood in this light, has no room for triumphalism; it contributes to removing the causes for religious animosity and the violence that often goes with it. Hospitality requires Christians to accept others as created in the image of God, knowing that God may talk to us through others to teach and transform us, even as God may use us to transform others.

43. The biblical narrative and experiences in the ecumenical ministry show that such mutual transformation is at the heart of authentic Christian witness. Openness to the 'other' can change the 'other', even as it can change us. It may give others new perspectives on Christianity and on the gospel; it may also enable them to understand their own faith from new perspectives. Such openness, and the transformation that comes from it, can in turn enrich our lives in surprising ways.

VI.   Salvation belongs to God

44. The religious traditions of humankind, in their great diversity, are 'journeys' or 'pilgrimages' towards human fulfilment in search for the truth about our existence. Even though we may be 'strangers' to each other, there are moments in which our paths intersect that call for 'religious hospitality'. Both our personal experiences today and historical moments in the past witness to the fact that such hospitality is possible and does take place in small ways.

45. Extending such hospitality is dependent on a theology that is hospitable to the 'other'. Our reflections on the nature of the biblical witness to God, what we believe God to have done in Christ, and the work of the Spirit shows that at the heart of the Christian faith lies an attitude of hospitality that embraces the 'other' in their otherness. It is this spirit that needs to inspire the theology of religions in a world that needs healing and reconciliation. And it is this spirit that may also bring about our solidarity with all who, irrespective of their religious beliefs, have been pushed to the margins of society.

46. We need to acknowledge that human limitations and limitations of language make it impossible for any community to have exhausted the mystery of the salvation God offers to humankind. All our theological reflections in the last analysis are limited by our own experience and cannot hope to deal with the scope of God's work of mending the world.

47. It is this humility that enables us to say that salvation belongs to God, God only. We do not possess salvation; we participate in it. We do not offer salvation; we witness to it. We do not decide who would be saved; we leave it to the providence of God. For our own salvation is an everlasting 'hospitality' that God has extended to us. It is God who is the 'host' of salvation. And yet, in the eschatological vision of the new heaven and the new earth, we also have the powerful symbol of God becoming both a 'host' and a 'guest' among us: 'See, the home of God is among mortals. He will dwell with them as their God; they will be his peoples . . .' (Rev. 21.3).

NOTES

1 All the Peoples of God

1 Most Protestant churches recognize that the Bible consists of 39 books in (mainly) Hebrew making up the Old Testament and 27 books in Greek in the New Testament. These are the canonical scriptures. The Roman Catholic and the Eastern Orthodox churches include another seven books as well as some additions to the books of Esther and Daniel. After much dispute 27 books from the earliest period of Christianity came eventually to be recognized as canonical scripture; the Easter Festal Letter of St Athanasius in 367 gave the full list of the books Christians know as the New Testament today.

2 There were also extreme variations of this process: J. N. Darby (1800–82) developed an interpretation of the Bible known as 'dispensationalism', and many people find their way through the scriptures by using the Scofield Reference Bible, where the passages relevant to this form of 'salvation history' are printed in red type.

3 *Christ and Time,* ET of *Christus und Zeit,* appeared in English in 1949, published in the USA by Westminster Press and in Britain by SCM Press, p. 117.

4 I am grateful to D. Preman Niles for calling attention to this passage from Oscar Cullmann, *From East and West: Rethinking Christian Mission,* Chalice Press, 2004, p. 121.

5 *Christ and Time,* p. 116.

6 *Ibid.,* p. 123.

7 *Ibid.,* p. 128.

8 *From East and West,* p. 122.

9 *Ibid.,* p. 123.

10 Quoted by Jacques Dupuis, *Toward a Christian Theology of Religious Pluralism,* Orbis, 1997, p. 10.

11 See the first part of Appendix 1, Ambivalent Theology and Ambivalent Policy, for the implications of this.

12 Cf. Oscar Cullmann, 'In his very first position within creation man appears, so to speak as the representative of creation. This is shown first in his Lordship over creation, but then above all in the fact, of which we have spoken, that the entire creation becomes involved in the curse', *Christ and Time,* pp. 115–16. We may note that even where the doctrine of creation is being thought about afresh the primary concern is with ecology, and not with the created order of the peoples, cf. Jürgen Moltmann, *God in Creation: A New Theology of Creation and the*

Spirit of God, Harper & Row, 1985, and the writings of Colin Gunton, especially *The Triune Creator: A Historical and Systematic Study,* Eerdmans, 1998.

13 *Not Without my Neighbour: Issues in Interfaith Relations,* Geneva, WCC Publications, 1999, p. 115.

14 For these quotations from Maurice see Kenneth Cracknell, *Justice, Courtesy and Love: Theologians and Missionaries Encountering World Religions* 1846–1914, Epworth, 1995, pp. 41–51.

15 F. D. Maurice, *The Religions of the World,* Macmillan, 1846, p. 192.

16 *Ibid.,* p. 193.

17 K. Barth, *Church Dogmatics,* III/1: *The Doctrine of Creation,* Part One, T & T Clark, 1958, p. xi.

18 *Ibid.,* p. 366. Note that this self-revelation is intensely important: 'It is not self-evident that the reality which surrounds man . . . is a reflection of the One to whom it owes its reality. In and for itself it is certainly not this. Menacing evil, or a polluted source of no less evil than good or menace than promise, might equally underlie it as the benevolence of the Creator', *ibid.,* p. 38.

19 *Ibid.,* p. 97.

20 D. T. Niles of Sri Lanka met Karl Barth for the first time in 1935. In the course of conversation Barth said, 'Other religions are just unbelief.' Niles asked, 'How many Hindus, Dr Barth, have you met?' Barth answered, 'None.' Niles said, 'How then do you know that Hinduism is unbelief?' Barth replied, 'A priori.' Niles concluded, 'I simply shook my head and smiled.' In D. T. Niles, 'Karl Barth: A Personal Memory', *The S E Asia Journal of Theology* 11 (Autumn 1969), pp. 10–11. I retell the story as it is in the notes to Gerald H. Anderson's 'Religion and Christian Mission', in *Christian Faith in a Religiously Plural World,* ed. D. G. Dawe and J. B. Carman, Orbis Books, 1978, p. 114.

21 The NRSV does the reader a disservice by translating toledoth as descendants in these verses, rather than as generations.

22 For a detailed discussion of the etymology of the name Noah see the commentaries. The NT sees Noah as a herald of righteousness, 2 Peter 4.5. Cf. Ben Sirach 44.16–17.

23 Karl Barth has some important things to say about Genesis 9 as a covenant of 'redemption'. See *Church Dogmatics,* IV/1, T & T Clark, 1956, pp. 26ff.

24 The bow, *qeshet,* is the archer's bow.

25 'God binds himself with a covenant as a sign of his repentance as well as his promise. The covenant is thus the reality of God's pain-love for his creation', *Third Eye Theology,* Lutterworth Press, 1979, p. 70. Throughout this work Song calls the love of God, 'the pain-love' of God.

26 For a survey of these two interpretations see Bernhard W. Anderson, 'Unity and Diversity in God's Creation', *Currents in Theology and Mission* 5 (1978), pp. 69–81. For the Jewish exegesis see Josephus, the Jewish historian of the first century.

27 Niles quoting an unknown source, *From the East and West,* p. 151.

28 *Ibid.,* p. 152.

29 Among Western scholars who have adopted the second pattern of interpreting the Babel story was S. R. Driver, who remarked that it 'shows how the distribution of mankind into nations, and diversity of languages are elements in [God's] providential plan for the development and progress of humanity'. In this context C. S. Song writes, 'very few exegetes have understood dispersion in the world not as God's punishment for human pride but as fulfillment of God's command', *The Compassionate God,* Orbis, 1982, pp. 22ff.

30 Though it is not our primary concern now we must remind ourselves that the Christian preoccupation with 'saving acts' and 'salvation-history' has often led to an under-emphasis on the biblical sense of God as universal creator and sustainer, concerned with all living things. In our time renewed attention is being paid to such words as, 'For every wild animal of the forest is mine, the cattle on a thousand hills. I know all birds of the air, and all that moves in the field is mine' (Ps. 50.10–11).

31 From the article on 'Nations' by S. Amsler, in *Vocabulary of the Bible,* ed. J. J. von Allmen, Lutterworth Press, 1958, p. 300.

32 See E. Jacob, *Theology of the Old Testament,* Hodder & Stoughton, 1958, p. 222.

33 For a Jewish concurring in this interpretation see Jonathan Magonet, *Form and Meaning,* Almond Press, 1983. He writes in his conclusion: 'If . . . we may extract a theme which seems to have become clarified by our analysis, it is precisely the freedom of God to be beyond any definition by which man would limit Him. God is not contained in Jonah's categories. He is free to deal with Nineveh as He wants, not as Jonah wants. It may be that as regards Nineveh, Jonah wants "justice" — the destruction of the wicked, but God is ready to accept their repentance. Jonah wants his own relationship to God (a controlling one!) to be maintained (whether this is Jonah's egoism or Israel's particularism) — but God is free both to maintain this privileged relationship (though on His terms) yet extend His concern at the same time to all mankind, and all creation' (p. 122).

34 Jacob, *Theology of the Old Testament,* p. 222.

35 See for example the NIV, ad loc.

36 H. H. Rowley, *The Missionary Message of the Old Testament,* Carey Kingsgate Press, 1944, p. 73.

37 The pioneer in the rediscovery was Jean Daniélou, in *Les saints 'paiens' de l'Ancient Testament,* Seuil, 1956, ET *Holy Pagans in the Old Testament,* Longmans, Green, 1957. For an evaluation of Daniélou's work, see Tord Fornberg, *The Problem of Christianity in Multi-Religious Societies of Today: The Bible in a World of Many Faiths,* Edward Mellen Press, 1995.

38 Melchizedek is the high priest of cosmic religion. He gathers in himself all the religious wealth of sacrifices offered from the beginning of the world until now and attests that these were all acceptable to God.

39 E. A Speyser, *The Anchor Bible: Genesis,* Doubleday, 3rd edn 1981, pp. 99–109.

40 *Ibid.*

41 Carroll Stuhlmueller, in Donald Senior and Carroll Stuhlmueller, *The Biblical Foundations for Mission,* SCM Press, 1983, pp. 17–18. Stuhlmueller wrote the Old Testament section.

42 H. H. Rowley, *The Rediscovery of the Old Testament,* James Clarke, 1945, p. 79.

43 J. H. Hertz, *The Pentateuch and Haftorahs,* Soncino Press, 1938, p. 670.

44 See *Ancient Near Eastern Texts,* ed. J. B. Pritchard, Princeton University Press, 2nd edn 1955, p. 150.

45 Dupuis, *Towards a Christian Theology of Religious Pluralism,* p. 36.

46 Lucien Legrand, cited by Jacques Dupuis, *ibid.,* pp. 40–1.

47 The Greek construction here is an appositive genitive and means 'the lost sheep/the house of Israel'. In Matthew's account we should note that the restriction of Jesus' mission to Israel is theologically important (cf. 15.24): only after the resurrection was the mission extended to all the nations.

48 See the work of Wilfred Cantwell Smith on the difference between 'faith' and belief, notably: *Faith and Belief and the Difference Between Them,* Oneworld, 1998, or, conveniently, in Kenneth Cracknell (ed.), *Wilfred Cantwell Smith: A Reader,* Oneworld, 2001, pp. 129–49.

49 The Greek expressions are *eusebēs kai phoboumenos ton theon* (Acts 10.2); his prayers and alms *anabēsan eis mnēmsunon emprosthen tou theou* (10.4). In 10.35 he is described as *ergazomenos dikaiosunēn* and *dektos* to God. Geoffrey Lampe says, 'Biblical language is thought by Luke to be appropriate for so "devout" a Gentile', *Peake's Commentary on the Bible,* Nelson, 1962, p. 900.

50 In *Faith in the Midst of Faiths,* ed. S. J. Samartha, WCC, 1977, pp. 124–5.

51 M. Eugene Boring and Fred B. Craddock, *People's Commentary on the New Testament,* Westminster John Knox Press, 2004, p. 414.

52 So R. Marett, *The Sacraments of Simple Folk,* Oxford University Press, 1933.

53 Justin Taylor suggests this in *The International Bible Commentary,* ed. William R. Farmer, Litugical Press, 1998, p. 15.

54 This word is the comparative form of the adjective formed from *deisidaimonia,* 'fear of the gods'. It is used in both senses in Greek literature, and also in a neutral way. In Acts 25.19 Festus uses *deisidaimonia* to describe the Jewish faith. It is hardly likely that Luke thought that Festus would have called Judaism a 'superstition' in addressing Herod and Bernice, both of whom needed the goodwill of their people, even if they were scarcely committed to the ancestral faith themselves.

55 F. D. Maurice saw this clearly: 'The language you see, assumed that the Athenians were in search of God, that they were ignorantly worshipping him,

that they had a sense of his being a Father; that they wanted some one living image of him, to supplant those images of him which they had made for themselves.' *The Religions of the World,* p. 220.

56 From the *Phaenomena* 1.5.

57 *Ad Jovem,* line 4.

58 For a discussion of these texts see Martin Dibelius, *Studies in the Acts of the Apostles,* SCM Press, 1956, pp. 47–52.

59 An early twentieth-century example of this kind of exposition is found in Sir William Ramsay: 'It would appear that Paul was disappointed and perhaps disillusioned by his experience in Athens. He felt that he had gone at least as far as was right in the way of presenting his doctrine in a form suited to the current philosophy, and the result had been little more than naught. When he went on from Athens to Corinth, he no longer spoke in the philosophical style. In replying to the unfavourable comparison between his preaching and the more philosophical style of Apollos, he told the Corinthians that, when he came among them, he "determined not to know anything save Jesus Christ, and Him crucified" (1 Cor. 2.1–2); and nowhere throughout his writings is he so hard on the wise, the philosophers and the dialecticians, as when he defends the way he had presented Christianity at Corinth', *St Paul the Traveller and Roman Citizen,* Hodder & Stoughton, 6th edn 1902, p. 252.

60 This way of telling the story is contrary to much of both NT interpretation and resulting missiological theory in the twentieth century. For example the German exegete Martin Dibelius wrote that the Areopagus speech is 'as alien to the New Testament (apart from Acts 14.15–17), as it is familiar to Hellenistic, particularly Stoic, philosophy' (*Studies in the Acts of the Apostles,* p. 63), and he distinguished 'the Paul of the Acts of the Apostles from the real Paul' (p. 62). He also wrote that Acts 17.31 is 'the *one Christian* sentence in the Areopagus speech' (p. 56, the italics are his). His countryman Ferdinand Hahn wrote, much more constructively, about both Acts 14.15–17 and Acts 17.22–31, 'The preaching to the Gentiles presupposes, not the covenant with and the promises to the fathers, but the care of the Creator', *Mission in the New Testament,* SCM Press, 1965, p. 135.

61 M. Eugene Boring and Fred B. Craddock suggest that the way to handle the book of Revelation in the life of a congregation is to read it in a setting of worship. After joining briefly in praise and prayer, they say, 'have a good reader (or several) read aloud the whole text without interruption or comment. This takes about an hour and a quarter', *People's Commentary on the New Testament,* p. 760.

62 For this see M. Eugene Boring, *Revelation,* John Knox Press, 1989.

63 Boring and Craddock, *People's Commentary on the New Testament,* p. 7.

64 George B. Caird, *A Commentary on the Revelation of St John the Divine,* Blackie/Harper & Row, 1966, p. 280.

65 N. Turner, *Peake's Commentary on the Bible,* ed. Matthew Black and H. H. Rowley, Nelson, 1962, p. 1059.

2 The Universal Presence of the Word

1 Paul F. Knitter, *Introducing Theologies of Religions,* Orbis, 2002; and Martin Forward, *An Inter-religious Dialogue: Short Introduction,* Oneworld, 2001. Alan Race's pioneering work, *Christians and Religious Pluralism: Patterns in the Christian Theology of Religions,* SCM/Orbis, 1982, is still very useful as an introduction. Amos Yong, *Beyond the Impasse: Toward a Pneumatological Theology of Religions,* Paternoster/Baker Academic, 2003, has incisive comments on recent theologies, as does Gavin d'Costa's *The Meeting of Religions and the Trinity,* Orbis Books, 2000.

2 Notice that the NRSV's translation here of '*amon* is speculative; there is a slightly differing reading in Aquila's version of the Hebrew (post-LXX) that uses the term 'nursling', and this comports well with the idea of a playful child in the words that follow.

3 See Craig Evans, *Word and Glory: On the Exegetical and Theological Background of John's Prologue,* Sheffield Academic Press, 1993, p. 103, and James D. G. Dunn, *Christology in the Making: A New Testament Inquiry into the Origins of the Doctrine of the Incarnation,* Westminster Press, 1980, p. 226.

4 There are other parallels within the targumic and midrashic literature where the Word, in Aramaic *memra,* is active in creation, and is associated with light.

5 The legend is found in *the Tosephta Sukka* 3.11. Philo also identified the rock with Wisdom.

6 'The absence of the definite article, "Son" seems quite purposeful. As a general rule in Greek, the presence of the definite article serves to identify; its absence serves to qualify. In other words, what is the quality or nature of God's speaking? It is through the person of a Son.' So M. Eugene Boring and Fred B. Craddock, *The People's New Testament Commentary,* Westminster John Knox Press, 2004, p. 685.

7 *Ibid.,* p. 653.

8 Cf. this one: 'Hills of the North Rejoice, Isles of the Southern Seas . . . Though absent long your Lord is nigh/ He judgment brings and victory.'

9 See Susan J. White, *Whatever Happened to the Father: The Jesus Heresy in Modern Worship,* Methodist Sacramental Fellowship, 2001.

10 'Mission, Dialogue and God's Will for Us', *International Review of Mission* 78/307 (July 1988), p. 361, n. 1.

11 Cf. Tertullian, *Apology,* ch. 47, and Theophilus, *Ad Autolycum.*

12 Jacques Dupuis, *Toward a Christian Theology of Religious Pluralism,* Orbis, 1997, p. 60. Dupuis here pertinently to the theme of this book quotes

Eric Osborn: 'here the history of the Logos is a history of salvation. The climax of Heilsgeschichte is the coming of the Christ who was known to all as reason and become present in fullness by his incarnation', in 'Justin Martyr and the Logos spermatikos', in 'Theology of Religion', Vol. 42 of *Studia Missionalia,* pp. 143–53.

13 For the far-reacing effects of Karl Rahner's theology of religions see Paul F. Knitter, *Introducing Theologies of Religions,* Orbis, 2002, pp. 68–75.

14 See O. Cullmann, *Christ and Time,* SCM Press, 1952, pp. 56–7. Cf., above pp. 2–30.

15 *Adv. Haer.* 4.20.6.

16 *Ibid.*

17 *Adv. Haer.* 2.61.

18 *Stromateis* 5.12, Ante Nicene Fathers 2, p. 464.

19 *Stromateis* 1.5.1–3, Ante Nicene Fathers 2, p. 305.

20 *Stromateis* 1.15, Ante Nicene Fathers 2, p. 316.

21 *Protreptikos* 11.112, Ante Nicene Fathers 2, p. 203.

22 *De Incarn. Verbi,* ch. 9: 'As when a mighty king entering some great city, although he occupies but one of its houses, positively confers great honour upon the whole city, and no enemy or robber any longer throws it into confusion by his assaults, but on account of the presence of the king in one of its houses, the city is rather thought worthy of being guarded with the greatest care. So also it is the case of Him who is Lord over all. For when he came into our country and dwelt in the body of one like ourselves, thenceforth the very plot of the enemy was defeated and the corruption of death that formerly operated to destroy men lost its power.'

23 Henry Scott Holland, *Logic and Life, with other Sermons,* quoted by A. V. G. Allen, in *The Continuity of Christian Thought,* Ward, Lock & Bowden, new edn 1894, pp. 18–19.

24 *Justice, Courtesy and Love: Theologians and Missionaries Encountering World Religions* 1846–1914, Epworth, 1995, is my account of how that happened.

25 Thomas figures prominently in non-Western church history. The *Acts of St Thomas* (second century) states that Jesus sent him specifically to India. This story is a fundamental credo of the Mar Thoma Christians of India and is accepted by many Roman Catholic and Protestant authorities, see Kenneth Scott Latourette, *A History of the Expansion of Christianity,* Eyre and Spottiswood, vol. i, 1938, pp. 107–8. There is much evidence of lively trade between the Roman empire and India and Sri Lanka in the first century, and there are no historical circumstances that count against the presence of Thomas in India in the first century. Roy C. Amore has examined the links in the centuries immediately before and after the birth of Jesus in relation to the interaction of Christian and Buddhist teaching in his *Two Masters, One Message,* Abingdon, 1978, and has demonstrated the commercial and cultural contacts between the Mediterranean area and the Indian

subcontinent. It is not inconceivable the writer of the Fourth Gospel knew that Thomas was both apostle and martyr.

26 The references are to William Temple, *Readings in St John's Gospel* (First and Second Series), Macmillan, 1961; C. K. Barrett, *The Gospel according to St John: An Introduction with Commentary and Notes on the Greek Text*, SPCK 1955, p. 382; F. C. Grant, *Nelson's Bible Commentary*, vol. vi, Nelson, 1962, p. 386, p. 222; Lesslie Newbigin, *The Light has Come*, Eerdmans 1982, p. 27; and A. J. Gossip's words are from *The Interpreter's Bible*, Abingdon Press, 1952, vol. viii, pp. 700–1.

27 Docetism: its 'distinctive thesis, which gave it its name (*dokein* = to seem), was that Christ's humanity, and hence his sufferings, were unreal, phantasmal' see J. N. D. Kelly, *Early Christian Doctrines*, Black, 4th edn 1968, p. 141; and the conjuring trick refers to the early suggestions, such as that another man was substituted on the cross to die in Jesus' place, or that Jesus was given some powerful drug which induced the appearance of death, see e.g. the *Apocryphal Gospel of Peter*, 4.11.

28 David van Daalen, *The Real Resurrection*, Collins, 1979, p. 18.

29 F. J. A. Hort, *The Way, the Truth, the Life*, Macmillan, 1893, p. 20.

30 *Ibid.*, pp. 20–1.

31 One of these is the period we have recently passed though, that of 'dialectical' theology associated particularly with the names of Karl Barth and Emil Brunner. See W. N. Pittenger, *The Word Incarnate*, Nisbet, 1959, for a criticism of this: he refers to Brunner, who wrote that Christ is the Revelation, 'absolutely different from all other events in history, from all other forms of religious and moral human development'. Pittenger continues, 'While it is true that the "neo-orthodox" theology was valuable in emphasizing once again the great fact of God's transcendent majesty and glory, it has obtained its victory at the expense of destroying the significance of the world which God loved enough to "enter" and to redeem. It is a hard saying, but I believe this theology is much further from the Christian gospel than the liberal school which it so despises', *ibid.*, p. 144.

32 See *God was in Christ*, Faber, 1948, 2nd edn 1955, pp. 114–15.

33 *Ibid.*, p. 117.

34 Arnuph Camps, *Partners in Dialogue*, Orbis Books, 1983, p. 84.

35 Lionel Blue, *To Heaven with Scribes and Pharisees*, Darton, Longman & Todd, 1975, p. 33. Maimonides' *Guide for the Perplexed* (Heb. *Moreh Nevukhim*) marks the high point of the 'golden age of Jewish learning' in the twelfth century of the Christian era. Maimonides was born in 1135, and worked with Aristotelian philosophy in order to give a rational basis for revelation and faith.

36 A. J. Arberry, *The Koran Interpreted*, Allen & Unwin, 1955; Oxford Paperback, 1983.

37 For a brief discussion for the non-specialist Christian reader, see Paul D. Clasper, *Eastern Paths and the Christian Way*, Orbis Books, 1980, pp. 17–32.

38 So M. A. Amaladoss in his essay 'An Indian Reads St John's Gospel', in *India's Search for Reality and the Relevance of the Gospel of John,* ed. C. Duraisingh and C. Hargreaves, ISPCK, 1975, p. 12.

39 The translation is that of Geoffrey Parrinder, in *The Bhagavad Gita: A Verse Translation,* Sheldon Press, 1974.

40 The most engaging recent introduction to Buddhism is Elizabeth Harris, *What Buddhists Believe,* Oneworld, 1998, in which many different Buddhists are allowed to speak for themselves.

41 *Sacred Books of the World: A Universal Anthology,* ed. Ninian Smart and Richard D. Hecht, Crossroad, 1990, p. 268.

42 Sulak Sivaraksa in Harris, *What Buddhists Believe,* p. 32.

43 Jotiya Dhirasekera in 'God at the Head of Religion: A Search through Buddhism' in *God — the Contemporary Discussion,* ed. F. Sontag and M. D. Bryant, Rose of Sharon Press 1982, pp. 74–5.

44 B. F. Westcott, *The Gospel according to St John,* John Murray, 1896; reissued James Clarke, 1958, p. 202. Westcott is very clear in this context, 'It does not follow that everyone who is guided by Christ is directly conscious of his guidance.'

45 C. S. Song, *Third-Eye Theology: Theology in Formation in Asian Settings,* Lutterworth Press, 1980, p. 17.

46 *The Interpretation of the Fourth Gospel,* Cambridge University Press, 1968, p. 19.

47 This is not to say that all Christians agree with the view of Joachim Jeremias that Jesus' use of the term *abba* was 'something unique and unheard of', so much evidence including that we consider later counts against this. Nor do we have to concede that Jesus meant by *abba* 'Daddy'. *Abba* was also a term used widely by adults. See J. H. Charlesworth, 'A Caveat on Textual Transmission and the Meaning of Abba', in J. H. Charlesworth, *The Lord's Prayer and Other Prayer Texts from the Greco-Roman Era,* Trinity Press International, 1994, pp. 8–9.

48 Hans-Joachim Schoeps, *The Jewish Christian Argument,* Faber, 1955, pp. 141–2.

49 Quoted in *ibid.,* p. 142.

50 See Charlesworth, 'A Caveat on Textual Transmission and the Meaning of Abba', pp. 1–14.

51 See Kenneth Cracknell, 'Christian Theology after the Holocaust', in *The Way* (January 1997), pp. 64–72.

52 George Appleton, *The Oxford Book of Prayer,* Oxford University Press, 1985, pp. 269–357, conveniently has a section, 'Prayers from Other Traditions of Faith' that reveals many other examples: Jewish at nos. 837, 838 and 846; Indian, nos. 859, 866, 874, 893, 909 ('Mother'); Muslim, no. 1050; African, nos. 1056, 1064, 1065, 1067; Canadian Indian, no. 1068 ('Grandfather'); Japanese Shinto, nos. 1081–3 ('God our parent'). Choosing just to look for parental expressions

takes no account of the tone and feeling of many others of the prayers in this section in which there is a profound sense of the intimate relation of God to his human children.

53 Hendrik Kraemer, *The Christian Message in a Non-Christian World,* Edinburgh House Press, 1938, p. 102.

54 W. Owen Cole, *The Guru in Sikhism,* Darton, Longman & Todd, 1982, pp. 15–16.

55 See Rudolf Otto, *Christianity and the Indian Religion of Grace,* CLS, 1929. Otto defined this as 'faith in salvation through an eternal God and through a saving fellowship with Him', p. 29.

56 *Bhagavad-Gita* 11.43, in Parrinder, *The Bhagavad Gita,* p. 67.

57 8.65–6, in *ibid.,* p. 101.

58 8.65–6, in *ibid.,* p. 101. Parrinder comments on this: 'The favourite final verse held to be the climax and summary of the Gita.'

59 A. J. Appasamy (ed.), *Temple Bells: Readings from Hindu Religious Literature,* Association Press, 1930, p. 47.

60 Cited in W. S. Deming, *Selections from Tukaram,* CLS, 1932, p. 23. Deming comments: 'yet here again, as a *bhakta,* Tukaram approximates to the Christian position, when he thinks of salvation as release from the power of sin, rather than as release from the bondage of *karma'.*

61 Appasamy, *Temple Bells,* p. 55, 'Save as Thy servant I am nought', is of the same spirit as Harriet Auber.

62 Appasamy, *Temple Bells,* p. 62.

63 The *Gitanjali,* a collection of prose translations made by the author from the original Bengali, were published in the UK by Macmillan in 1913 with an introduction by W. B. Yeats. I am told that many of these songs form the regular hymnology of the Bengali Christian church, though Tagore never became a Christian himself, or, at least, 'a Christian like us'.

64 *Gitanjali,* Macmillan, 1996, song 36, p. 28, quoted by S. Wesley Ariarajah, *Not without My Neighbour: Issues in Interfaith Relations,* WCC, 1999, p. 33. Ariarajah used this in a Christian workshop on prayer and asked the participants to identify its source. Several attributed it to St Francis. Others suggested St Teresa of Avila, Martin Luther and from a hymn by Charles Wesley.

65 Cf. Kenneth Cracknell, 'ISKCON and Interfaith Dialogue', *ISKCON Communications Journal, a Journal of Dialogue* 8/1 (June 2000).

66 See for this Wilfred Cantwell Smith, *The Meaning and End of Religion: A New Approach to the Religious Traditions of Mankind,* Macmillan, 1963; or the selection, pp. 160–76 'Conferring Names Where They Did Not Exist', in Kenneth Cracknell, *Wilfred Cantwell Smith: A Reader,* Oneworld, 2001.

67 The pioneering work in this area did not come until Edwin W. Smith in the twentieth century. See W. John Young, *The Quiet Wise Spirit: Edwin W. Smith 1876–1957 and Africa,* Epworth, 2002.

68 Just a selection of recent work on African religious traditions by Africans themselves may be mentioned here: K. A. Dickson and P. Ellingworth (eds),

Biblical Revelation and African Beliefs, Lutterworth, 1969; J. S. Mbiti, *Concepts of God in Africa,* SPCK, 1970; G. I. Metuh, *God and Man in African Religion,* Chapman, 1981. For a vivid example of what happens if the Christian missionary takes African knowledge of God seriously, see Vincent Donovan, *Christianity Rediscovered: An Epistle from the Masai,* SCM Press, 1982.

69 John S. Mbiti, *The Prayers of African Religion,* SPCK, 1975, cf. his *Concepts of God in Africa,* SPCK, 1970, pp. 64–70, and his *African Religions and Philosophy,* Heinemann, 1969, esp. pp. 61–8. But note also Mbiti's telling comment from the last-named book: 'As for the love of God, there are practically no sayings that God loves. This is something reflected in the daily lives of African peoples, in which it is rare to hear people talking about love. A person shows his love for another more through action than through words. So, in the same way, people experience the love of God in concrete acts and blessings; and they assume that He loves them, otherwise He would not have created them', p. 38.

70 *Sacred Books of the World: A Universal Anthology,* ed. Ninian Smart and Richard D. Hecht, Crossroad, 1990, p. 348.

71 John Mbiti, *The Prayers of African Religion,* SPCK, 1975, p. 129.

72 Lamin Sanneh has recently written: 'African religions as the carriers of the names were in relevant aspects anticipations of Christianity . . . It suggests that theologically God had preceded the missionary, a fact that Bible translation clinched with decisive authority.' *Whose Religion is Christianity? The Gospel beyond the West,* Eerdmans, 2003, p. 32.

73 *Missions from the Modern Point of View,* Revell, 1905, p. 203.

74 See C. F. D. Moule, *The Birth of the New Testament,* Black, 1962, p. 167: 'The Epistles to the Colossians and to the Hebrews both contain a "logos-doctrine" in all but the actual term.' Cf. A. T. Hanson in *The Image of the Invisible God,* SCM Press, 1982, p. 88: 'Colossians is particularly interesting because it has what is virtually a Logos doctrine without using the word Logos.'

75 A. C. Bouquet, Christian *Faith and Non-Christian Religions,* Nisbet, 1959, p. 160. We should be grateful to Bouquet for other sharp perceptions of the New Testament writers' basic stance, e.g. in Acts 28.8, *autoi kai akousontai.* The gentiles will listen to the message of salvation. 'Why', asks Alan Bouquet, 'should the *goyim* do this?' *ibid.,* p. 159.

76 *Ibid.,* p. 157.

77 Dodd, *The Interpretation of the Fourth Gospel,* p. 9. Dodd was certainly not so emphatic as Bouquet that the Logos reference was intended for the Stoics. He thought that John's work revealed a much wider range of reference to the many strands of religious thinking that would be present in the varied and cosmopolitan society of a great Hellenistic city such as Ephesus.

78 Cf. the sharp criticism of W. Norman Pittenger in *The Word Incarnate,* Nisbet, 1959, of 'neo-orthodox' Christologies as based upon 'an irrational philosophy, a sceptical epistemology, and a dialectic theology'. He continues, 'It is a hard saying, but I believe that this theology is much farther from the Christian gospel than the liberal school which it so despises. For even if man is in sin, he is

still God's; of that fundamental fact Christian faith can never lose sight, and the "liberals" were at least near the truth in this. They did not cast away as rubbish the world which God created; nor did they despair utterly of the potential goodness of the men and women whom Christ came to save, the simple people whom he was not ashamed to call his brethren' (pp. 144–5).

79 Cf. these words of Norman Pittenger: 'the only way to understand the Incarnation of God in Christ is in the context of an incarnational presence and operation of the Word of God in nature, in history and human life. What is "diffused" elsewhere, "at sundry times and in divers portions" is "focused" in our Lord Jesus Christ. There is always union between God and man, of some sort and in some way: in Jesus Christ there is the union towards which all others point and from which they are seen in all their rich potentiality yet in all their tragic failure.' *The Word Incarnate,* p. 12, emphasis his.

80 *Readings in St John's Gospel,* St Martin's Library edition, Macmillan, 1961, p. 9.

81 William Temple, *Christus Veritas,* Macmillan, 1924, p. 140.

82 In 'Jesus and the World Religions' in John Hick (ed.), *The Myth of God Incarnate,* SCM Press, 1977, p. 181, and reprinted in John Hick, *God Has Many Names,* Macmillan 1980, p. 75. It is from the latter that the citation is taken.

83 Cf. Irenaeus' phrase: 'the measure of the unmeasured godhead' and the subtitle of Kenneth Cragg's book on religious pluralism, *The Christian and Other Religions: The Measure of Christ,* Mowbray, 1977.

84 'One of a kind' is a better translation of *monogenēs* than 'only begotten', and has the immense advantage of obviating the Muslim criticism that 'God is not begotten neither does he beget'.

85 See John Wesley's wise words about what salvation means, in his *Farther Appeal to Men of Religion and Reason.* 'By salvation I mean, not barely, according to the vulgar notion, deliverance from hell, or going to heaven; but a present deliverance from sin, a restoration of the soul to its primitive health, its original purity; a recovery of the divine nature; the renewal of our souls after the image of God, in righteousness and true holiness, in justice, mercy, and truth. This implies all holy and heavenly tempers, and, by consequence, all holiness of conversation' *Works of John Wesley,* vol. xi, Oxford University Press, 1975, p. 106.

86 Geoffrey Lampe, *God as Spirit,* Oxford University Press, 1977, reissued SCM Press, 1983, p. 31. Lampe continues, 'Through the life and death, the words and deeds of Jesus, and his personal character, the power of the Kingdom of God, which is the creating and saving power of God as Spirit, was released into the world with new strength. Decisive as the act of God in Jesus was, it was not discontinuous with the creating and saving work through the entire historical process.'

3   In Order to Friendship

1 See Hans Küng, *Global Responsibility: In Search of a New World Ethic,* Crossroad, 1991.

2 See Appendix 1: Ambivalent Theology and Ambivalent Policy: The World Council of Churches and Interfaith Dialogue 1938–1999.

3 F. D. Maurice, *The Religions of the World,* Macmillan, 6th edn 1886, p. 96.

4 Cf. the Qur'anic statement: '[the Jews] slew him not nor crucified, but it appeared so unto them: and lo! those who disagree concerning it are in doubt thereof; they have no knowledge thereof save pursuit of a conjecture, they slew him not for certain. But Allah took him up unto himself' (Sura 4.157).

5 My history of the earliest encounters of Western missionaries with people of other faiths, *Justice, Courtesy and Love: Theologians and Missionaries Encountering World Religions* 1846–1914, Epworth, 1995, has scores of examples of these close friendships. One example will stand for many. It is that of Charles Freer Andrews' relationship with a Muslim scholar and mathematician Zuka Ullah. '"What is the use of argument and controversy?" my old Mussulman friend once said to me, "Tell me your beautiful names for God and I will tell you mine"' (pp. 175–6). For the story of Henry Martyn, see later in this book, pp. 167–9.

6 'The Rules of the Game' are included in Raimon Panikkar's *The Intrareligious Dialogue,* Paulist Press, rev. edn 1999, pp. 66–71.

7 Among the best known in English are: *The Unknown Christ of Hinduism,* Darton, Longman & Todd, 1964, 2nd edn 1981; *The Trinity and the Religious Experience of Man,* Darton, Longman and Todd, 1973; *Worship and Secular Man,* Darton, Longman & Todd, 1972; and *Myth, Faith and Hermeneutic,* Paulist Press, 1979.

8 In Wilfred Cantwell Smith, *Questions of Religious Truth,* Gollancz, 1967, p. 71.

9 Smith was profoundly influenced by Martin Buber and used him often as a model of contemporary Jewish mission to Christians, e.g. 'Here was a Jew, profoundly Jewish, who had something to say to Christendom, and said it. Christians agreed that he had something to say, and read him studiously and with profit. They learned from him, or should we, rather, say learned through him, about God, about themselves, about the Christian tradition in which they were participants. They welcomed him, applauded him, asked him to come back to give them more. I nominate Martin Buber as the model of a modern missionary par excellence' in Kenneth Cracknell (ed.), *Wilfred Cantwell Smith: A Reader,* Oneworld, 2001, p. 230.

10 *Faith and Belief,* Princeton University Press, 1979, p. 420.

11 From the new preface to *Patterns of Faith around the World,* Oneworld, 1998, a revised republication of *The Faith of Other Men.*

12 *The Intrareligious Dialogue,* Paulist Press, rev. edn 1999, p. 65.

13 *Towards a World Theology,* Macmillan, 1981, p. 74.

14 The recent Bossey Declaration, printed as Appendix 2, uses as an equivalent idea 'hospitality', see p. 219.

15 John Macmurray, *The Self as Agent,* Faber 1957, reissued 1969, pp.14–15.

16 See for this Appendix 1, pp. 194ff.

17 Karl Barth, *Church Dogmatics,* ET, T & T Clark, IV/3, p. 773. Note the comment of a German missiologist: 'On the other hand the kerygmatic antithesis set over against everything religious in this period still functions as a detectable handicap for the missionary encounter with the other religions.' Horst Bürkle, Missionstheologie, Kohlhammer, 1979, p. 19 (my translation).

18 Cf. Appendix 1.

19 Paul Weller, *Religions in the UK Directory,* 2001–3, published by the Multi-faith Centre at the University of Derby in Association with the Interfaith Network of the United Kingdom, 2001.

20 *Current Dialogue* is available from the Team for Interreligious Relations and Dialgue, WCC, 150 Route de Ferney, PO Box 2100, 1211 Geneva, Switzerland.

21 See the bibliographies by Eleanor Forfang Brockman on the website: http://www.brite.tcu.edu/directory/cracknell/index.htm

22 From the Jewish traditions, the words of Hillel: 'that which is hateful to you do not do to your neighbour' through to the Analects of Confucius, 'Do not unto others what you would not have them do to you.'

23 Wesley Ariarajah, *Not Without my Neighbour: Issues in Interfaith Relations,* WCC Publications, 1999, p. 55.

24 Martin Forward, *Religion: A Beginner's Guide,* Oneworld, 2001, p. 150.

25 *Ibid.,* p. 151.

26 Raimon Panikkar, *The Intrareligious Dialogue,* Paulist Press, rev. edn 1999, p. 65.

27 Lesslie Newbigin, *The Open Secret,* SPCK, 1978, p. 43.

28 Stanley Samartha, *Courage for Dialogue,* WCC, 1981, p. 57.

29 Such learning requires, of course, a certain humility . . . and respect *vis-à-vis* men and women of other cultures, a humility that . . . neither Christians nor Western secularists regularly had. Sceptic and believer, at loggerheads at home, joined company to feel superior when they looked abroad: the one presuming that the religious faith of all humankind was superstitious error, the other that that of the non-Christian was. At the very least, both for a time lacked that humility that recognizes that one can learn about oneself and about one's own world from other civilizations.' *Towards a World Theology,* p. 77.

30 *Towards a World Theology,* p. 203.

31 'Mission, Dialogue and God's Will for Us', *International Review of Mission* 78/307 (July 1988), p. 373.

4   Is Your Heart Right with My Heart?

1   See 'Spirituality', in *A New Dictionary of Christian Theology*, ed. Alan Richardson and John Bowden, SCM Press, 1983, p. 549.

2   Hans Conzelmann described the situation in Corinth perceptively: 'Paul attests the community's wealth of knowledge . . . But Christianity is on the way to being transformed into a mystery religion of the ancient style. Faith is oriented not to the death of Christ but to his heavenly glory. In the sway of the Spirit the believer experiences his own participation in this glory and hovers above the world.' *History of Primitive Christianity*, Darton, Longman & Todd, 1973, p. 103.

3   'Spirituality', in Gordon Wakefield (ed.), *A Dictionary of Christian Spirituality*, SCM Press, 1983, p. 363.

4   The sermon 'Catholic Spirit' from which all these quotations are taken is number 39 in Albert Outler (ed.), *The Works of John Wesley*, vol. 2, Abingdon Press, 1985, pp. 79–95.

5   Kenneth Cracknell and Susan J. White, *An Introduction to World Methodism*, Cambridge University Press, 2005, goes into some detail about this, see pp. 257ff.

6   In *Can We Pray Together? Guidelines on Worship in a Multi-Faith Society*, BCC, 1983, p. 17.

7   See 'Silence', in Wakefield, *A Dictionary of Christian Spirituality*.

8   *Hindu–Christian Meeting Point*, rev. edn, ISPCK, 1976,   p. xiii.

9   *Ibid.*

10   *Guru and Disciple*, SPCK, 1974.

11   Abhishiktananda, *The Further Shore*, ISPCK, 1975; and *Saccidananda: A Christian Approach to Advaitic Experience*, ISPCK, 1974.

12   Abhishiktananda, *Hindu–Christian Meeting Point*, p. viii.

13   Bede Griffiths, *Christian Ashram: Essays Towards a Hindu–Christian Dialogue*, Darton, Longman & Todd, 1966, p. 63.

14   William Johnston, *The Inner Eye of Love*, Collins, 1978, p. 10.

15   *Ibid.*

16   *Ibid.*, p. 68.

17   *Ibid.*, p. 69.

18   Bernard Lonergan, *Method in Theology*, Darton, Longman & Todd, 1977, p. 112, quoted by Johnston, *ibid.*, p. 70.

19   *Ibid.*

20   See 'Spirituality', in Wakefield, *A Dictionary of Christian Spirituality*, p. 363.

21   For our theme Dunne's most relevant books are *The Way of All the Earth: An Encounter with Eastern Religions*, Sheldon Press, 1973; and *The Reason of the Heart*, SCM Press, 1978. The latter contains a closing essay, 'A Note on Method', in which he says, 'my method is my journey' (p. 151). 'It became a kind

of odyssey, passing over into the great religions and coming home again to Christianity and my own life' (p. 152).

22 Gustave Warneck at the New York Mission Conference in 1900 told the delegates that the Great Commission did not say, 'Go into all the world and teach them English.'

23 The Prologue to Ecclesiasticus (Ben Sirach).

24 Lamin Sanneh, *Whose Christianity Is It? The Gospel Beyond the West*, Eerdmans, 2002, p. 124.

25 This judgement may have to be revised. We are seeing increasingly the phenomenon of 'multiple religious participation', known as MRP: to the challenge to people that appear to belong in two religious traditions that 'you can only speak one language', they are replying, 'But we are doing it.'

26 Monica Furlong, *Merton: A Biography*, Collins, 1980, p. 339.

27 William Walsh, *The Use of Imagination: Educational Thought and the Literary Mind*, Chatto & Windus, 1959, p. 86.

28 *The Letters of John Keats*, selected by Frederick Page, Oxford University Press, 1954, p. 53.

29 *Ibid.*, p. 80.

30 Walsh, *The Use of Imagination*, p. 89.

31 W. H. Auden in *Thank You, Fog*, Faber, 1974, p. 29.

32 *Voices of Varanasi; Uncharted Journey;* and *Journey into Varanasi,* all published by the Church Missionary Society during 1973–9. Later Hooker published his matured reflections on this experience in a large work, *Themes in Hinduism and Christianity: A Comparative Study,* Peter Lang, 1989.

33 Hooker, *Voices of Varanasi,* p. 12.

34 *Ibid.*, pp. 10–11.

35 *Ibid.*

36 For comparative religion see Eric J. Sharpe, *Comparative Religion: A History,* Duckworth, 1975. Sharpe elsewhere writes of the distinction between the Comparative Study of Religion (CSR) and the theological task I am concerned with throughout this book: 'Let me make it quite clear I have no quarrel whatsoever with the attempt from the side of the Christian Church to work out a theology of confrontation with other religions; in view of the actual situation of the Church in many parts of the world, this is an imperative necessity and methodologically perfectly legitimate, providing always it is made quite explicit on what criteria the Christian is passing judgment. But in this, theological college and secular university part company, it is a confessional concern, and I hold no brief for Christian apologetics masquerading as CSR.' 'The Comparative Study of Religion in Historical Perspective', in Whitfield Foy (ed.), *Man's Religious Quest,* Croom Helm, 1978, p. 20. For 'bracketing', see also Sharpe, *Comparative Religion,* p. 224.

37 These are some of the relevant books by these authors: Francis X. Clooney, *Theology after Vedanta: An Experiment in Comparative Theology,* State Uni-

versity of New York Press, 1993; *Seeing Through Texts: Doing Theology among the Srivaisnavas of South India,* State University of New York Press, 1996; *Hindu Wisdom for All God's Children,* Orbis, 1998; and *Hindu God, Christian God: How Reason Helps Break Down the Boundaries between Religions,* Oxford University Press, 2001; Leo D. Lefebure, *The Buddha and the Christ: Explorations in Buddhist and Christian Dialogue,* Orbis Books, 1993; John P. Keenan, *The Meaning of Christ: A Mahayana Theology,* Orbis, 1989; Aloysius Pieris, *Love Meets Wisdom: A Christian Experience of Buddhism,* Orbis, 1988; *An Asian Theology of Liberation,* Orbis, 1988; *Fire and Water: Basic Issues in Asian Buddhism and Christianity,* Orbis, 1996; and James Fredericks, *Faith among Faiths: Christian Theology and the Non-Christian Religions,* Paulist Press, 2001.

38 Paul F. Knitter, *Introducing Theologies of Religion,* Orbis, 2002, pp. 205–6.

39 *Theology after Vedanta,* pp. 187–93.

40 Fredericks quoted in Knitter, *Introducing Theologies of Religion,* p. 209.

41 See the range of books already in existence, in note 37.

42 Fredericks uses the word *philia* for this love: it represents genuine appreciation for the particular qualities experienced in the other person, rather than the *agape* of generalized benevolence. See his *Faith among Faiths,* pp. 173–9.

43 In Hebrew, the *tikkun 'olam* is the mending of creation, the task of all human beings.

44 Wakefield, *A Dictionary of Christian Spirtuality.*

45 'The Pater Noster as an Eschatological Prayer', in *New Testament Essays,* Chapman, 1967, p. 239.

46 Bishop David Brown, in *Towards a Theology for Interfaith Dialogue,* CIO Publishing, 1984, p. 35.

47 Monica Furlong, *Merton: A Biography,* p. 329.

48 See on these themes Pieris, *Love Meets Wisdom: A Christian Experience of Buddhism; An Asian Theology of Liberation; Fire and Water: Basic Issues in Asian Buddhism and Christianity.*

49 *The Meaning and End of Religion,* Macmillan, 1963; SPCK, 1978, p. 201.

5 To Bear an Authentic Witness

1 The view of Lesslie Newbigin, who insisted that both were needed, see Wesley Ariarajah, *Not Without my Neighbour: Issues in Interfaith Dialogue,* WCC Publications, 1999, p. 44. Ariarajah comments, 'It would appear that each time a Hindu meets a Christian he or she must ask "what mood are you in?" before deciding to continue the conversation.'

2 Apparently the position of the distinguished British theologian John Macquarrie, *Principles of Christian Theology,* 2nd edn, SCM Press/Scribners, 1977, p. 446.

3 Although as I write these words there is a form of American imperialism involved in the self-appointed mission of the USA to bring freedom and democracy to the Middle East.

4 There is no need to spell this history out, though I felt it necessary so to do in 1986, in *Towards a New Relationship,* pp. 22–4, where I referred to 'Macaulay's Minute' that made English the language of Indian education under the Raj. Arguing for this, Macaulay wrote: 'What then shall that language be? . . . I have no knowledge of either Sanskrit or Arabic . . . I am quite ready to take the oriental learning at the valuation of the Orientalists themselves. I have never found one of them who could deny that a single shelf of a good European library was worth the whole native literature of India and Arabia.' In contrast, the English language 'stands pre-eminent even among the languages of the West'. The die was cast: English was to be the imperial language not only in the British expansion but also of American imperialism. To be sure a fuller account of the nineteenth century would have to make it clear that there is another side of this picture. There were colonial administrators who behaved with profound sympathy for the cultural aspirations and values of those among whom they worked. There were missionaries from William Carey onwards who saw beyond the misconceptions and prejudices with which they had arrived in their new countries. Kenneth Cracknell, *Justice, Courtesy and Love: Theologians and Missionaries Encountering World Religions 1846–1914,* Epworth, 1995.

5 Cited by Robert T. Handy, *A Christian America: Protestant Hopes and Historical Realities,* Oxford University Press, 1971, p. 126.

6 In *ibid.,* pp. 105–6.

7 See Jerald Gort, 'Distress, Salvation and the Mediation of Salvation', in *Missiology: An Ecumenical Introduction: Texts and Contexts of Global Christianity,* ed. A. Camps, F. Verstraelen and M. Spindler, Eerdmans, 1995, p. 208. Gort writes that the Church 'has a duty to insure that its witness is not shaped wrongly, in such a way that it hinders God's action and blocks the kingdom. Looking at the practice of the past one is struck by the fact that church has frequently given witness to the gospel "with might and main," exhibiting a crusading rather than a crucified mind. And in many situations this remains true even now.' *Ibid.,* p. 208.

8 Thomas Thanagaraj, *The Common Task: A Theology of the Christian Mission,* Abingdon, 1999, p. 28.

9 *Ibid.,* pp. 28–9.

10 Lamin Sanneh, *Whose Religion is Christianity? The Gospel beyond the West,* Eerdmans, 2003, p. 39.

11 Hans Georg Gadamer, *Truth and Method,* Crossroad, 1992, pp. 337, 341, cited in Thanagaraj, *The Common Task,* p. 32.

12 *The Common Task,* p. 32.

13 In Kenneth Cracknell and Christopher Lamb (eds), *Theology on Full Alert,* BCC, 1986, cited by David Bosch in *Transforming Mission: Paradigm Shifts in the Theology of Mission,* Orbis, 1991, p. 477.

14 Bosch, *Transforming Mission*, p. 483.

15 According to Gerald Anderson, David Bosch was himself the person who drafted these lines, see 'The Theology of Religions: The Epitome of Mission Theology', in Willem Saayman and Klippes Kritzinger (eds), *Mission in Bold Humility: David Bosch's Work Reconsidered*, Orbis, 1996, p. 119. Anderson gives these words his own conservative imprimatur: 'There has been no better statement for a theology of religion from any church or mission agency since the San Antonio Conference, and it was due in large part to David Bosch', see p. 20.

16 Bosch, *Transforming Mission*, p. 489.

17 Saayman and Kritzinger, *Mission in Bold Humility*, pp. 118ff.

18 'The Great Commission' is the heading for these verses in the KJV: as a title it has no other authority.

19 John Wesley, *Explanatory Notes upon the New Testament*, Epworth, 1976, p. 138. Cf. James C. Logan, 'The Evangelical Imperative: A Wesleyan Perspective', in James C. Logan (ed.), *Theology and Evangelism in the Wesleyan Heritage*, Kingswood, 1995, pp. 21ff.

20 See Cracknell, *Justice, Courtesy and Love*, p. 287, note 5.

21 The Dutch Reformed scholar Johannes van den Berg has described this form of Calvinism: it was, he said, 'one sided in its rigidity; the sovereign character of God's free grace was emphasized at the expense of human responsibility, and man was taught to wait in complete passivity on God', *Constrained by Jesu's Love: An Inquiry into the Motives of the Missionary Awakening in Great Britain in the Period between 1698 and 1815*, Kok, 1956.

22 For brief background to this see Cracknell, *Justice, Courtesy and Love*, pp. 20ff. and especially the endnotes for that page.

23 See also Cracknell, *Justice, Courtesy and Love*, p. 286, n. 5.

24 Perhaps the worst case is from the ending supplied by an unknown writer to the Gospel of Mark: 'Go into all the world and proclaim the gospel to the whole creation. The one who believes and is baptized will be saved; but the one who does not believe will be condemned' (Mark 16.16).

25 *Transforming Mission*, p. 57.

26 M. Eugene Boring and Fred B. Craddock, *People's Commentary on the New Testament*, Westminster John Knox Press, 2004, p. 103.

27 The appearance of Christ here is depicted as being both post-resurrection and post-ascension. Jesus has according to the pattern of ancient Near Eastern kingship been chosen, exalted, presented, and enthroned (see Dan. 7.13). This has just happened — see the force of the ingressive aorist *edothe*, 'has [just] been given me'. 'All authority' is the translation of *kol-hashultan* of Dan. 7.13, a much stronger conception than the Greek, *pasa exousia*.

28 Western translations of Matt. 28.19 from the Vulgate onwards without exception have the strong imperative form 'Go'.

29 For an example of discipling a people rather than individuals, see, very vividly, Vincent Donovan, *Christianity Rediscovered*, Orbis, reprinted 2001. He is recounting how he came to an end of preparing a group of Masai people for

baptism by selecting those who should be baptized: 'So I stood in front of the assembled community and began: "This old man sitting here has missed too many of our instruction meetings. He was always out herding cattle. He will not be baptized with the rest. These two on this side will be baptized because they always attended and understood very well what we talked about. So did this young mother. But that man there has obviously not understood the instructions. And that lady there has scarcely believed the gospel message. They cannot be baptized. And this warrior has not shown enough effort . . .' The old man, Ndangoya, stopped me politely by firmly. "Padri, why are you trying to break us up and separate us? During this whole year that you have been with us, we have talked about these things when you were not here, at night round the fire. Yes, there have been lazy ones in this community. But they have been helped by those with much energy. There are stupid ones in this community, but they have been helped by those who are intelligent. Yes, there are ones with little faith in this village, but they have been helped by those with much faith. Would you turn out and drive off the lazy ones and the ones with little faith and the stupid ones. From the first day I have spoken for these people. And I speak for them now. Now, on this day one year later, I can declare for them and all this community, that we have reached the step in our lives where we can say, We believe."' (pp. 91–2).

30 *Transforming Mission;* p. 66. That some Christians have preferred the emotional ecstasy of the Spirit to obedience to Christ has been manifest in the Church since the earliest times, see 1 Corinthians 4.8ff.

31 See his *Evangelism in the Early Church,* Hodder & Stoughton, 1970, p. 173. Green's actual sentence is: 'They went everywhere gossiping the gospel; they did it naturally, enthusiastically, and with the conviction of those who are not paid to say that sort of thing.'

32 There is one obvious objection to describing the nation as a corporate entity. How can a 'nation' or 'people-group' be baptized: baptism is surely an individual initiation rite, performed upon the profession of faith. But 'baptism' is also used as a metaphor in the NT, cf. Mark 10.33, 39; Luke 12.50, and particularly 1 Cor. 10.2, the Israelites were all 'baptized into Moses'. Since 'baptizing them' (*autous*) refers grammatically to the nations (not 'disciples' or 'converts'), we should consider that the 'baptism in the name of the Father, the Son and the Holy Spirit' may well be a metaphor, this time a baptism into the qualities represented by the Father, the Son and the Holy Spirit. Jane Schaberg's *The Father and the Son and the Holy Spirit,* Scholars Press, 1982, is useful in suggesting a way of interpreting the Trinitarian formula. We may note, incidentally, that if Jesus commanded baptism in the threefold name, the first-century Christian Church took no notice of its Lord, see Acts 2.38; 11.48 and other examples.

33 One NT scholar who has paid this incident some attention is Elisabeth Schüssler Fiorenza in her introductory chapter called 'Aspects of Religious Propaganda', in a collection of papers she edited, *Judaism and Early Christianity,* University of Notre Dame Press, 1976, p. 9: 'However, after some slanderous

attacks and opposition from the side of the Jews, Paul separated the Christians from the Synagogue and established an independent Christian congregation. The new place for the Christian assembly was no longer the synagogue but the hall of Tyrannus. The new location served to foster the image of the Christian community as a philosophical school and to depict Paul as a teacher in dialogue with not only the Jews but also the Greeks.'

34 The English translations in common use a whole range of as variants: 'disputing' (KJV), 'reasoning' (Revised Version), 'using argument' and 'continued to hold discussions' (New English Bible), 'held discussions' (Good News Bible), 'argued persuasively' (Jerusalem Bible). We must remember however that the KJV 'disputing' referred to the practice of medieval and renaissance scholars in their 'disputations', their formal academic exercises.

35 The first definition in the *Encarta Dictionary* (1999) captures this precisely: '*Argue:* express disagreement, to express disagreement with somebody, especially continuously or angrily.'

36 The missionary motivation of Hudson Taylor, the founder of the China Inland Mission, whose words these are. See Cracknell, *Justice, Courtesy and Love,* pp. 11–14 and the criticism of T. E. Slater on p. 113.

37 Paul may be counted as one of the earliest instances of 'multiple religious belonging': he is both Jew and Christian.

38 These are the words of the Kaddish, a prayer central to present-day Judaism: though we are unclear about synagogue worship before 70 CE we cannot neglect the parallels between the Kaddish and the Lord's Prayer, see Raymond A. Brown, 'The Pater Noster as an Eschatological Prayer' in *New Testament Essays,* Geoffrey Chapman, 1967, pp. 217–53, and more recently James H. Charlesworth with Mark Harding and Mark Kiley, *The Lord's Prayer and Other Texts from the Greco-Roman Era,* Trinity Press International, 1994, pp. 1–27.

39 Kenneth Cracknell, *Towards a New Relationship: Christians and People of Other Faith,* Epworth, 1986, p. 28.

40 There are some grounds for supposing Ephesus to be the place of origin of the Letter to the Colossians, where such expressions are used, see J. D. G. Dunn, *The Epistles to Colossians and Philemon,* Eerdmans, 1996, p. 40. An earlier NT scholar, C. F. D. Moule, wrote once that the identification of Jesus, 'the crucified Nazarene, within thirty years of his death as the subject of such terminology is staggering, and fairly cries of for some explanation', *The Epistles of Paul the Apostle to the Colossians and to Philemon,* Cambridge University Press, 1957, p. 19. It could well be that part of the explanation is the two-year period spent in the school of Tyrannus.

41 Some New Testament scholars (Conzelmann, John Knox) have suggested that there was a quite definite 'school of Paul', where his ideas were worked on by a group of early Christian thinkers. Conzelmann suggested that this would have been centred in Ephesus, and cited the presence of Apollos, Aquila and Prisca, and the 'dialogues' in the *scholē* of Tyrannus. We do know that Ephesus became

'the city of dialogue' by the end of the century. The judgement of Raymond Brown about the provenance of the Fourth Gospel is also important: 'Ephesus still remains the primary contender for identification as the place where John was composed. Besides the almost unanimous voice of the ancient witnesses who speak of the subject, we have an argument from the parallels between John and Revelation, for the latter work clearly belongs to the area of Ephesus.'

42 I use the term 'Asiarchs' rather than the colourless expression of the NRSV: 'some officials of the province of Asia'. Note this definition of 'Asiarch': 'Each of the cities of proconsular Asia, at the autumnal equinox, assembled its most honourable and opulent citizens, in order to select one to preside over the games to be exhibited that year, at his expense, in honour of the gods and the Roman Emperor. Thereupon each city reported the name of the person selected to a general assembly held in some leading city, as Ephesus, Smyrna, Sardis.' Grimm-Thayer, *Greek–English Lexicon of the New Testament, ad loc.*, p. 80. Note Elisabeth Schüssler Fiorenza's comment: 'The second part of the story (19.29– 34) demonstrates the support of the Asiarchs, the cultic officials of the Roman civil religion in Asia Minor, for the Christian missionary, Paul. Luke's point is quite clear: a sect, whose leader had such friends, cannot be at all dangerous to the Roman Empire', *Judaism and Early Christianity*, p. 17.

43 The Dutch missiologist Johannes Verkuyl suggested this in his *Inleiding in de Nieuwere Zendingswetenschap*, J. H. Kok, 1975, p. 234. Verkuyl went on to remark that Paul points here to the fact of experience, that whoever shares the gospel with someone else, receives it again, freshly and with deeper meaning.

44 Vincent Donovan, whom we quoted at length, has a couple of important sentences on this subject: 'One of the effects of passing on an already interpreted Gospel to a people is the effect such a process has on you. You can easily come to think that the interpretation you pass on is the only interpretation possible', *Christianity Rediscovered*, p. 122.

45 *The Cross-Cultural Process in Christian History*, T & T Clark and Orbis, 2002, pp. 40–1.

46 *Ibid.*, p. 41.

47 For a galaxy of other examples see Cracknell, *Justice, Courtesy and Love.*

48 The most important recent study in English is Brijraj Singh, *The First Protestant Missionary to India: Bartholomaeus Ziegenbalg* (1683–1719), Oxford University Press, 1999.

49 *Ibid.*, p. 105. Brijraj Singh is basing this assessment on a manuscript which Ziegenbalg completed in 1711. The English version of the title can be read as *The complete description of the heathendom of Malabar wherein, from their own writings, their precepts and doctrines in theology as well as philosophy are set out in detail and are communicated for the useful instruction of beloved Europe.* He sent this home to A. H. Francke in Halle, who refused to print it. Only in 1927 was the full text published, and it has never been translated into English. There

is also a later document, completed in 1713, that did appear in English as *The Genealogy of the South-Indian God* (1868). Francke also refused to publish this, writing that 'Missionaries were sent out to extirpate Hinduism, and not to spread heathenist nonsense in Europe.'

50 I think, for example, of Sir William Jones (1746–94) working in Calcutta. His references to Indians are full of condescension about their supineness and indolence.

51 Singh, *The First Protestant Missionary to India,* p. 120.

52 *Ibid.,* pp. 122–3.

53 *Ibid.,* p. 128.

54 For a brief but cogent introduction see Clinton Bennett, 'Henry Martyn 1781–1878: Scholarship in the Service of Mission', in Gerald Anderson, Robert T. Coote, Norman A. Horner and James M. Phillips (eds), *Mission Legacies: Biographical Studies of the Leaders of the Modern Missionary Movement,* Orbis, 1994, pp. 264–70. Martyn's story is well-known through popular works like Constance Padwick, *Henry Martyn: Confessor of the Faith,* SCM Press, 1922.

55 *Biographical Dictionary of the Christian Mission,* Macmillan, 1998, p. 438.

56 S. Wilberforce, *Journals and Letters of Henry Martyn,* London: R. B. Seeley and W. Burnside, 1837, vol. ii, p. 55. By 'the recesses of the sanctuary' Martyn meant 'the deepest spiritual experiences, normally never discussed by Englishmen'.

57 In Padwick, *Henry Martyn.*

58 For more about Slater, see my *Justice, Courtesy and Love,* pp. 108–19.

59 *The Philosophy of Modern Missions: A Present Day Plea,* James Clarke, 1882, pp. 47–8.

60 Paul F. Knitter has recently made it his all-embracing term for inclusive theologies like those of Karl Rahner and Jacques Dupuis, see *An Introduction to the Theology of Religion,* Orbis, 2004.

61 *The Philosophy of Modern Missions,* p. 112.

62 *The Higher Hinduism in Relation to Christianity: Certain Aspects of Hindu Thought from a Christian Standpoint,* Elliott Stock, 1902, p. 291.

63 *Ibid.*

64 See J. J. E. van Lin, *Protestantse Theologie der Godsdiensten van Edinburgh naar Tambaram 1910–1938,* Van Gorcum, 1974, now in English as *Shaking the Fundamentals: Religious Plurality and the Ecumenical Movement,* Rodopi, 2002.

65 *The Christian Message in a Non-Christian World,* Edinburgh House Press, 1938. It was reprinted several times in both Britain and the USA in the 1950s.

66 Kraemer was a complex and multi-layered thinker and he went on writing for almost another thirty years. For an excellent brief introduction see Libertus A. Hoedemaker, 'Hendrik Kraemer, 1888–1965: Biblical Realism Applied to Mission', in Gerald Anderson et al., pp. 508–15. Hoedemaker also highlights the

idea of 'the missionary as point of contact', remarking that this concept connects Kraemer's thought 'very fruitfully to later developments in the theology of religions and of dialogue', p. 514.

67 This reputation is often justified. See for example his references to Islam as 'a great syncretistic body' and to its 'iron rigidity', pp. 215, 353, and to Hinduism as 'exclusively individualistic and essentially eudaemonistic', p. 140.

68 *Ibid.*, p. 298.

69 *Ibid.*, p. 356.

70 *Ibid.*, pp. 354–5.

71 *Ibid.*, p. 140.

72 See Kenneth Cracknell, *Wilfred Cantwell Smith: A Reader,* Oneworld, 2001, and for a convenient introduction to Smith's writings, its introductory essay.

73 'Can Religions be True or False?' in *Questions of Religious Truth,* Gollancz, 1967, p. 89.

74 On all this see most conveniently chapter 7 of *Faith and Belief,* Princeton University Press, 1979, now reprinted as *Faith and Belief: The Difference Between Them,* Oneworld, 1998.

75 *The International Review of Mission* 77/307 (July 1988), p. 265.

76 This first appeared in the *Occasional Bulletin* of the Missionary Research Library, New York, 20/4 (1969), pp. 1–13, and has been reprinted in abridged form in Gerald H. Anderson and Thomas F. Stransky (eds), *Mission Trends* No. 2, Paulist Press and Eerdmans, 1975.

77 The vision set out in his *Toward a World Theology,* Macmillan, 1981.

78 Cracknell, *Towards a New Relationship,* p. 6.

79 1 Peter 3.15 seems to be a key verse for interfaith conversation: always be ready to make your defence (*apologia*) to anyone who asks about the hope that is in you, but with gentleness and reverence: and the NRSV captures perfectly the force of *alla meta prautētos kai phobou.*

Appendix 1

1 This is the theme of my 1995 book, *Justice, Courtesy and Love: Theologians and Missionaries encountering World Religions 1846–1914.*

2 *The Missionary Message in Relation to the Non-Christian Religions,* 1910, p. 267.

3 *Ibid.* For the evidence before Commission Four see *Justice, Courtesy and Love,* pp. 181–227.

4 For these quotations see vol. i of the Jerusalem Report: *The Christian Life and Message in Relation to Non-Christian Systems,* pp. 491–2.

5 The first use of the term dialogue in English for friendly interfaith encounter is from the early 1960s.

6 Origen Vasantha Jathanna, *The Decisiveness of the Christ Event and the Universality of Christianity, with special reference to Hendrik Kraemer and Alfred*

George Hogg as well as to William Ernest Hocking and Pandipeddi Chenchiah,
Peter Lang, 1981, p. 509.

7 'Findings and Recommendations' in its report *The World Mission of the Church,* p. 46, italics mine.

8 *The Decisiveness of the Christ Event and the Universality of Christianity,* p. 510, italics his.

9 *Ibid.*

10 *Between Two Cultures: Ecumenical Ministry in a Pluralist World,* WCC, 1996, p. 39.

11 Published by the IMC at its Edinburgh House Press in 1938, and reprinted several times after the Second World War. My quotations are from the third edition, James Clarke, 1965.

12 *Ibid.* p. 298.

13 *Ibid.*

14 *Ibid.,* pp. 214–16.

15 *Ibid.,* p. 353.

16 Samartha, *Between Two Cultures,* p. 34.

17 *The Christian Message,* p. 161.

18 *Ibid.,* p. 172.

19 *Ibid.,* p. 160.

20 *Hindus and Christians: A Century of Protestant Ecumenical Thought,* Eerdmans/Rodopi, 1991, p. 169.

21 *Ibid.*

22 'Findings and Recommendations', in *The World Mission of the Church,* p. 51; cf. The Authority of the Church, vol. i, p. 194.

23 *Ibid.*

24 Since we shall often find criticisms in what follows of the Euro-centricity of this theology, let me make it clear it represented a massive achievement wrought by giant spirits and thinkers who had confronted and overcome one of the greatest challenges that the Church has ever faced, namely the perversion of Christianity by the Nazis.

25 *The Church's Witness to God's Design,* 1948, p. 213.

26 It was at this time that the Dutch missiologist J. C. Hoekendijk protested about the church-centredess of so much missiology.

27 See Dirk C. Mulder, 'A History of the Sub Unit on Dialogue of the World Council of Churches', in *Studies in Interreligious Dialogue* 2/2 (1992), pp. 136–7.

28 Norman C. Goodall (ed.), *The Uppsala '68 Report: Official Report of the Fourth Assembly of the WCC,* 1968, p. 29.

29 Printed in the *International Review of Mission* 59/236 (October 1970) and in *Living Faiths and the Ecumenical Movement,* WCC, 1971.

30 Note the title of the 'book of the conference', of the Colombo Consultation: *Towards World Community: The Colombo Papers,* WCC, 1975.

31 'Christians in Dialogue with Men of Other Faiths: the Zurich Aide Memoire', in S.J. Samartha (ed.), *Living Faiths and the Ecumenical Movement,* p.33.

32 Samartha, *Between Two Cultures,* p. 105, italics his.

33 Mulder, 'A History of the Sub Unit on Dialogue', p. 146.

34 Ans van der Bent, *Vital Ecumenical Concerns: Sixteen Documentary Surveys,* WCC, 1986, p. 55.

35 *Ibid.,* p. 56.

36 *Minutes of the Third Meeting of the Working Group, Trinidad, May 1978,* p. 97. There is a catena of quotations of church responses on pp. 99–102.

37 It does not detract from the significance of the Central Committee's action to point out that these words are in the document presented to the Central Committee by the DFI, see *Minutes,* p. 124. Fine words have to emerge from somewhere.

38 For my own comments at the time see K. Cracknell, *Why Dialogue? A First British Comment on the WCC Guidelines,* BCC, 1978.

39 Trinidad Meeting *Minutes,* p. 98.

40 *Guidelines on Dialogue,* p. 13.

41 See David Gill (ed.), *Gathered for Life: Official Report, VIth Assembly, World Council of Churches, Vancouver, Canada,* 24 July–10 August, 1983, Eerdmans/WCC, pp. 31–42. These words appear on p. 40.

42 *Ibid.,* p. 41.

43 This had been the dream of the Central Committee when it met in Geneva in July 1982: 'For the future work of the DFI after Vancouver it is suggested that great attention should be paid to the theological issues involved in Christian relations with people of other faiths . . . and that this should be undertaken in cooperation with Faith and Order and CWME', *Minutes,* p. 59.

44 In her summary report of the Working Group meeting, Diana L. Eck, the Moderator, notes more neutrally: 'The Dialogue sub-unit did not meet with Faith and Order, for lack of time.' *Minutes of the Seventh Meeting of the Working Group,* Potsdam/GDR, July 1986, p. 72.

45 Ariarajah, *Hindus and Christians,* p. 196.

46 Cf. his article 'San Antonio and Other Faiths', *Current Dialogue 16* (August 1989), pp. 3–8.

47 *International Bulletin of Missionary Research* 13/2 (1989), p. 54.

48 For one account of the negotiations, pointing to the role played by the late David Bosch of South Africa, who was asked to draft the Final Report, see Gerald Anderson, 'Theology of Religions: The Epitome of Mission Theology', in Willem Saayman and Klippies Kritzinger (eds), *Mission in Bold Humility: David Bosch's Work Considered,* Orbis, 1996, pp. 94–120.

49 Happily now preserved within the excellent collection by Michael Kinnamon and Brian Cope: *The Ecumenical Movement: An Anthology of Key Texts and Voices,* WCC/Eerdmans 1997. For a long time it was only available in the WCC Sub-unit on Dialogue's limited circulation newsletter *Current Dialogue* 18 (July 1990) and reprinted in the following issue.

50 Minutes of the Central Committee, Geneva 9–18 July 1984, p. 42.

51 See his 'Notes on Interreligious Dialogue', *Current Dialogue* 7 (Autumn 1984), pp. 13–15.

52 *Ibid.*, p. 15.

53 *Current Dialogue* 19 (January 1991), pp. 32–40.

54 *Ibid.*, p. 40.

55 Her complete speech is in Michael Kinnamon (ed.), *Signs of the Spirit: Official Report of the Seventh Assembly,* WCC, 1991, pp. 37–47.

56 Kinnamon and Cope, *The Ecumenical Movement.*

57 See the 'Report on the Church and the Jewish People', in *New Directions in Faith and Order,* Bristol 1967 (Faith and Order Report No. 50), WCC, 1968, pp. 69–80.

58 Mulder, 'A History of the Sub Unit on Dialogue', p. 150.

59 *Between Two Cultures,* p. 41, italics his.

60 *To Be the Church: Challenges and Hopes for a New Millennium,* WCC, 1997, p. 21.

61 *Ibid.*, p. 23.

62 In an illuminating chapter 'The Impact of Interreligious Dialogue on the Ecumenical Movement', in John D'Arcy May (ed.), *Pluralism and the Religions: The Theological and Political Dimensions,* Cassell, 1998. This paper was first published in the *Ecumenical Review* 49/2 (1997), pp. 212–21.

FURTHER READING

This is only a selection, chosen for the variety of approaches represented by these authors. For full-scale annotated bibliographies see my web page: http://www.brite.tcu.edu/directory/cracknell/index.htm

Ariarajah, S. Wesley, *Not Without my Neighbour: Issues in Interfaith Relations,* Geneva, WCC Publications, 1999.

Cracknell, Kenneth, *Justice, Courtesy and Love: Theologians and Missionaries Encountering World Religions 1846–1914,* London, Epworth Press, 1995.

D'Costa, Gavin, *The Meeting of Religions and the Trinity,* Maryknoll, Orbis, 2000.

Dupuis, Jacques, *Toward a Christian Theology of Religious Pluralism,* Maryknoll, Orbis, 1997.

Eck, Diana L., *Encountering God: A Spiritual Journey from Bozeman to Banaras,* Boston, Beacon Press, 1993.

Forward, Martin, *Inter-religious Dialogue: A Short Introduction,* Oxford, Oneworld, 2001.

Heim, S. Mark, *The Depth of the Riches: A Trinitarian Theology of Religious Ends,* Grand Rapids, Eerdmans, 2001.

Knitter, Paul F., *Introducing Theologies of Religion,* Maryknoll, Orbis, 2002.

Küng, Hans, and Kuschel, Karl-Josef (eds), *A Global Ethics: The Declaration of the Parliament of the World's Religions,* London, SCM Press, 1993.

May, John D'Arcy (ed.), *Pluralism and the Religions: The Theological and the Political Dimensions,* London and Herndon VA, Cassell, 1998.

Niles, D. Preman, *From East and West: Rethinking Christian Mission for Today,* Saint Louis, Chalice Press, 2004.

Pinnock, Clark H., *A Wideness in God's Mercy: The Finality of Jesus Christ in a World of Religions,* Grand Rapids, Zondervan, 1992.

Smith, Wilfred Cantwell, *Patterns of Faith Around the World,* Oxford, Oneworld, 1998.

Smith, Wilfred Cantwell, *Wilfred Cantwell Smith: A Reader,* ed. Kenneth Cracknell, Oxford, Oneworld, 2001.

Suchocki, Marjorie Hewitt, *Divinity and Diversity: A Christian Affirmation of Religious Pluralism,* Nashville, Abingdon Press, 2003.

Thangaraj, M. Thomas, *The Common Task: A Theology of the Christian Mission,* Nashville: Abingdon, 1999.

Yong, Amos, *Beyond the Impasse: Toward a Pneumatological Theology of Religions,* Carlisle, Paternoster Press/Grand Rapids, Baker Academic, 2003.

Index of Scriptural References

Indexes of Names and Subjects